Flash 8 Essentials

Paul Barnes-Hoggett
Stephen Downs
Glen Rhodes
Craig Swann
Matt Voerman
Todd Yard

friendsof

DESIGNER TO DESIGNER™

an Apress® company

Flash 8 Essentials

ISBN (pbk): 1-59059-532-7

9 8 7 6 5 4 3 2 1

Distributed to the book trade worldwide by Springer-Verlag New York, Inc., 233 Spring Street, 6th Floor, New York, NY 10013. Phone 1-800-SPRINGER, fax 201-348-4505, e-mail orders-ny@springer-sbm.com, or visit www.springeronline.com.

For information on translations, please contact Apress directly at 2560 Ninth Street, Suite 219, Berkeley, CA 94710. Phone 510-549-5930, fax 510-549-5939, e-mail info@apress.com, or visit www.apress.com.

The source code for this book is freely available to readers at www.friendsofed.com in the Downloads section.

Credits

Additional Material	**Assistant Production Director**
Chris Mills	Kari Brooks-Copony
Lead Editor	**Production Editor**
Chris Mills	Katie Stence
Technical Reviewer	**Compositors**
Marco Casario	Dina Quan and
	Van Winkle Design Group
Editorial Board	
Steve Anglin, Dan Appleman,	**Proofreader**
Ewan Buckingham, Gary Cornell,	Elizabeth Berry
Tony Davis, Jason Gilmore,	
Jonathan Hassell, Chris Mills,	**Indexer**
Dominic Shakeshaft, Jim Sumser	Lucie Haskins
Project Manager	**Artist**
Kylie Johnston	April Milne
Copy Edit Manager	**Interior and Cover Designer**
Nicole LeClerc	Kurt Krames
Copy Editors	**Manufacturing Director**
Damon Larson, Julie Smith, Nicole LeClerc	Tom Debolski

CONTENTS AT A GLANCE

CONTENTS

CONTENTS

ABOUT THE AUTHORS

After studying architecture for seven years, **Paul Barnes-Hoggett** changed his mind and decided to spend his time designing the "intergoogle." He spent time as a lead developer at boxnewmedia, where he built award-winning sites for clients such as Select Model Management. (In his own words, he admits, "It's a tough job looking at pictures of beautiful people all day, but someone has to do it.")

He set up Eyefodder in 2003, which specializes in building rich Internet applications for the media industry, and has built solutions for clients including FHM, Adidas, Air Miles, and ITV. When not pushing pixels, Paul likes to eat, drink, and be merry. To get in contact with Paul, visit www.eyefodder.com.

Stephen Downs, aka Tink, has been a freelance Flash designer/developer for the past four years, and has a background in art, design, and photography. Based in London, England, he works on a wide range of projects, both for other companies and his own clients. The growth in his workload has recently lead to the startup of his own company, Tink Ltd. His primary focus is user interaction and interactive motion, which includes integrating design and development to any design specification using best practice methodologies. For contact info and work examples, visit www.tink.ws. For Tink's daily thoughts, visit www.tink.ws/blog.

Glen Rhodes is the CTO of CRASH!MEDIA, located in Toronto, Canada. He's also a Flash game developer and has authored over ten books, including *Macromedia Flash MX 2004 Game Development*, *Flash MX 2004 Games Most Wanted*, and *Flash MX Designer's ActionScript Reference*. He's also a regular writer for several computer magazines, including *Web Designer* and *Practical Web Projects*. Glen has developed dozens of games for many platforms, including Windows PC, PlayStation, and these days, Macromedia Flash. He has developed many Flash games, including *The Black Knight* for Arcade Town, *Domino Dementia* at www.shockwave.com, and "W.R.A.X." at www.superdudes.net. He's the founder of www.flashgamecoders.com, and currently runs this Flash game development community website. Glen's website is www.glenrhodes.com.

In addition to his Flash work, Glen also writes and records music with Canadian singer-songwriter Lisa Angela (www.lisaangela.com). Together, their music has had much success, including regular air play on the Oprah Winfrey Show.

Craig Swann is founder of the award winning interactive agency CRASH!MEDIA (crashmedia.com). Craig has been working in the online space since 1995 and has been a core part of the Flash community since it's inception. As an educator, curator, speaker and writer of new media technologies Craig has given 20 International talks on Flash, written and contributed to 7 Flash books and currated over a dozen new media events featuring some of the world's brightest Flash and interactive developers. His flash work at CRASH! has received over a dozen awards and has been featured in both print and television. Craig's interactive audio work has developed into the multi-award winning online music application Looplabs.com which has been used by such clients as Coca-Cola, Miller, Bacardi, Calvin Klein, Toyota, Sony and others. When not plugged into the matrix, Craig enjoys travelling the world and questioning everything.

Certified Macromedia master instructor, Team Macromedia member, internationally published author, and active Flash/Flex community participant, **Matt Voerman** has been using Flash since its inception as Future Splash. He has over ten years professional web and multimedia industry experience, and has worked with national digital marketing agencies, state government departments, and international finance sector clients. Based out of Perth, Australia, Matt has worked with Macromedia on a number of levels, most recently as a subject matter expert (SME), helping to develop the official Macromedia Flash Developer Certification Exam.

Todd Yard is currently a Flash developer at Brightcove in Cambridge, Massachusetts, where he moved early in 2005 in the middle of a blizzard. Previously, he was in New York City, working with EGO7 on its Flash content management system and community software. He has contributed to a number of friends of ED books, of which his favorites were *Flash MX Studio* and *Flash MX Application and Interface Design*, though he feels the most useful was *Extending Flash MX 2004: Complete Guide and Reference to JavaScript Flash*. His personal site (which he used to update all the time, he fondly remembers) is www.27Bobs.com.

ABOUT THE TECHNICAL REVIEWER

Marco Casario is currently one of the most dynamic developers in the Macromedia world. A Certified Flex Instructor and Certified Flash and Dreamweaver Professional, he collaborates with Macromedia Italy as a speaker and promoter for several events and conferences, in addition to developing challenging rich Internet applications himself.

A Flash Lite evangelist, he has also founded a Flash Lite Yahoo Group (http://groups.yahoo. com/group/FlashLite) and often deals with this new mobile technology on his blog pages at http://casario.blogs.com.

Marco recently founded Comtaste (www.comtaste.com), a company dedicated to exploring new frontiers in the rich Internet and mobile applications fields.

INTRODUCTION

Hello, and welcome to *Flash 8 Essentials*, the result of a collaboration between friends of ED and some of the most talented Flash developers in the world today. It's been a long, hard road getting here, but we've done it, and we're very proud of our creation. We designed this book to serve a number of purposes. It's an essential guide to all of the great new features available in Flash 8, it's a reference guide for you to look up all those fiddly details, and it's also a gallery of inspirational examples to help you go further in your work, allowing you to create more beautiful, breathtaking designs and more usable applications.

As you've no doubt realized if you've started to experiment with Flash 8, Flash has come a very long way since the days of Flash 3 and 4. Some of you will remember even earlier than that. (Remember what Flash was like before ActionScript? OK, let's not go there . . .)

This book is broken down into ten chapters and an appendix. Each chapter deals with a different new area of Flash 8, getting you up to speed as quickly as possible with the new features, using a combination of easy-to-follow tutorials, reference material, and inspirational examples. The appendix is a gallery of fully-functional examples—some of the stuff is touched upon in previous chapters, and some isn't. The chapters are as follows:

- In **Chapter 1**, Matt Voerman introduces you to the world of Flash 8, summarizing the new features and setting the scene nicely for the rest of the book.

- **Chapter 2** sees Craig Swann and Glen Rhodes playing with blend modes—blending movie clips together for some exciting graphical effects, the likes of which were previously only available in graphics packages like Photoshop.

- **Chapter 3** sees Craig and Glen again take the helm, looking at the all-new filter effects, another set of functionality that has been borrowed from graphics packages. Filters allow you to apply effects such as drop shadows to text or movie clips easily— what previously required a lot of hard work can now be achieved with a few clicks on the Flash interface. And there's much more to discover than that, of course.

- Todd Yard looks at Flash 8 drawing improvements in **Chapter 4**, covering Object Drawing mode, gradient enhancements, and much more.

- In **Chapter 5**, Craig and Glen are back to give you the lowdown on the exciting advances made with video in Flash 8, all thanks to the new On2 VP6 codec. Coverage includes some exciting ActionScript video manipulation, and a great game that makes use of the new video alpha channel!

- Matt returns to the scene in **Chapter 6** to explore Flash 8's `TextField` improvements, including smoother text using Saffron and text anti-aliasing using both the IDE and ActionScript classes.

- In **Chapter 7**, friends of ED's very own Chris Mills demonstrates the new Flash 8 performance-enhancing features, including bitmap caching and the Show Redraw Regions option.

- **Chapter 8** is the domain of Paul Barnes-Hoggett, who dives deep into the exciting new `BitmapData` API. He shows you how all the important methods work before following up with some exciting applied examples.

- **Chapter 9** sees Todd return to present some of his amazing work with the new Flash 8 features—getting creative with filters, masks, and animation. Some of the effects presented here are easier to achieve using Flash 8 than previous versions; some were nearly impossible in previous versions!

- In **Chapter 10**, as you get close to the crescendo of the book, Craig and Glen give you an introduction to the `ExternalInterface` API, which allows your SWFs to easily and effectively communicate with host applications written in Java, C#, etc., for some interesting advanced application development techniques.

- Last but certainly not least, Stephen Downs (aka Tink) presents a gallery of inspirational examples in the **Appendix**, which includes a few features not covered in the rest of the book, such as the `FileReference` object. He also revisits a plethora of examples introduced earlier, with breathtaking results.

Who this book is for

Simple—this book is for anyone with previous experience in Flash who wants to get up to speed with the new features introduced in Flash 8 as soon as possible. We won't waste time looking at timeline basics and tweens, as we think it will be insulting to your intelligence. We know how anxious you must be to further your knowledge with a minimum of time investment and get back to your work, fully harnessing the power of Flash 8. These are busy times for Flash-using professionals.

Do I need to have Flash 8?

In a word, yes. This book won't be much use to you if you haven't upgraded to Flash 8. If you want to buy this book as a guide and check out the new features of Flash 8 before you decide to make that investment, you can always download a 30-day trial version from www.macromedia.com/cfusion/tdrc/index.cfm?product=flashpro. We would also recommend going for Flash 8 Professional rather than Flash 8 Basic. While Basic is still a competent product, you'll be missing out on some of the amazing new features that are only available in Professional—video alpha channel support, the stand-alone video encoder, blend modes, and filters, to name just a few. Go to www.macromedia.com/software/flash/flashpro/productinfo/features for more information about the new features and their availability in the different versions.

Support for this book

All the necessary files for this book can be downloaded from www.friendsofed.com. If you run into a problem with any of the instructions, check the errata page for this book at www.friendsofed.com/books/1590595327, or post a question in the friends of ED forum at www.friendsofed.com/forums, and we'll try to help you as quickly as possible. If you post to the forum, please be as precise as you can about the nature of the problem. We've made our very best efforts to ensure that all of the content presented in this book is error free, but mistakes do occasionally slip through— it's just a sad fact of life. We do apologize in advance for any you find.

1 FLASH 8 OVERVIEW

by Matt Voerman

From little things, big things grow. When John Gay and Robert Tatsumi first developed their computer-illustration tool SmartSketch back in 1993, they never imagined that 12 years and eight versions later their humble application would be the tool of choice of over 1 million rich-media developers worldwide.

SmartSketch went on to be known as FutureSplash, until its parent company (FutureWave) was bought out by Macromedia in 1996. Macromedia then changed FutureSplash's name to Flash. Fast-forward to April 2005, and Adobe Systems announces its intention to purchase Macromedia in a deal valued at $3.4 billion. Flash, and its global ubiquity, was one of the main motivators behind Adobe's acquisition of Macromedia.

Code-named 8Ball during its development phase, Macromedia Flash 8 has now evolved into the industry standard for creating (and delivering) web-based rich-media content and applications.

Flash 8 contains a plethora of new features and functionality, with a large portion of them targeted squarely toward web designers and animators, as well as video and interactive media professionals. That's not to say that rich Internet application developers have been left out in the cold. With its new lightweight, cross-platform runtime and mobile device authoring features, the Flash Platform (www.macromedia.com/platform) is still the ideal choice for the development of rich enterprise and mobile applications.

What's new in both versions of Flash 8

In 2004, Macromedia took the step of splitting Flash into two distinct versions to cater for their wide designer and developer audience. Flash 8 continues this tradition by creating a clearer distinction between the two versions with the release of Flash Basic 8 and Flash Professional 8.

Flash Basic 8 is ideal for web and new-media designers who have elementary requirements with regard to importing and manipulating various types of media. Flash Basic 8 designers still gain access to all of Flash's foundation functionality (including several new workspace enhancements), but not some of the newer power features of the latest release.

For designers and developers looking to utilize the majority of the new feature sets of Flash 8, Flash Professional 8 is the preferred option. Flash Professional 8 offers a substantial number of features not found in its sibling's version, such as graphics effect filters, alpha channel video support, and custom text anti-aliasing.

The following pages outline the new features available in both versions of Flash 8.

Bitmap caching

Just as web pages are cached in your web browser to assist with the speedy retrieval of page data, runtime bitmap caching allows you to specify movie clips or buttons that can be cached within Flash Player (at runtime) to speed up screen redraw. By declaring that these symbols be cached as bitmaps, the Flash Player doesn't have to redraw them constantly from vector data. This provides a significant speed and performance enhancement. Chapter 7 outlines the details of Flash 8's speed improvements.

For example, let's say you've created an animation that uses a complex physics algorithm to sequentially draw a series of cubes on the screen. Rather than having to execute the algorithm on a static cube that has already been rendered to the stage, you can use run-time bitmap caching to effectively freeze these prerendered cubes. This ability to freeze a static portion of a symbol that isn't being updated reduces the number of times Flash Player has to perform a redraw operation. If a region changes onstage, vector data is used to update the bitmap cache accordingly.

Bitmap smoothing

In previous versions of Flash, there was often a marked difference in the quality of bitmap images when viewed in the authoring environment than when viewed in Flash Player. The new bitmap smoothing feature addresses this issue by allowing designers to apply anti-aliasing to imported images so that they render comparably in both environments. Figures 1-1 and 1-2 demonstrate the bitmap smoothing feature.

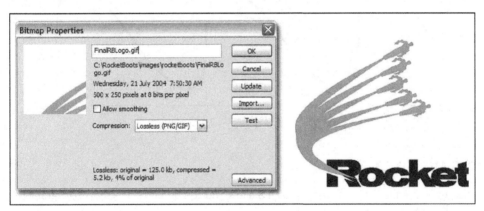

Figure 1-1. A bitmap image with smoothing not enabled

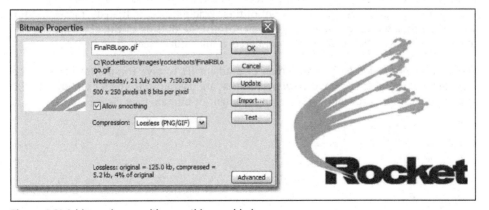

Figure 1-2. A bitmap image with smoothing enabled

New curve algorithm

The new curve algorithm feature allows designers to modify the amount of smoothing applied to curves drawn with the Brush and Pencil tools. Using the new Optimize Curves dialog box (see Figure 1-3), you can increase (or decrease) the number of points used to calculate a curve. The downside of this new feature is that using more points results in larger SWF files. You can choose to apply this feature to a shape you've drawn by selecting Modify ➤ Shape ➤ Optimize.

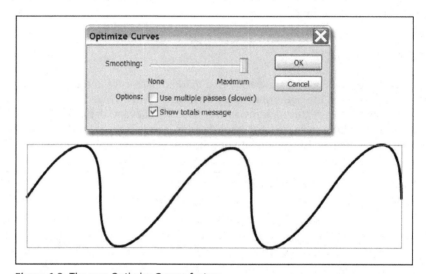

Figure 1-3. The new Optimize Curves feature

Gradient enhancements

The gradient enhancements within Flash 8 allow you to add up to 16 colors to a gradient, as well as use a bitmap as a gradient fill.

A gradient focal point feature has also been added to Flash 8 to give designers greater control over the direction and focal point of their gradients. Using the Fill Transform tool, you simply drag the focal point of the gradient from the outside of the object you're filling to manipulate how the gradient is rendered within your object.

Flash 8 also allows you to lock a bitmap or gradient fill to give the impression that the fill extends over the entire stage. New objects that are painted with the locked gradient fill appear as masks that reveal the underlying gradient or bitmap. (See Figure 1-4.)

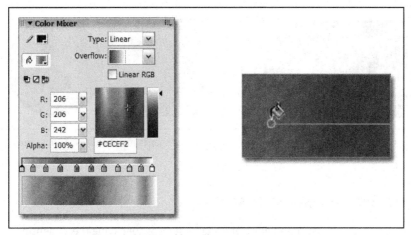

Figure 1-4. Enhanced gradients, including the new gradient focal point

Object Drawing model

In previous versions of Flash, when you used the Brush, Line, Oval, Pencil, or Rectangle tool to draw an intersecting line (or shape) across another line (or shape), the overlapping objects would be divided into segments at the point of intersection. Then, using the Selection tool, you could select, move, or manipulate each segment individually. This mode of illustration subtraction is known as the Merge Drawing model (see Figure 1-5).

Flash 8 introduces the Object Drawing model, which allows designers to create shapes and lines directly on the stage as separate objects. So, unlike the Merge Drawing model, these new shapes and lines don't interfere with other pre-existing shapes on the stage (see Figure 1-6). This allows you to safely overlay objects that are on the same layer without fear of merging or dissecting parts of other objects on the stage. Activating Object Drawing is as simple as clicking the Object Drawing button found among the options for each tool in the Tools panel.

> *Flash 8's drawing enhancements are covered in more detail in Chapter 4 of this book.*

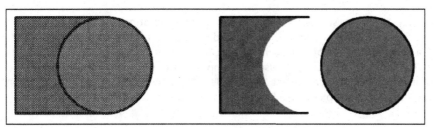

Figure 1-5. The traditional Merge Drawing model

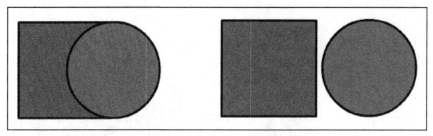

Figure 1-6. The new Object Drawing model, in which shapes maintain their forms when overlaid

Oval and Rectangle tool settings

To assist designers with common illustration tasks such as specifying the dimensions of frequently drawn objects, Macromedia has introduced a new dialog box, Rectangle Settings (see Figure 1-7), that allows designers to specify the width and height of ovals and rectangles, as well as the corner radius of rectangles.

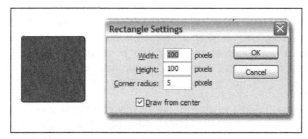

Figure 1-7. The new Oval and Rectangle tool settings

Return of Normal Mode scripting

When Macromedia removed Normal Mode scripting from Flash MX 2004, there was an outcry from the design community. Many designers who weren't familiar with ActionScript syntax relied heavily on Normal Mode scripting to add interactivity to their Flash content.

Thankfully, Macromedia believes in listening to its users, and it has returned Normal Mode scripting to Flash 8, but this time under the moniker of Script Assist.

Essentially, Script Assist is identical to Normal Mode scripting, but with a few enhancements. Script Assist allows you to search and replace text, view script line numbers, and save a script in the Script pane when you click away from the object or frame (this is known as **pinning**). You can also use the Jump menu to go to any script on any object in the current frame. You can select and deselect Script Assist by clicking the Script Assist button on the Actions panel (see Figure 1-8).

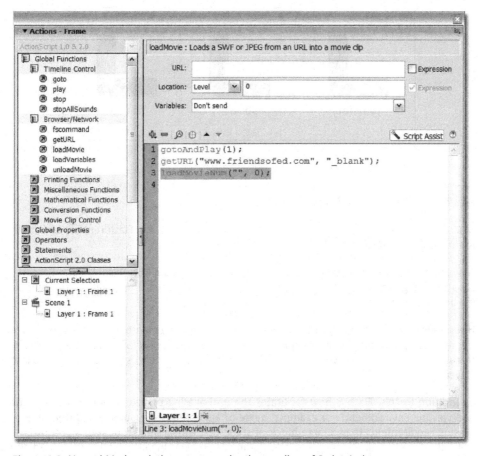

Figure 1-8. Normal Mode scripting returns under the moniker of Script Assist.

Improved strokes

Flash 8 has improved the way in which designers can work with paths and strokes. No longer are you subjected to dealing with only one type of path end (cap); you now have the option of using either rounded or square caps.

Joins (i.e., the points at which two paths meet) have also received a makeover, with designers now having the choice of using either Bevel, Miter, or Round joins (see Figure 1-9). These are chosen from the Join drop-down menu, found sitting proudly on the Property Inspector.

Strokes can now be colored using a gradient, and their maximum size has been increased from 10 to 200 pixels.

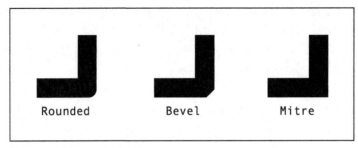

Figure 1-9. New stroke joins

TextField improvements

Macromedia has made some significant improvements to the way Flash renders text (both in the authoring environment and within Flash Player).

New Saffron text-rendering technology has been licensed from Mitsubishi Electric Research Labs and integrated into Flash Player 8. Saffron greatly improves the quality of the rendering of small font sizes.

Historically, text that was rendered within the Flash authoring environment has varied considerably from that rendered within Flash Player. Flash 8's new WYSIWYG text anti-aliasing feature ensures that what you see in the authoring environment is what you get in Flash Player.

In addition to this, Flash 8 now facilitates the anti-aliasing of text based on the specific end-viewing environment. For example, a line of animated text would have different anti-aliasing requirements than a large block of static text with a small font size. If you use the Anti-alias for animation text option, the alignment and kerning information is ignored and the text is rendered as smoothly as possible.

> *TextField improvements are covered in much more detail in Chapter 6 of this book.*

Security enhancements

Security of Flash Player and the SWF format has always been paramount for Macromedia. This view has been further consolidated in Flash 8 with the release of a new Local or Network Security model. The new model helps prevent SWF files from being used maliciously to access local file information and transmit that information over a network.

Contained within the Publish Settings dialog box (accessed via File ➤ Publish Settings), developers now have the option of specifying either a local or a network security model for their SWF files. Files that have been granted network access permission won't be able to access local file data, and vice versa.

SWF file metadata

One of the major bugbears developers have had since Flash's inception was the product's inability to produce to SWFs that could be indexed by search engines such as Google. This was due to their inability to included embedded metadata within the SWF.

Flash 8 has addressed this issue by adding the capability to import metadata into SWFs in XML format. This metadata is based on the RDF (Resource Description Framework; see `www.w3.org/RDF`) and XMP (Extensible Metadata Platform; see `www.adobe.com/products/xmp/in-depth.html`) specifications, and is stored within Flash in a W3C-compliant format.

Video improvements

The encoding and workflow of video within Flash 8 has been substantially enhanced via the introduction of On2's VP6 video codec. This new codec is part of the core Flash Player upgrade, and it substantially improves video playback, quality, and encoding. Unlike Flash Professional, Flash Basic allows only the encoding of embedded video via the Import Video option. Additionally, encoding to VP6 within Flash Basic is restricted to three presets, none of which can be modified.

> *Flash 8 video improvements are covered in greater detail in Chapter 5 of this book.*

Workspace enhancements

This section covers all the workspace enhancements present in Flash 8, added in response to the reams and reams of valuable feedback given to Macromedia by all you Flash developers and designers out there. Talk about a community effort!

Exporting keyboard shortcuts as HTML

Flash keyboard shortcuts can now be exported as HTML files that can be viewed and printed using a standard web browser. This is done by opening the Keyboard Shortcuts dialog box (Edit ➤ Keyboard Shortcut on the PC, or Flash 8 Professional/Basic ➤ Keyboard Shortcuts on the Mac) and then selecting the Export As HTML button at the top-right corner.

Library enhancements

The following list describes the enhancements to the Flash Library:

- **Single library panel**: In previous versions of Flash, separate library panels were required to view the library items of multiple Flash files. Library panel enhancements in Flash 8 now allow users to view the library items of multiple Flash files simultaneously in the same single panel (see Figure 1-10).

- **Library panel state memory**: This was allegedly one of the most requested enhancements for this version of Flash, but strictly speaking, this is more a bug-fix than an enhancement. In previous versions of Flash, when you opened (or closed) library panels in a document you were working on, and then closed that document, you would expect the library panels to be in the same place/order/sequence when you reopened the document again. Alas, this was not the case. This "undocumented feature" has been addressed, and library panels now remember the state they were left in.

- **Drag-and-drop library components**: When working with components in previous versions of Flash, in order to add components to the library of a Flash file, you first had to place them onto the stage and then delete them. Flash 8 has addressed this issue, and you can now place components directly into the library without first having to place them onto the stage.

Figure 1-10.
Multiple document libraries
in a single panel

Macintosh Document Tabs

Mac users can now open and easily navigate through multiple Flash documents within the same window. This is accomplished via the new Macintosh Document Tabs feature, located at the top of the workspace (see Figure 1-11).

Figure 1-11.
The new Document Tabs feature

Object-based Undo and Redo commands

Flash 8 users now have the option of tracking changes from either a document or an object level. Using the object-based Undo/Redo command lets users undo the changes made to an object without having to undo changes to other objects (as is the case with the document-level Undo/Redo option).

Expanded stage pasteboard

The pasteboard is the gray region located around the outside boundary of the stage. Historically, designers have used this area to place graphics or components they want to include within a Flash movie, but don't necessarily want to appear onstage during playback (or want them to appear at a later point in an animation). Flash 8 has increased the size of the pasteboard, giving designers more screen real estate to work with.

XML-to-UI extensibility

Historically, customizing user interfaces (UIs) so they work across the various operating platforms, such as Windows and Macintosh, has been a developer's nightmare. To help ease some of this pain, Netscape and Mozilla teamed up to develop XUL (pronounced "zool")—XML User Interface Language.

Using a subset of XUL and some custom Flash tags, XML-to-UI extensibility allows developers to extend and automate the Flash 8 IDE to perform common and repetitive tasks/actions. These include behaviors, commands (JavaScript API), effects, and tools.

The XML-to-UI engine works with each of these extensibility features to create custom modal dialog boxes if the extension either requires or accepts parameters. These *modal* dialog boxes are required to be dismissed (either accepted or cancelled) by the user before the application can continue.

New Flash Professional 8–specific features

Flash Professional 8 contains the same feature set as Flash Basic 8, plus an abundance of new features that are specific only to the Professional edition.

Blend modes

Blend modes allow designers to apply compositing effects to objects located on the stage (see Figure 1-12). **Compositing** refers to the process of varying (or blending) the color (or transparency) of an object on one layer with an object located on a layer below it.

Designers who are familiar with other graphics applications such as Photoshop will instantly recognize some of the 14 new blend modes available in Flash Professional 8, which include Multiply, Difference, Saturation, and Hue.

> *Blend modes are discussed in more detail in Chapter 2 of this book.*

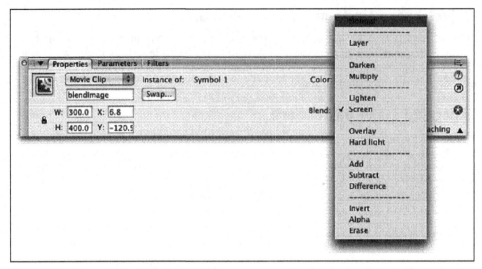

Figure 1-12. The new object blend modes

Custom easing controls

Offering a two-dimensional graph to represent the start and end points of a tweened animation, Flash Professional 8's new custom easing controls give designers the ability to precisely manipulate the speed and complexity of the rate at which their animations ease in or out. This helps create more realistic movement within animations.

The best way to get to grips with this new feature is to experiment! Try creating a simple tween animation such as a bouncing ball, and compare the old familiar easing controls with the new custom easing controls. You can access the new controls by clicking the new Edit button found next to the familiar controls, which opens up the screen shown in Figure 1-13. You'll be impressed.

Graphics effects filters

One of the most heralded new features of Flash Professional 8 allows designers to apply graphics effects filters—such as the Drop Shadow, Blur, Glow, Bevel, Gradient Bevel, and Adjust Color filters—to objects located on the stage.

The filter process is performed by passing the object's image data through a series of algorithms that filter (and subsequently render) the data in a predefined way.

Filters are covered in more detail in Chapter 3 of this book.

Filters can be applied to MovieClips, TextFields, and button symbols, and are rendered in real time by Flash Player. Filter effects can be applied either via the Filters tab located in the Properties panel or programmatically via ActionScript.

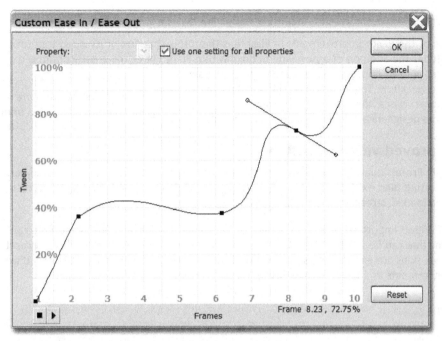

Figure 1-13. The new Custom Ease In/Ease Out controls

More TextField enhancements

Along with the new WYSIWYG Anti-alias for readability **and** Anti-alias for animation options contained within Flash Basic 8, Flash Professional 8 has a Custom anti-alias **feature** that allows you to customize the sharpness and thickness of your text (see Figure 1-14).

The Sharpness option determines the degree of smoothness between the text edges and the background, while the Thickness option allows you to tweak the degree of text edge blend with the background.

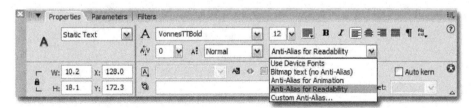

Figure 1-14. The new WYSIWYG text anti-aliasing feature

The anti-aliasing options are also covered in more detail in Chapter 6 of this book.

More video improvements

One of the major improvements in Flash 8 is the turbo-charging of its video tool set. This includes the addition of a new video codec within Flash Player for greatly optimized playback, and an improved video encoder for streamlined workflow. The inclusion of video alpha channel support raises the bar even further, giving rich-media designers a new level of creative freedom.

> *These new video features are covered in greater detail in Chapter 5 of this book.*

Improved video workflow

Flash Professional 8's Video Import Wizard has been improved to assist designers in importing (and exporting) video in a variety of formats (such as embedded, progressively downloaded, streamed, or linked).

The Video Import Wizard also contains an enhanced library of predesigned video player skins that can be used as playback shells for your imported videos when they're exported. These skins are exported as separate SWFs and can be customized to suit your individual requirements as a designer (see Figure 1-15).

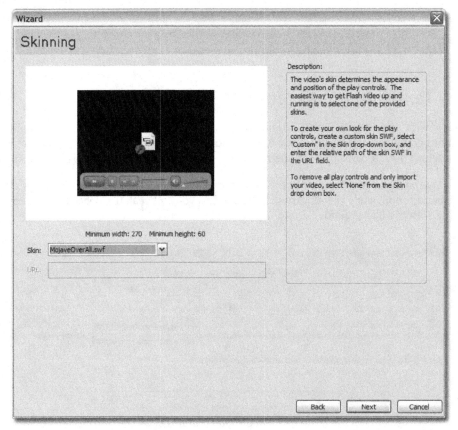

Figure 1-15. Custom skins for FLV controls

Alpha channel support

One of the most eagerly awaited features of Flash Professional 8 is its new video alpha channel support. Using On2's V6 video codec, Flash Player 8 now offers support for run-time alpha channels. This new feature allows designers to import video that has been captured in front of a blue (or green) screen. Using the new alpha channel support, this video can then be overlaid on still images or live video, allowing for multilayered compositing.

For example, imagine you've captured some video footage of a woman, filmed in front of a blue (or green) background (see Figure 1-16). You then import this video into Flash Professional 8 and overlay it on a static (or animated) image of a shopping mall. Using the alpha channel support, you specify the background green color of the first video as an alpha channel. This effectively renders the green background (of the woman video) into a transparent background, which in turn reveals the static image of the shopping mall on the layer below. Voilá—you've just instantly created a special effect of a woman hovering through a shopping mall (see Figure 1-17)!

Figure 1-16.
A video filmed with a green screen alpha channel

Figure 1-17.
The same video, with a shopping mall animation composited into the alpha channel

Embedded cue points

Tucked away within the advanced tabs of the new Video Import Wizard is a feature for adding embedded cue points to your Flash video (FLV). **Cue points** are markers that are inserted into your video and can be used to dynamically trigger events during playback.

Cue points come in two flavors: **navigation** and **event**. Navigation cue points can be used for something as simple as a scene selection menu, whereas event cue points can be used for something more complex, such as triggering an event to display a separate animation or on-screen textual definition of an item being discussed within a movie. See Figure 1-18.

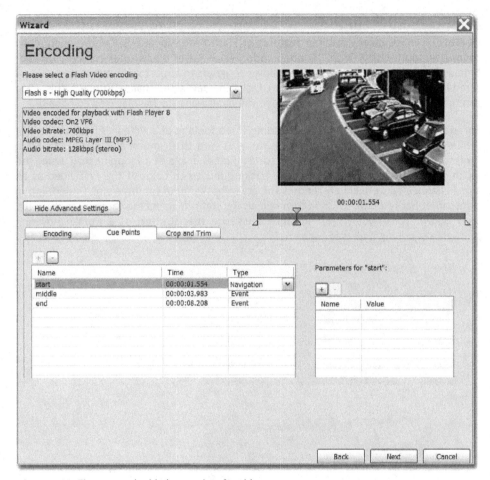

Figure 1-18. The new embedded cue points for video

Stand-alone FLV encoder

The Flash Professional 8 ships with an external FLV video encoder. This stand-alone encoder, which can be installed on a separate, dedicated PC, provides video professionals who prefer to work outside the Flash authoring environment with the facility to encode FLV files.

The stand-alone encoder contains the same features as the authoring environment encoder, but with the added advantage of including batch-processing capabilities that allow developers to encode multiple video files at once.

FLV QuickTime Export plug-in

Now more than ever, leading third-party video applications are supporting the FLV format. This is further highlighted by the release of the FLV QuickTime Export plug-in, which, when used in conjunction with video applications from companies such as Avid, Adobe, and Apple, provides FLV export capabilities from within their software.

Advanced settings for On2 V6 video encoding

To provide designers with increased control over their video encoding, Flash Professional 8 has a new feature that allows the manipulation of advanced settings of On2 V6 video encoding.

Located within the Video Import Wizard, the Advanced Settings encoding option allows you to modify video encoding elements such as frame and data rates, keyframe placement, video and audio quality, and file dimensions.

Flash mobile enhancements

Flash Professional 8 contains a new mobile device emulator to allow developers to test and view their Flash Lite applications (see Figure 1-19). Content created for output via either Flash Lite 1.0 or 1.1 can now be viewed and tested via a series of new device templates that display and interact with content as they would on the selected phone.

The Flash Lite emulator also generates error and warning messages to help debug your applications.

Figure 1-19. Flash Lite mobile emulator

Summary

Despite the fact that Flash 8 may be the last version of Flash to ship under the Macromedia corporate moniker, Macromedia has endeavored to deliver the most (design) feature-rich version of Flash to date. The core of this latest release is (as is the case with most Macromedia products) built around the features and functionality requested by the designers and developers who use the products regularly, and it therefore makes sense that the following chapters are written by some of the world's best Flashers!

2 BLENDING MODES

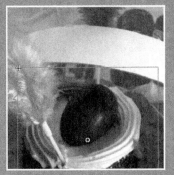

by Glen Rhodes and Craig Swann

Since the introduction of Flash as a tool for interactive development, it has widely been used as a creative tool. From online design, art, and animation, Flash has been adopted by both designers and creative people worldwide, in order to bring their visions to the world via the Internet. However, in the last few iterations of this incredible software package there was a significant movement into the world of application design and **R**ich **I**nternet **A**pplication (**RIA**) development. As Flash grew, it became integrated and geared more towards the developer than the artist, but this is changing dramatically in Macromedia Flash Basic 8 and Macromedia Flash Professional 8!

It is clear, as will be demonstrated throughout this book, that the focus of this version is to return to the roots of visual design, for both designers and developers alike. You'll find many incredible advancements in visual display when you explore Macromedia Flash 8, including Filters, Drawing Improvements, Video, and the new Image API. But first we'll take a look at blending modes. It's time, once again, to get visual with Flash!

So, what, exactly, are blending modes?

Blending modes are used to take pixel color values from two separate movie clips or buttons and then perform a set of calculations to create a new hybrid image. This hybrid image is a result of the calculations made on the two overlapping objects.

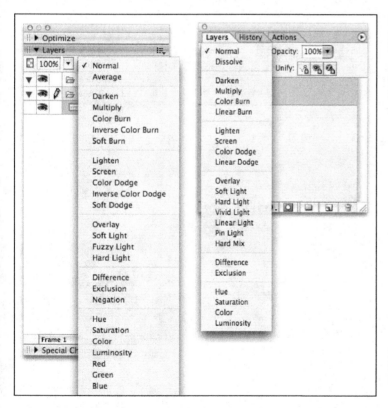

If you are familiar with graphic editing programs like Fireworks or Photoshop, then there is a good chance you have encountered and used blending modes before in your graphic work. Figure 2-1 is an example of the blending modes available in these applications.

Figure 2-1.
Layer palettes in Photoshop and Fireworks

In these applications, blending modes are used between two images which are found on adjacent layers. Flash, however, has a completely different approach to stacking images, Sprites, movie clips, and objects in the authoring environment. Of course, you have the power to control your structure any way you like and you can easily drop a single instance of an image or object on its own independent layer. However, Flash also allows you the opportunity to place multiple objects on a single layer as well as the ability to attach and duplicate movie clips dynamically with code (which relies on levels and not layers). This is an important concept to understand, because with Flash, blending modes are operated on the movie clip, sprite, or button found immediately below the movie clip, button, or sprite to which the blending mode is applied.

> *It is important to understand that blending modes can only be applied to movie clips or buttons. Of course, you can use static or dynamic text, video files, or live camera images, but you need to ensure that these types of content are embedded into a movie clip which you can then use to apply blending modes. Also, only the top or source of the blending needs to be a movie clip. When this movie clip is blended it will impact whatever is below it, whether it is a movie clip, text, or symbol on the stage.*

Blending modes supported by Flash 8

Due to the complexity of some blending modes used in other popular imaging applications, such as "Hue" and "Luminosity" (which requires a color space change and thus extra processing power which does not allow for the real-time display in the Flash environment), Flash 8 uses a subset of the most common and popular blending modes.

Before getting into the nuts and bolts of each of the available blending modes and the visuals that can be produced with them, let's quickly get an overview of the sort of blends that we can access and utilize with Flash 8.

Flash 8-supported blending modes include:

- Normal
- Darken
- Multiply
- Lighten
- Screen
- Overlay
- Hard Light

- Add
- Subtract
- Difference
- Invert
- Layer*
- Alpha*
- Erase*

> ** These last three are special blending modes that you may not be familiar with and that require a different set of circumstances to use. These will be covered independently later in the chapter.*

The other great thing about the addition of blending modes in Flash 8 is the ability to access and control them using both the Flash 8 IDE and the ActionScript API. This allows you to utilize interesting visual effects, either through direct manipulation on the stage via the Property Inspector or through ActionScript by modifying a movie clip's `blendmode` property. We'll take a look at the ActionScript method in a little bit. For now, let's focus on applying blends with the Flash IDE, so that we can see exactly what these blends look like.

Applying blends using the Flash 8 IDE

In Flash 8, the Property Inspector has been overhauled, allowing for a whole range of new visual options and parameters, and including Blends and Filters (which we will cover in the following chapter). You can now directly apply blends to movie clips with the newly added Blend drop-down menu, accessible in the Property Inspector and shown in Figure 2-2.

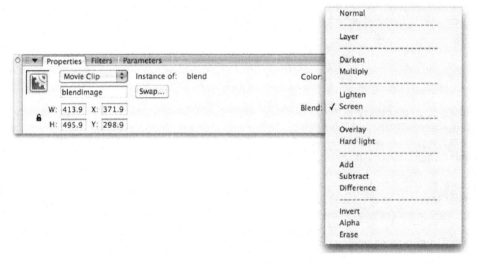

Figure 2-2. Blending modes can now be applied directly to a movie clip using the Property Inspector.

To help you understand the impact that blending modes have on images, we'll go through each of the possible modes and describe how the blending mode works, as well as demonstrate each with an example. If you are going through this book with your computer nearby, you can open the `BlendingModes.fla` and work through these examples in real-time. If, however, you are enjoying a sunny day and sitting in a park learning about the wonders of Flash 8—sigh—lucky you. You can easily follow along without a computer and see what these new blends hold in store for you.

If you are super anxious to see blending modes in action, you can skip down to the Applying blends using ActionScript section. You can also download the file `BlendingModesAS.fla` from `www.friendsofed.com`, which allows you to dynamically swap blending modes to quickly see the new power in visual expression using blending.

But let's start at the beginning. Opening the BlendingModes.fla file will reveal a simple Timeline architecture with two layers. Two image movie clips have already been created and placed on their own layers, so you can immediately start playing with blending. You'll notice that the top layer and subsequent movie clip are labeled sourceMC, and the bottom layer and movie clip are correspondingly labeled destinationMC. Since blending modes are applied in a top-down fashion, it is the pixel information of the sourceMC that will be *applied* to the destinationMC. For those free from the chains of a computer, you can see the sourceMC and destinationMC being used in the examples shown in Figure 2-3.

Figure 2-3. The sourceMC and destinationMC images used for the following blending examples

Normal mode

When accessing the Blend drop-down menu (see Figure 2-2) in the General tab of the Property Inspector the default mode will always be Normal. This mode does not mix or combine pixels of the source image with the destination image in any way. Thus, in normal blending mode, if you test the BlendingModes.fla file, you will generate the image shown in Figure 2-4.

Figure 2-4.
BlendingModes.fla output with sourceMC set to Normal. No pixels are combined.

Darken mode

This mode is used to punch through the darker colors in the source image onto the destination image. When performing the Darken blending mode, pixel colors from both sourceMC and destinationMC are compared and only the values in the sourceMC that are darker than the pixel in the destinationMC are used in the updated image.

If you change the blending mode of sourceMC in the Property Inspector to Darken you will create the new, combined image shown in Figure 2-5.

Figure 2-5.
Affected image when Darken blending mode is applied from sourceMC to destinationMC

You can clearly see that the chocolate egg in the sourceMC is now visible (as is the other chocolate goodness) over the church in the destinationMC. This mode can generate an interesting result when the source image is black and white or contains high contrast. By now, even if you are not familiar with blending operations, you should start to see the new creative possibilities that exist in leveraging assets in Flash to create wonderful new compositions.

Multiply mode

Similar to the Darken mode, Multiply mode does just what you might expect it to do. It multiplies the pixels in both the sourceMC and destinationMC. Unlike Darken, which substitutes and displays the darker of the two overlapping pixels, the Multiply mode multiplies the two color values. The resulting color will always be as dark as either of the two colors from both sourceMC and destinationMC (shown in Figure 2-6).

Figure 2-6.
Affected image when Darken blending mode is applied from sourceMC to destinationMC

This image looks very similar to the last example using Darken; however, you should be able to see that some areas have become darker still as a result of the multiplying effect. Keep in mind that multiplying a color with black will always result in having black in the resulting image, while multiplying with white will always leave the destinationMC colors unchanged.

Lighten mode

As expected, the Lighten mode will do the exact opposite of the Darken mode. Here, the lighter color of both the sourceMC and destinationMC are chosen. If the sourceMC is lighter than the pixel beneath the destinationMC, this color is transferred to the destinationMC in the resulting image—otherwise it is left unchanged (shown in Figure 2-7).

Figure 2-7.
Affected image when Lighten blending mode is applied from sourceMC to destinationMC

In Figure 2-7 you can clearly see that only the lighter elements from the sourceMC (in this case, the icing and feather) are displayed over the building. This type of effect is often used in superimposing text and titles over images and video, in order to create more fluid and soft-edged type treatments.

Screen mode

Just as the Lighten blending mode is the opposite of the Darken blending mode, so is the Screen mode opposite to the previously demonstrated Multiply mode. Thus, screening a color with white will produce white (as black did with Multiply) and screening with black will leave the color unchanged. Technically, the colors from both sourceMC and destinationMC are complemented and then multiplied before the destination image is replaced with the resulting image. A picture tells a thousand words, so take a look at the resulting image, shown in Figure 2-8, when Screen mode is applied to the sourceMC.

Figure 2-8.
An example of an image when Screen blending mode is applied from sourceMC to destinationMC

Although it's similar to the Lighten blending mode, you can see how the images take on more of an ethereal and soft look when this blending mode is applied. This is an excellent blending mode to use when you need to create highlights or apply a lens flare dynamically to an image.

Overlay mode

The Overlay blending mode either multiplies or screens the colors, depending on the destination color you've chosen. The effect is that the sourceMC will be overlayed over the destinationMC while maintaining all of its highlights and shadows. The resulting composition generally will contain more of the destinationMC image, as shown in Figure 2-9.

This effect looks similar to having both images on transparency. The color values will be overlayed and create a blend of colors between source and destination. However, unlike transparency, highlights from the source image will remain in the resulting image.

Figure 2-9.
An example of an image when
Overlay blending mode is applied
from sourceMC to destinationMC

This mode is often used in digital cartooning and coloring. Artists will often take the outlined illustration, apply the coloring on another layer, and use the Overlay mode to create the two separate layers. It is an interesting way to combine pen-sketch illustrations and digital coloring techniques.

Hard Light mode

Hard Light blending mode operates very similarly to the previous Overlay mode, with the exception that color values from sourceMC are used instead of destinationMC for determining whether overlapping pixels are screened or multiplied. For instance, if the sourceMC color is lighter than 0.5, the destinationMC is lightened through screening. If the sourceMC color is darker than 0.5 than the destinationMC is darkened through multiplying. Subsequently using pure black or pure white will maintain color values as shown in Figure 2-10.

Figure 2-10.
Example of image when Hard
Light blending mode is applied
from sourceMC to destinationMC

Just as Overlay generally maintained more of the destinationMC image, you can see from Figure 2-10 that the sourceMC becomes more prevalent when you're using the Hard Light blending mode.

Add mode

The Add blending mode adds the sourceMC to the destinationMC color values to create the resulting image. The general result is a soft, bright image, which can be useful when creating dissolves between images as well as for accomplishing lighting type effects (see Figure 2-11).

Figure 2-11.
Affected image when Add blending mode is applied from sourceMC to destinationMC

Subtract mode

With the Subtract blending mode, the reverse of the Add blending mode is calculated and the sourceMC is subtracted to the destinationMC. This blending mode can be used for shadow-type effects, as shown in Figure 2-12.

Figure 2-12.
Affected image when Subtract blending mode is applied from sourceMC to destinationMC

Difference mode

This unique blending mode often creates surprising results. The Difference blending mode operates by determining the darker of the two colors in sourceMC and destinationMC and then subtracting the darker of the two from the lighter one. This way, white will always invert the destination color and black in the sourceMC will create no change. Generally this effect will create the vibrant saturated colors shown in Figure 2-13.

Figure 2-13.
An example of an image when Difference blending mode is applied from sourceMC to destinationMC

Invert Mode

Invert mode is a common image manipulation in many graphic applications and involves inverting the colors of the destinationMC image. However, you can't apply this blending mode to a single destinationMC. Here, the sourceMC is used merely to represent the area of the destinationMC that you wish to invert. Similar to a mask, only the overlapping areas will invert the destinationMC (see Figure 2-14).

Figure 2-14.
An example of an image when Invert blending mode is applied from sourceMC to destinationMC

It's important to know that this blending mode is affected differently with regards to the alpha of the sourceMC. The strength of the sourceMC determines the level of invert on the destinationMC. Applying an alpha level of 100 to the sourceMC creates a full invert; however if you try adjusting the alpha of the sourceMC to 50% you will notice that the entire image goes grey, and that reducing it further will reduce the invert to 0%, which will create no invert whatsoever. This is a significant difference from the use of the mask and you should be aware of this if you plan to animate MovieClips with alpha while using an invert blending mode.

Now that you are familiar with what will ultimately be the most familiar blending modes available in Flash 8, it's time to take a look at several more blending modes, all of which operate a little differently than the modes covered so far. To access the Alpha, Erase, and Layer blending modes we need to create a Composition clip to properly achieve the blending effects.

Applying Layer, Alpha, and Erase blending modes

With the addition of these new blending modes comes a special set of operations that have been long awaited. For years, creating a soft mask in Flash has been no easy task. Creating mask layers with alpha has never produced the soft-faded mask that you might have expected—instead it has always assumed the shape of the object and not the alpha information it contains. However, many wishes have been fulfilled with the addition of the new Layer blending mode, which finally allows you to create soft-feathered masks using alpha gradients.

Using the Layer blending mode, however, involves a few more steps than the blending modes covered so far, but the payoff is well worth it. So, let's get on with it.

Layer blending mode

As mentioned, using the Layer blending mode requires some additional steps to generate the desired effects, and uses both Alpha and Erase blending modes. These sets of blending modes can work in conjunction, but they require the creation of an additional MovieClip for compositing the final result.

The reason this extra composition movie clip is required is because unlike an imaging application that uses a layer hierarchy, such as Fireworks or Photoshop, Flash uses an entirely different hierarchical structure for managing elements and objects on the stage. For this reason, the use of Alpha and Erase require that an additional parent movie clip is set to the Layer blending mode. Flash treats this movie clip as a new canvas where embedded blending modes are calculated and then parent clips are redrawn using normal mode. This process is necessary because Flash can't modify the opacity of the main or root timeline and both of these blending modes use opacity and thus alpha modifiers.

But enough with the technical explanations—no doubt you are anxious to see how easily we can create soft masks!

Alpha mode: Creating soft masks

The purpose of the Alpha blending mode is to utilize the alpha information of the applied movie clip inside the composition Layer movie clip in displaying the destinationMC image. Any area in the movie clip that is transparent (using alpha values) will cause the same area in the destinationMC to be transparent, allowing the sourceMC image to show through. This may seem confusing at first, so let's take a look at the following example which clearly illustrates the proper structure required to use the Alpha blending mode. When completed, you will have a feathered circle mask displaying the destinationMC through the sourceMC.

Start by opening BlendingModes.fla, which is the file you used in the previous examples. You will be modifying this file yourself, in order to familiarize yourself with the concept of using Layer and Alpha blending modes. If you want to jump right ahead and see the finished product, you can take a look at the AlphaBlending.fla which is the completed file created by following the steps below.

Creating a composition movie clip using the Layer blending mode

The first thing that you need to do is modify the existing sourceMC blend and transform it into a precomposition movie clip.

1. Select sourceMC, which is located on the top layer (you may want to lock the destinationMC layer, as you won't need to modify it in this example) and change the blending mode to Layer using the Blend drop-down menu on the Property Inspector.

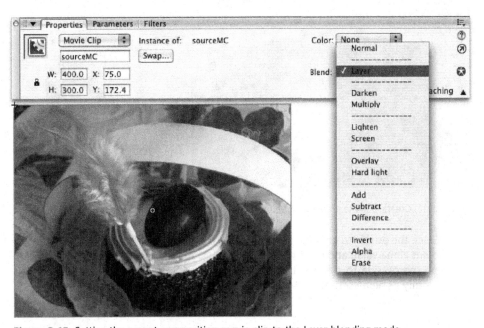

Figure 2-15. Setting the parent composition movie clip to the Layer blending mode

You'll notice that it appears the same as it would in the Normal blending mode. Your sourceMC image is the only thing visible blocking out the destinationMC image that lies beneath it.

2. With sourceMC set to the Layer blending mode, double-click on sourceMC to enter "Edit in Place" mode, and add a new layer on top and label it sourceMask.

Figure 2-16. Creating a layer for Alpha blending mode to be applied to sourceMC Timeline

The sourceMask layer is the layer that will contain the masking movie clip you will create next.

3. With the sourceMask layer selected, draw a circle on the stage. Look for the Color Mixer palette. If you can't find it, open the Color Mixer palette using *SHIFT+F9* and you'll find it at the right side of the screen. With the newly drawn circle selected, use the Color Mixer palette and set the fill to Radial.

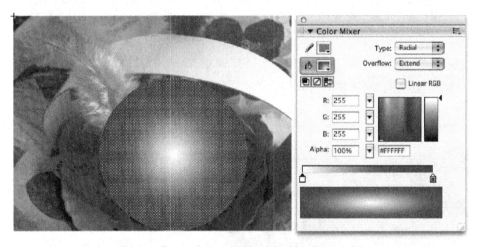

Figure 2-17. Creating Alpha gradient to be used with Alpha blending mode

4. Since the goal is to create a soft feathered mask, you need to adjust the inner gradient alpha value and set it to 0. By doing this, the gradient fades from full opacity on the outside to a transparent center region. Select the left gradient color and modify its alpha setting to 0.

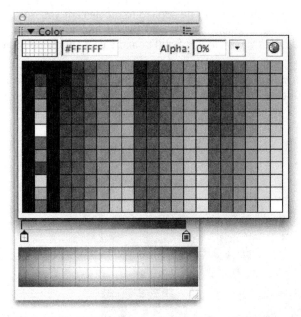

Figure 2-18. Setting inner gradient alpha level to 0% for displaying destinationMC

Your new gradient circle should now have an alpha fade and provide a preview of the final effect.

Figure 2-19.
Preview of feathered mask region inside the sourceMC

However, this preview of the alpha mask is currently over your sourceMC image, which is not what we want. Remember, the object is to mask the destinationMC image through this newly created mask. The next steps are crucial for achieving this.

5. Since blending modes can only be applied to movie clips you must now select your newly created alpha gradient circle and turn it into a movie clip. Once selected choose Modify ➤ Convert to Symbol (F8) and give it the name sourceMask.

6. To utilize this alpha information, you must now select your newly created sourceMask movie clip and change its blending mode to Alpha in the Property Inspector. Once you have done this, you'll notice that sourceMask is now invisible on the stage, with only its bounding box showing.

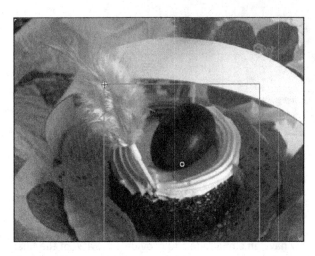

Figure 2-20.
How the sourceMask appears inside sourceMC when set to Alpha blending mode

Fear not! Although the destinationMC clip appears invisible inside of the sourceMC movie clip, if you return back to the main Timeline by selecting the Scene1 link, you'll see that the same destinationMC clip is now being displayed through the alpha gradient clip that you created.

Figure 2-21.
Final completed Alpha blend effect when previewed on main Timeline

It's as easy at that! This is just the beginning of the interesting and creative things that can be done with this fabulous new blending mode. For instance, with this file, try creating different sourceMask clips containing different shapes, sizes, and alpha gradients. Experiment! Explore!

Another beautiful aspect of utilizing the Alpha blending mode is that you can animate them as well. For instance, in your sourceMC Timeline, try animating your newly created sourceMask clip. Try scaling or moving it and note how the alpha information is transferred to the destinationMC when you test your movie. With luck, this will be the beginning of a whole new world of creative possibilities for your Flash projects.

Erase mode

With the Erase blending mode, you use the same process that you used with the Alpha mode—which, as you'll remember, requires the creation of a parent composition MovieClip set to a Layer blending mode.

The generated effect, however, is the opposite of what was seen with the Alpha blending mode. When you use Erase, the opaque areas of the alpha gradient remove areas of the destinationMC. Areas with low alpha will allow the destinationMC to be seen through the sourceMC. You can see this opposite effect in the following image.

Figure 2-22.
Final completed Erase blend effect when previewed on main Timeline

Although the blending modes demonstrated so far in this chapter have been done manually in the Flash IDE, blending modes are also available as a MovieClip property and can be accessed via ActionScript—and it couldn't be easier!

Applying blends using ActionScript

In Flash 8, the ability to access blending modes has been extended beyond the IDE and is now accessible through ActionScript. You can now modify a movie clip's blending mode by altering the new blendMode property. Macromedia defines this new property by saying that `blendMode` is "The blending mode for this movie clip. The blending mode affects the appearance of the movie clip when it is in a layer above another object on-screen."

1. Reopen the `BlendingModes.fla`, if you don't still have it open.

2. Create a new layer and label it Actions

3. On frame 1, create a frame action with the following code:

```
sourceMC.blendMode = "darken";
```

If you test this movie now, you will see that this code will override whatever existing blending mode was set manually in the Property Inspector. The blendMode property accepts both strings and numbers (1–14) as values, so if you are using a string, ensure that you have it within quotations. For instance for the Multiply blend you can either use:

```
sourceMC.blendMode = "multiply";
sourceMC.blendMode = 3;
```

If you'd like to be able to see how all the blending modes look quickly, open up the `BlendingModesAS.fla` file. This file is the same as `BlendingModes.fla` with the addition of a `ComboBox` component which dynamically will change the blending mode of the sourceMC movie clip when a new selection is made from the `ComboBox`.

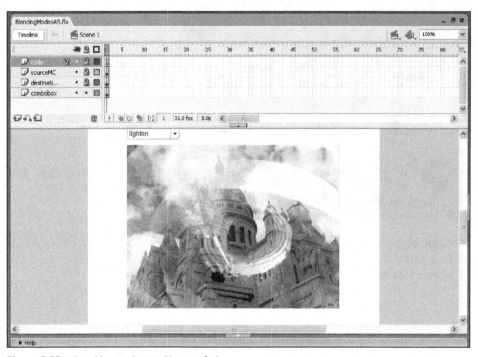

Figure 2-23. `BlendingModeAS.fla`, ready to go.

The additional code used to perform this is also very simple as you can see:

```
modeChangeListener = new Object(); // Create the listener object
// define the 'change' event
modeChangeListener.change = function(evtObj)
{
    // Set the blendMode to the value of the label
    //of the selected item in the blend_cb comboBox
    sourceMC.blendMode = evtObj.target.selectedItem.label;
}
// Assign the change event to blend_cb
blend_cb.addEventListener("change", modeChangeListener);
```

The ComboBox component is merely passing on the label which is a string to the blendMode property in the function called when a selection is made in the ComboBox.

Summary

And so concludes today's lesson on the incredible and amazing blending modes now supported in Flash 8. However, this is just the tip of the iceberg, with regards to the new visual enhancements available within Flash 8, as you'll soon see. In the next chapter you will discover the wonderful new world of Flash filters.

Table 2-1. The summary of the different blending modes

blendMode	Result of sourcePixel and destPixel
Normal	`sourcePixel`

Darken	`if (sourcePixel < destPixel)`
	`    sourcePixel`
	`else`
	`   destPixel`

Multiply	`sourcePixel x destPixel`

Lighten	`if (sourcePixel > destPixel)`
	`    sourcePixel`
	`else`
	`   destPixel`

Screen	`1 - (1-sourcePixel) x (1-destPixel)`

Overlay	`if (sourcePixel < 0.5)`
	`    Multiply sourcePixel with destPixel`
	`Else`
	`    Screen sourcePixel with destPixel`

Continued

37

Table 2-1. The summary of the different blending modes *(continued)*

blendMode	Result of sourcePixel and destPixel

Hard Light	```if (destPixel < 0.5)```
	``` Multiply sourcePixel with destPixel```
	```Else```
	``` Screen sourcePixel with destPixel```

Add	```sourcePixel + destPixel```
Subtract	```(sourcePixel + destPixel) - 1```
Difference	```| sourcePixel - destPixel |```
Invert	```1 - destPixel```

Note that, in all cases, the math is performed on the red, green, and blue component values separately, to create final pixel red, green, and blue components. So, Multiply actually does the following:

```
    newRed = sourceRed x destRed
    newGreen = sourceGreen x destGreen
    newBlue = sourceBlue x destBlue
final pixel is newRed, newGreen, newBlue
```

Though values are represented as a number from 0 to 255 digitally, they are actually treated as if they are in the range of 0 to 1 when the blend operations take place. This way, multiplying 128×128, which would normally be 16,384, would actually be treated as 0.5×0.5, which would result in 0.25, and then digitally that would be 64.

In some cases, for example with Add and Subtract, where a resulting value is greater than 1 (255) or less than 0, then the value is simply clamped and set to 255 or 0.

3 FILTERS

by Glenn Rhodes and Craig Swann

As you have seen in the previous chapter there are plenty of new creative ways to work with visual assets in Flash 8. However, blending modes is just the beginning! As you will see in this chapter, there are some very powerful new possibilities to be discovered through the use of the new Filters that are available.

More than likely, if you have ever worked with image assets in Fireworks or Photoshop you are familiar with filters. In these imaging applications, filters such as Blur, Glow and Bevel are common (if not overused). These same filters, as well as many more, can now be harnessed directly inside of Flash 8. Although at times it may be better to treat images and text in an imaging application first, in order to save on processing power, the ability to use filters inside of the Flash environment is an indispensable way to create quick, easy, and often powerful visual effects.

As with the previously covered blending modes, filters can be accessed and manipulated through both the Flash 8 IDE as well as directly through ActionScript. The big difference between filters and blends is that filters can be animated! This opens up even more options for both the designer and developer using Flash. Let's first take a look at the filters that are now available in Flash 8.

Remember that you can download all the code examples featured in this chapter from http://www.friendsofed.com.

Filters available in Flash IDE

The following filters are available in Flash IDE:

- **Drop Shadow:** Places a black shadow beneath an object giving it the appearance of "floating" above the stage.
- **Blur:** Defocuses an object, giving it the appearance of looking through smudged glass, or a poorly focused lens.
- **Glow:** Creates a slight glowing outline around an object, following the contours and curves of the object perfectly.
- **Bevel:** Creates a shadow and a highlight on opposite edges of an object, giving the illusion that it is 3D. Bevel is very common, and most user interface buttons in regular applications have a Bevel filter.
- **Gradient Glow:** Similar to the Glow filter, except the glow itself may follow a gradient of color from the inner to the outer edge.
- **Gradient Bevel:** Similar to the Bevel filter, except you can specify a gradient color on the shadow and highlights of the beveled edges.
- **Adjust Color:** Allows you to adjust the brightness, hue, and saturation of an object.

ActionScript filters

The following filters are available in Actionscript:

- **Color Matrix:** Allows you to perform several color tricks, including all those accessible in the previously mentioned Adjust Color filter, as well as effects similar to the `setTransform` method of the `Color` object.
- **Displacement Map:** Allows you to move pixels by a certain amount, both horizontally and vertically, and independent of each other. Creates popular effects like warp, bend, water ripples, and more.
- **Convolution:** A filter that allows you to perform various effects by performing adjustments to pixels, based on the color of their adjacent pixels.

As you can see, there is a lot to play with. You will also notice that the previous list is broken down to include filters specific to ActionScript. Convolution, Color Matrix and Displacement Map are very powerful and complex filters, which are available only through the use of ActionScript. Keep in mind though, that while all filters can be accessed directly through ActionScript, the Convolution, Color Matrix, and Displacement Map filters can *only* be used in conjunction with ActionScript. Don't fret—as complex as this may sound, the examples later in this chapter will give you the knowledge necessary to begin using these filters—even if you are not a hardcore ActionScript developer.

This chapter will cover both methods of applying filters, but let's start with the most direct way of adding filters to your Flash projects—through the Flash 8 IDE.

Applying filters using the Flash 8 IDE

Unlike blending modes there is a little more flexibility when using filters. You can apply a filter to either a movie clip, button, or TextField (whether static or dynamic). Filters are available in the Flash Authoring Environment in the Property Inspector. A new tab has been added to this Inspector called Filters, as seen in Figure 3-1, which is where you will find the filters that are accessible through the IDE. Let's dive right in and start exploring how easy it is to apply Filters.

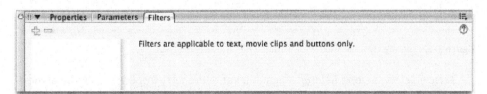

Figure 3-1. New Filters tab in the Property Inspector for applying filters to text, movie clips, and buttons

Drop Shadow

Creating soft drop shadows in previous versions of Flash was not always possible. Generally you could create alpha gradients and use the Soften Fill Edges (Modify ➤ Shape ➤ Soften Fill Edges...) to create a simulated effect, or create them using Photoshop, then import them. However, this was often not very useful because you could never use this with dynamic movie clips or Dynamic Text, which might change shape or size. The ability to use the now-available **Drop Shadow** filter makes it a snap to instantly add a realistic drop shadow to any existing object on stage, whether it's text, movie clip or button. If you're interested, take a look at http://www.flashkit.com/tutorials/Text_Effects/DropShad-Loudboy-913/index.php to see how you *used* to have to add drop shadows in Flash. It wasn't pretty, and it wasn't fun.

Let's start off by adding a drop shadow to dynamic text.

Adding a drop shadow to dynamic text

For this example, you will add a Drop Shadow to some Dynamic Text. As you'll soon see, there's nothing to it!

With a new Document open complete the following steps:

1. Select the Text tool, click it on stage and type "Flash 8 Rocks!" (OK, OK, feel free to type in whatever you like, if you feel so inclined, but Flash 8 does rock.)

2. With the text selected, open the Property Inspector, and make sure to select Dynamic Text for the type of text and give it the instance name dynamicText. You'll need this a little later, and it should look something like the following:

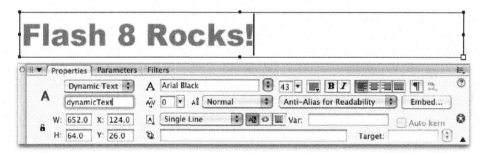

Figure 3-2. Creating Dynamic Text with instance name `dynamicText`

3. Now Select the text field on stage and in the Property Inspector click the all-new-for-Flash-8 Filters tab.

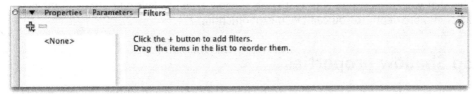

Figure 3-3. New Filters tab in the Property Inspector for adding filters.

You will notice there is an option to add new filters using the Add Filter (+ button).

4. Click the Add Filter (+ button) in the Filters tab and then, from the drop-down menu, select the Drop Shadow option.

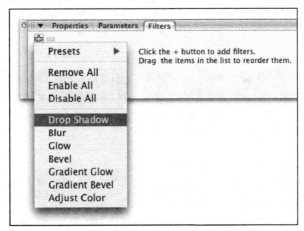

Figure 3-4. New filters available through the Filters tab in the Property Inspector.

You will notice as soon as you do this that the text will instantly take on some default properties and that you are provided with the full Drop Shadow properties, available to be modified to your every whim. Our dynamic text now looks like the image below with the properties visible in the Property Inspector.

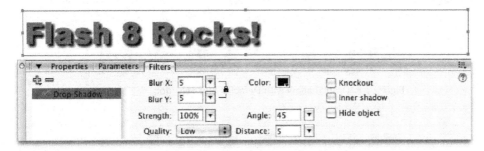

Figure 3-5. Adding a Drop Shadow through the Filters tab in the Property Inspector.

Now that you have created your first Drop Shadow example, let's take a look at the properties in more depth so you can begin experimenting.

Drop Shadow properties

The following modifiable properties exist within the Drop Shadow filter.

Blur X and Blur Y

`Blur X` and `Blur Y` affect the amount of the blur that the drop shadow receives. By default, these are set to be constrained using the small lock icon next to the property input fields. Quite often this generates the most realistic drop shadow effect, however you can also unlock the constraints by clicking the lock icon and set individual values (0-100) for both the X and Y Blur values. Don't forget that this property, like all others, can be animated on the Timeline to create lighting effects (see Figures 3-6 and 3-7).

Figure 3-6. Drop Shadow with Default Blur values of Blur X = 5 and Blur Y = 5.

Figure 3-7. Drop Shadow with Modified Blur values of Blur X = 5 and Blur Y = 20

Color

The `Color` property works just as the other Color palette options in the Flash environment do. This property sets the color to be used for the drop shadow. You'll also notice that this `Color` property includes an alpha value, which can be used to create softer drop shadows when the alpha value approaches 0. You can see some examples in Figures 3-8 and 3-9.

Figure 3-8. Drop Shadow with Default Color Selection

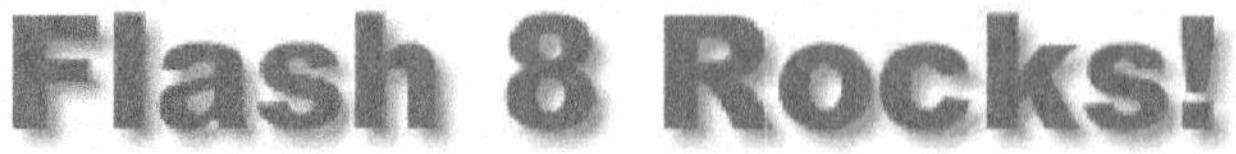

Flash 8 Rocks!

Figure 3-9. Drop Shadow with Color settings modified to a hex value of #FF9999 and an alpha value of 50%

Strength

The Strength property represents the filter strength being used, and creates effects very similar to those created when you change the alpha value in the Color property. This property will accept values between 0-1000%. Generally values between 0-100% will suffice, but there may be times when you can generate interesting results by using the upper regions of the property. Like all new things in Flash 8, it's best if you experiment and see how these different properties work for you in your own Flash projects, as shown in Figures 3-10 and 3-11.

Figure 3-10. Drop Shadow with Default Settings of Strength = 100%

Figure 3-11. Drop Shadow with Modified Settings of Strength = 1000%

Angle

The Angle property does just what you think it does, which is set the angle (0-360) that the light source is coming from. By modifying the Angle, you can adjust the direction and ultimate position of the drop shadow which is generated. As this property can also be animated on the timeline (or in ActionScript as you will see later) you can use this to create the illusion of a moving light source. See Figures 3-12 and 3-13 for more details.

Figure 3-12. Drop Shadow with Default Angle setting of 45

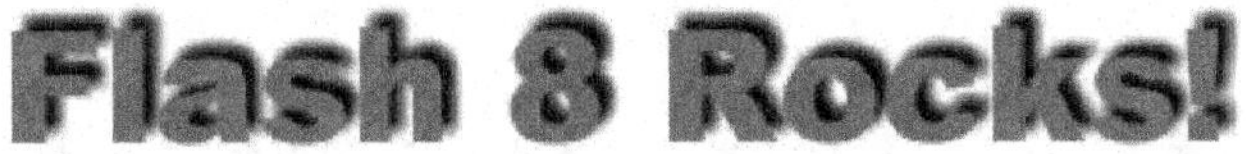

Figure 3-13. Drop Shadow with Modified Angle setting of 315

Distance

The Distance property works in conjunction with the Angle property. Based on the angle of the light source used to create the drop shadow, the Distance value (-32 – +32) sets how far the drop shadow should be placed from the object being applied with it. Negative values will move the drop shadow closer to the calculated light source and positive values will move the drop shadow further away. As it's another property that can be animated, Distance, in conjunction with other changing property values, can greatly enhance the realistic illusion of light sources moving. You'll see what we mean in Figures 3-14 and 3-15.

Figure 3-14. Drop Shadow with default Distance setting of 5

Figure 3-15. Drop Shadow with default Distance setting of 15

Quality

Quality is used to apply the quality level of the drop shadow. If you try toggling this value, you will see that there are subtle differences in the quality of the visual representation. Be aware, however, that using a Quality setting of High will require more processing power to apply. When animating or using motion on objects that have filters applied to them, it is best to keep the Quality setting to Low. You'll find that at this setting, you can still create quality effects.

Knockout

Knockout is a property that can be toggled on and off and is used to knock out the source image. Take a look at Figures 3-16 and 3-17 to see the difference that is made when this property is turned on and off.

Figure 3-16. Drop Shadow with Knockout deselected

Figure 3-17. Drop Shadow with Knockout selected

Inner Shadow

The Inner Shadow property is used to create a cutout of the source object being applied and then place the drop shadow inside of the object. You can clearly see the effect in Figures 3-18 and 3-19.

Flash 8 Rocks!

Figure 3-18. Drop Shadow with Inner Shadow deselected

Flash 8 Rocks!

Figure 3-19. Drop Shadow with Inner Shadow selected

Hide Object

The final available property for Drop Shadow is Hide Object, which is used to completely keep the original object from being rendered to screen and, instead, only shows the final Drop Shadow filter effect. You'll see some examples in Figures 3-20 and 3-21.

Flash 8 Rocks!

Figure 3-20. Drop Shadow with original settings

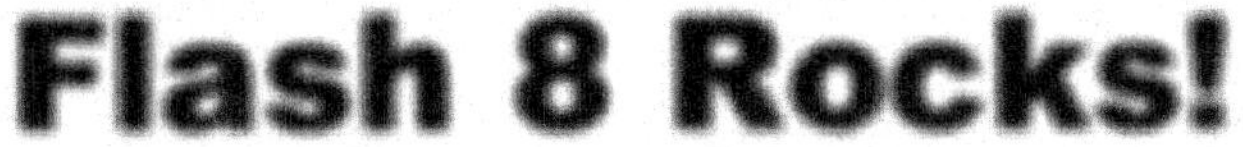

Flash 8 Rocks!

Figure 3-21. Drop Shadow with Hide Object selected

As you can see, there is a vast range of visual options for you to choose from when using the Drop Shadow filter. Spend some time experimenting with all the properties and finding combinations that you like. Before we move on to the Blur filter though, as promised, let's prove that all of these funky new effects can be applied to text dynamically, using ActionScript.

Modifying the Dynamic Text

Create a button on the stage, above your `dynamicText` field from earlier, and give it an instance name my_btn.

Create a new layer in the timeline, click on the first frame, and then enter the following code:

```
// Create an array of 3 phrases
var words:Array = ["Flash 8 Rocks!","Who would have thought!",
                                "OMG Dynamic Drop Shadows"];
// Attach code to the button
my_btn.onPress=function(){
    // Choose a random number from 0 to the number of elements
    // in the array.
    var randomWord:Number = Math.floor(Math.random()*words.length);
    // Fill the text field with the word that corresponds to
    // the randomWord number
    dynamicText.text = words[randomWord];
}
```

Test the movie with *CTRL/CMD+ENTER* and click the button.

The small snippet of code that was added creates an array of different phrases which are dynamically placed in the dynamic text instance. As you can see when you test this movie, all of the applied Drop Shadow effects remain and only the text changes. This is a complete godsend if you work with dynamic content. This means that all the content you create can have the same visual impact that your static elements have. Hallelujah!

Drop shadows are only the beginning of what is available when we look under the hood of filters. Let's next take a closer look at the Blur filter.

Blur filter

Blur is a common filter in imaging applications and is a powerful new tool for creating interactive environments in Flash. Blurs can be used to generate a whole slew of interesting effects. You can use blurs to demonstrate motion and speed, which is particularly useful when creating games. You can also use blur to create much more realistic 3D environments, where objects further away are slightly blurred to create a stronger sense of depth of view. Of course, it can also be used for straight text and advanced shadow effects in your Flash layouts.

The Blur filter blurs the edges of a movie clip using just two properties: `Blur X` and `Blur Y`. As you can guess, these two properties will affect the amount of blur on both the X (horizontal) and Y (vertical) axis.

To see this filter in action you can continue using the Drop Shadow example with Dynamic text or try using this filter with an image. Remember you must use a button, text field, or movie clip to apply a filter. You can see some examples in Figures 3-22 and 3-23.

Applying Blur to a Movie Clip

Figure 3-22. Default Imported Image with no Blur filter

Figure 3-23. Default Imported Image bounding area shown with Blur X and Blur Y value of 50

The basis for this example is an image that has been imported to the stage and then converted to a movie clip, as in Figure 3-22, by first selecting the imported image and then pressing *F8* to convert it to a symbol. A Blur filter is then applied to the movie clip, like Figure 3-23. The movie clip name and instance name do not matter.

Take note that in the previous image the blur goes beyond the actual dimensions of the original movie clip size (with no blur applied). It is also important to note, specifically when using ActionScript calculations, that although the rendered area of the movie clip has expanded when the Blur filter is applied, the registration points (the white dot) and the bounding box (the blue box) of the movie clip remain unchanged. This is something that needs to be taken into account if you're using dynamic ActionScript placement with movie clips that have been affected by a filter that expands outside of the original dimensions.

Spend some time experimenting with the blur values, but also try using them with Motion Tween animations. Like most filters, Blur is a great way to add interesting mouse interaction to buttons and clips in your interfaces. The true power from filters shines through when they're intelligently utilized in your animations, giving your interactive objects much more life and interest for the user.

The cool thing is, this effect will act on any type of movie clip. So, whether you create a vector animation or a cartoon character, it too will be fully blurred.

Glow filter

Next in our line-up of filters is the **Glow** filter. This filter acts very similar to the Drop Shadow filter. As you can see in Figure 3-24, the properties available are nearly identical, with the exception of the absence of the `Angle` and `Distance` property found in Drop Shadow.

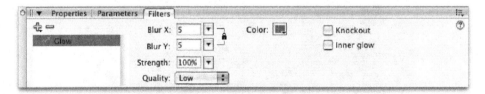

Figure 3-24. Glow filter parameters in Filters tab

The Glow filter acts equally on all sides of a movie clip instance. There is no one direction and thus the effect appears evenly around (or inside when Inner Glow is applied) the object.

Several examples of Glow settings are illustrated in Figure 3-25, in order to show the differences when using the default Glow setting as well as applying Knockout and Inner glow to a movie clip.

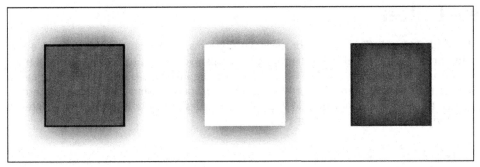

Figure 3-25. Three examples of applied Glow filters: Regular, Knockout, & Inner. Examples of the Glow filter with a (1) Blue blur with X and Y values of 50, (2) the same Glow settings with Knockout selected, and finally (3) with Inner Glow selected.

The new Glow filter is an excellent option for creating rollover states. By modifying the `blurX` and `blurY` values over timeline keyframes, you can create realistic and incredibly small file-sized animations of glowing objects that have a sense of life when the user interacts with them. Like all filters that use color, you can also control this property through animation.

To affect the intensity of the Glow, you can either adjust the `Strength` property or, in the Color Picker, modify the alpha level to create either stronger or more subtle glows.

Here's a simple yet cool example. Let's create a button that uses a glow in its rollover state.

1. Create a new movie.
2. On the stage, draw a white box with a black border. The box should be about 80 × 25.
3. Select the entire box (border and all), and press *F8* to convert it to a movie clip.
4. Give it the name `buttonFace`, and set the type to movie clip. Click OK.
5. With the new movie clip selected, press *F8* again, and this time set its type to Button, and name it `theButton`.
6. Double-click the button on the stage in order to edit it.
7. Press *F6* twice.
8. Click on the Over frame in the timeline.
9. Select the `buttonFace` movie clip and apply a default glow filter to it.
10. Return to the main timeline, and make a few copies of the button.
11. Test the movie with *CTRL/CMD+ENTER*

Amazing isn't it? Roll over the button and watch the glow appear, roll off and the glow disappears.

Figure 3-26.
Buttons with the Glow filter applied to their rollover state

Bevel filter

If you have ever built interfaces or navigation systems, than more than likely you've run into our friend the **Bevel** before. Although perhaps overused in today's world of interactivity, there is no escaping it. The Bevel is used on the interface elements of almost every application that is created. There are a number of properties which can be used in setting Bevels, as illustrated by taking a look at the Properties available when the Bevel filter is selected on a movie clip, in Figure 3-27.

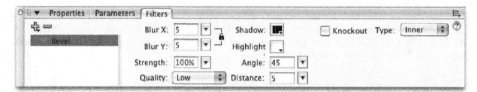

Figure 3-27. Properties available when the Bevel filter is used on a movie clip, button, or text field.

The Bevel filter creates an illusion of 3D depth by adding a shadow and highlight to the object. This subtle addition of tones creates a sense of depth. Inner Bevel gives an object the appearance of being cut-out or depressed, whereas the Out Bevel gives the object a sense of protrusion, as if it was standing out above its surroundings. The Bevel is often used on buttons, in order to give them a subtle 3D look. When Outer Bevel is applied, the button appears to be just waiting to be pressed, because of its illusion of being something protruding from the screen. When clicked, applying an Inner Bevel gives the button the impression it has been pressed. Take a look at the four examples in Figure 3-28 using No Bevel, Inner Bevel, Outer Bevel, and a combination of both.

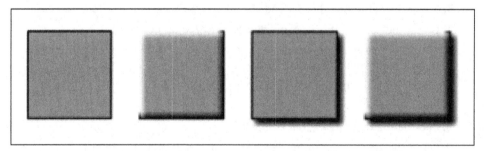

Figure 3-28. Default flat movie clip then modified using Inner, Outer, and Full Bevels.

The `Shadow` and `Highlight` properties allow you to customize the colors you use to generate the Bevel effect. Using `Black` and `White` are the default, as they best give the illusion of a subtle 3D effect, however like all new options available in Flash 8, it's best if you spend some time experimenting with different shapes, objects, and colors to see what kind of interesting examples you can come up with on your own.

Let's spend a few minutes creating an example application with buttons that are beveled at runtime. The finished example for this can be found in the file bevelButtons.fla. When you want a button that uses a Bevel for its 3D look, what you really want is a button that appears to protrude on the Over frame, and to be depressed on the Down frame. You simply need a movie clip on each frame of the button, with different bevel filter settings applied to it. Here's how to do it:

1. Start a new default Flash file of 550 × 400

2. Create a solid 90 × 90 square box with no border on the stage, in your favorite color. We chose #999999 because we love the number 9.

3. With the new box selected, press *F8* to convert to symbol. Make sure the type is set to Movie clip, and name it Square. Click OK.

4. With the newly created movie clip selected, press *F8* again and this time choose type Button, and name it squareButton.

5. From the stage, double-click on the newly created button, and you'll be editing frame 1 (the Up frame) of the button.

6. Select the Square movie clip, and flip to the Filters tab in the properties panel (opened with *CTRL+F3*).

7. Click on the + in the filters list, and choose Bevel from the menu that appears.

8. In the Bevel properties, set the Blur X and Blur Y to 1, and the distance to 1. Everything else should remain the same.

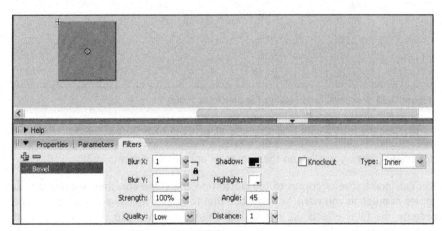

Figure 3-29. The Bevel filter settings for the Up frame

9. Press *F5* twice to stretch this frame onto the Over frame and the Down frame.

10. Click on the Down frame, and press *F6* to insert a keyframe.

11. Select the `Square` movie clip again, and go to the Filters tab in the Properties panel.

12. Change the distance to –1.

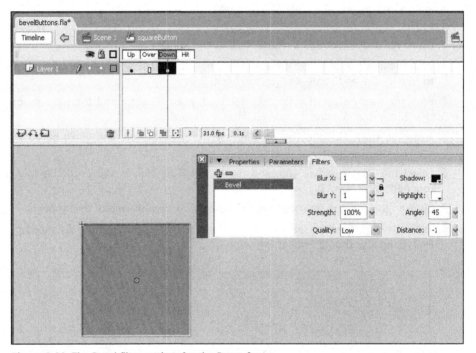

Figure 3-30. The Bevel filter settings for the Down frame

13. Test the movie with *CTRL/CMD+ENTER*, or Control ➤ Test Movie.

Notice that when you click on the button, it appears to depress in 3D.

You can make several copies of the button on the stage and then scale and resize those copies as much as you want. You'll notice that the bevel will always be nicely 1 pixel in size, because the filter effects are not scaled when the movie clip containing them is scaled. Look at Figure 3-31 to see how we've positioned and scaled several instances of the same button.

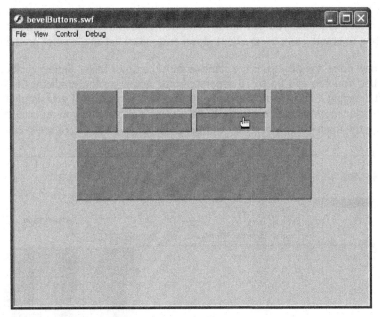

Figure 3-31. Several instances of the Bevel button

Gradient Glow Filter

The **Gradient Glow** filter is like a cross between the Glow and Drop Shadow filters previously covered, as you can see by taking a look at its properties (Figure 3-32).

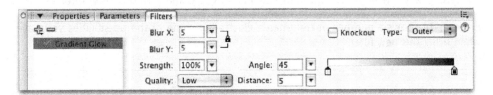

Figure 3-32. The Gradient Glow filter properties

With this filter, unlike the previous Glow filter, there is the addition of the Angle and Distance properties, which were found in the Drop Shadow filter. This allows for offsetting the glow as could be done with Drop Shadow. However, the significant new property in this filter, as the name implies, is the inclusion of a color gradient mixer.

Similar to the gradient mixer located in the Color Mixer, when this type of fill is set to Linear or Radial gradient, you can modify and add gradient nodes as well as change the color setting to create complex gradient glows, instead of flat single color gradients.

To add a new node, the process is the same as with the Color Mixer. Simply click below the gradient bar. You can add up to 15 separate color nodes on the gradient. Clicking on a node and dragging it away from the gradient mixer will remove it. If you simply click on a node, the color mixer will appear and offer the same options that you are accustomed to when using the main Color Mixer. You can see an example of this in Figure 3-33.

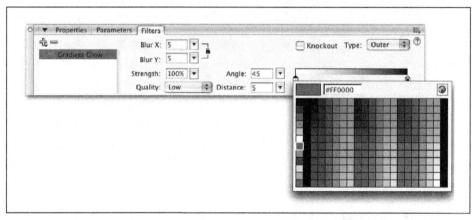

Figure 3-33. Adjusting gradient colors using the pop-up Color mixer in the Filter properties

As with the Glow filter, the Gradient Glow will allow you to select Knockout to remove the original selected object and view only the filtered effect. You also have options to select the Type of Glow from Inner, Outer, or Full, just as you could with the Bevel filter.

Figure 3-34 shows a number of treatments illustrating some of the possibilities you have when using this new filter.

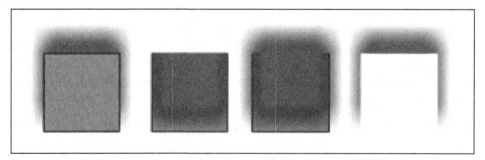

Figure 3-34. Examples of Gradient Glow: (1) Set to Type:Outer, (2) Set to Type:Inner, (3) Set to Type:Full, (4) Set to Type:Outer with Knockout selected

Gradient Bevel filter

This filter is also a combination of previous filters including the standard Bevel filter and the Gradient Glow filter. The significant difference in creating gradients with this filter is that by default there is always a transparent node set in the middle of the gradient, which can't be moved. The reason for this is because, if you recall, the Bevel filter uses a Highlight and Shadow color value.

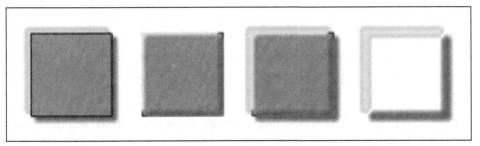

Figure 3-35. Examples of Bevel Gradient Glow from left to right: (1) Set to Type:Outer, (2) Set to Type:Inner, (3) Set to Type:Full, (4) Set to Type:Outer with Knockout selected

Notice that, in Figure 3-35, unlike the single gradient effect using the Gradient Glow Filter, this filter will generate gradients that contain distinct color regions for the Highlight and Shadow options. It may get confusing at times to decide which filter to use, but if you take some time to explore all of the options available for modifying and customizing the filters through their properties, you will soon have a good grasp of how to best utilize filters to get the desired effect.

Adjust Color filter

This final filter, which can be used through the Property Inspector, has been a long time coming in the Flash environment. You may already be familiar with the Advanced Color Effects available in the Property Inspector (Figures 3-36 and 3-37).

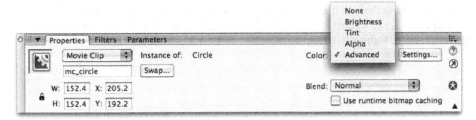

Figure 3-36. Where to find the Advanced Effect Color settings in the Property Inspector

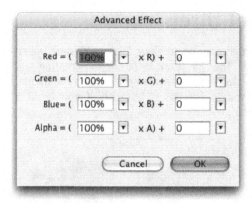

Figure 3-37. The Advanced Effect Color settings found in the Property Inspector

The Inspector in Figure 3-37 is used to generate advanced color effects on a movie clip, but it's a component, which can be hard to understand and use. Unlike components found in imaging applications such as Photoshop, this panel only allows for modifying the red, green, and blue channels separately, with no options to for adjusting Saturation or Hue.

Hallelujah for the new **Adjust Color** filter! In part because it bases its operations on imaging applications that many designers are already familiar with, this is an excellent filter to get the most out of your image elements in Flash, particularly bitmaps. This single filter, shown in Figure 3-38, allows for the modification of Brightness, Contrast, Saturation, and Hue properties in a movie clip and thus creates a vast array of varied color imaging effects.

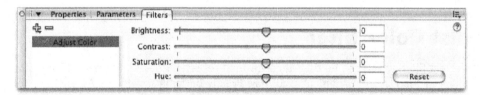

Figure 3-38. The new Adjust Color Filter Property Inspector

Have you ever wished that you could integrate both black and white and color images without the need to import separate images for both types? Well, take a look at the possible variations in Figures 3-39 through 3-43.

Figure 3-39. Original Image we will be applying the Adjust Color Filter to

Figure 3-40. Applying Saturation to the source image

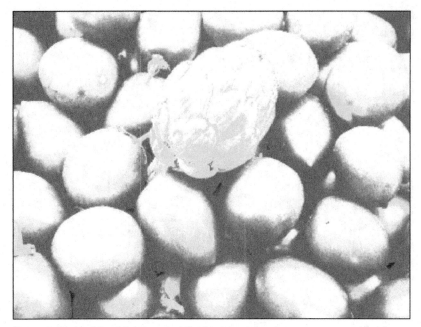

Figure 3-41. Applying Brightness and Contrast to source image

Figure 3-42. Desaturating source image to create black and white version

Figure 3-43. Creating smooth color shifts by modifying the Hue property of the source image

One of the greatest advantages to using this filter is the ability to do visually stunning animations and transitions. For instance, try creating a simple Motion Tween animation. In this case, make the second keyframe how you'd like the image to appear when the transition is complete, while in the first keyframe apply Adjust Color filter so that Brightness and Contrast are increased until the image appears pure white. When you preview and animate this tween, you'll see a beautiful soft blending transition from white to the ending image setting you've chosen. Try playing around with some animations. Cycle through the Hue spectrum, increase Saturation, modify Contrast and you are sure to be inspired to use this filter to create interesting new ways of displaying images and clips in your work!

So far, we've gone through and taken a look at the default filters and how they can be controlled through the Property Inspector in the Flash IDE. Still, the best is yet to come! All of these filters, plus the addition of Convolution, Displacement Map, and Color Matrix are now available through ActionScript directly. You are about to witness some truly amazing new effects through some straightforward ActionScript applications. Now's a good time to put on that pot of coffee, because things are about to get really interesting!

Applying filters using ActionScript

Before we get into some of the more advanced filters available such as Convolution and Displacement Maps, let's first recap some of the filters you are familiar with and look at how you can generate the same effects using nothing but a few lines of code!

Applying the Blur filter with ActionScript

In this first example, you will create a clip and then apply code so that based on the movement of the movie clip you have a corresponding level of blur. This simple example can be quite useful in the development of a host of other examples, particularly for interesting motion transitions, as well as for gaming. It's a simple process, and you should be up and running within a matter of minutes—ready to modify and use the code. Let's get cracking!

1. Create a new Flash document and then import an image to the stage (File ➤ Import ➤ Import to stage, or *CMD/CTRL+R*) or create some sort of graphic to form the basis of the movie clip that you want to apply the blur to.

2. With your new visual reference, select Modify ➤ Convert to Symbol (*F8*). Set the type to Movie clip.

3. Select the newly created movie clip on the stage and give it the instance name myMC.

4. Now that your movie clip is created, it's time to instantiate the code that you will use to control the Blur X and Blur Y properties. Create a new layer on the time-line, and call it Actions. In the first frame of the Actions layer add the following Frame code:

```
var blur:flash.filters.BlurFilter = new flash.filters.BlurFilter();
```

This code creates a new blur variable, which is set to Type flash.filters. BlurFilter. This is the new reference to the actual Blur filter. This step is always required when creating a new filter you want to apply to a movie clip. Of course nothing will happen yet—first you must add this new filter to your movie clip.

Add the following code below the line you've already added to apply the Blur filter to the myMC clip:

```
myMC.myFilterList = new Array(); // create new temporary Array
myMC.myFilterList.push(blur); // push blur filter reference to array
myMC.myFilterList[0].blurX = 15; // set default blurX value of 15
myMC.myFilterList[0].blurY = 15;  // set default blurY calue of 15
myMC.myFilterList[0].quality = 5; // set Filter quality to a value of 5
myMC.filters = myMC.myFilterList; // transfer the array to myMC.filters
```

The first step is to create a temporary array to store the filter in, using the first line of the previous code. Unfortunately, Flash does not allow for direct access to the Filters array of a movie clip, but instead requires the creation of a temporary array, which is then used as a bridge to the actual Filters array of the movie clip. For this reason, you need to create an array that we will then populate (push) with the filter and modify properties. Once parameters have been set up or modified we then make the actual filters array equal to the newly created bridge array.

After the new reference to the BlurFilter(), named blur, is pushed to the temporary array myFilterList, you can see that the three properties (blurX, blurY, and quality) you can control are modified using ActionScript. The default settings for blurX and blurY are 4, unlike the Property Inspector which defaults to a value of 5 for those properties.

Once you establish these new default properties to easily see the effect on stage, the last step is to transfer the temporary myFilterList array of myMC to the actual filter reference myMC.filters.

Save and test your movie now (*CMD/CTRL+ENTER*) and take a look at your clip on the stage. You'll notice that you have now created your first filter effect by blurring the myMC movie clip 15 pixels on both the X and Y axis! Now that you have the Blur filter set up and ready to use on your movie clip, it's time to put it into motion!

The last step is to create an onEnterFrame listener, which will detect the position of the mouse cursor, detect the distance from the current myMC location, and animate the myMC clip to this position while applying a dynamic blur to it. Add the following onEnterFrame code below your existing code:

```
//create onEnterFrame listener for myMC
myMC.onEnterFrame = function(){

    // Move towards the mouse cursor
    this.destx = _root._xmouse;
    this.desty = _root._ymouse;


    // Distance between where I am (myMC), and where
    // I want to be (the mouse cursor x,y position)
    var dx:Number = this.destx - this._x;
    var dy:Number = this.desty - this._y;

    // Move by 20% of that distance.
    this._x += dx * .5;
    this._y += dy * .5;

    // The blur is based on the amount of distance left
    (and therefore,
    //how fast myMC will be moving).
    tempFilterList = this.filters;
    tempFilterList [0].blurX = Math.abs(dx / 7);
    tempFilterList [0].blurY = Math.abs(dy / 7);
    this.filters = tempFilterList;
}
```

With this code entered correctly, you can now test your movie. Watch how myMC follows the mouse and, based on how fast the mouse moves, apply more or less blur. The entire source code is shown below:

```
var blur:flash.filters.BlurFilter = new flash.filters.BlurFilter();

myMC.myFilterList = new Array();
myMC.myFilterList.push(blur);
myMC.myFilterList[0].blurX = 15;
myMC.myFilterList[0].blurY = 15;
myMC.myFilterList[0].quality = 5;
```

```
myMC.filters = myMC.myFilterList;
var blur:flash.filters.BlurFilter = new flash.filters.BlurFilter();
//create onEnterFrame listener for myMC
myMC.onEnterFrame = function(){

    // Move towards the mouse cursor
    this.destx = _root._xmouse;
    this.desty = _root._ymouse;


// Distance between where I am (myMC), and where
// I want to be (the mouse cursor x,y position)
    var dx:Number = this.destx - this._x;
    var dy:Number = this.desty - this._y;

    // Move by 20% of that distance.
    this._x += dx * .5;
    this._y += dy * .5;

    // The blur is based on the amount of distance left
    (and therefore,
    //how fast myMC will be moving).
    tempFilterList = this.filters;
    tempFilterList [0].blurX = Math.abs(dx / 7);
    tempFilterList [0].blurY = Math.abs(dy / 7);
    this.filters = tempFilterList;
}
```

Figure 3-44 shows our final result. OK, it doesn't look very exciting here, so try the code out by yourself for the full effect!

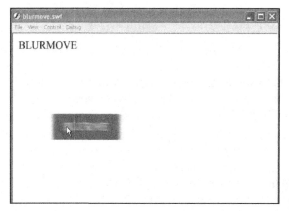

Figure 3-44. Screenshot of blurmove.fla with the object in motion

Pretty rad stuff! You can see how easy it is to set up and apply the Blur filter to a movie clip. The ability to add this effect via ActionScript opens up many new interactive possibilities, other than applying it strictly through the Filter tab in the Property Inspector. You can use this same general setup to apply blurring effects on movie clips that are animated via code. Imagine the possibilities for creating dynamic and realistic blurs to the elements that you animate in your Flash projects, for example, the ability to create interesting motion transitions on the movie clips you use in games! The possibilities are endless and open for you to explore and there is definitely nothing that you should be intimidated by. Once the filter has been declared and assigned via the temporary array to the movie clip, you can modify to your heart's content. Of course this is only the beginning; let's take a look at another dynamic example using the Drop Shadow filter with ActionScript. Also, take a look at Table 3-1 to see the Blur filter properties.

Table 3-1. Properties reference table for the Blur filter

Property	Definition
blurX: Number	The amount of horizontal blur along the X axis. Accepted value 0-100.
blurY: Number	The amount of vertical blur along the Y axis. Accepted value 0-100.
quality: Number	The quality value of the blur. Value range 0-15.

Casting dynamic Drop Shadows with ActionScript

Now that you have a basic understanding of how filters are used with ActionScript, this next example should be easy to follow. In this example, the main difference is that several movie clips will have code placed inside of them so that they can run simultaneously. The idea for this Drop Shadow example is to use the Mouse cursor as a light source of sorts. movie clip instances on the stage will watch the Mouse cursor, and, based on the position of the movie clip and the current X and Y position of the mouse, generate dynamic drop shadows that reflect the distance and angle.

Open the DropShadowLight.fla found in the code download for this chapter on www.friendsofed.com. Before taking a look at the code, test the movie to see the effect that is being created. You will notice that as you move the mouse across the stage, all instances of the movie clip create realistic drop shadows based on your position. Figure 3-45 shows the effect when the mouse is located to the left and to the right of the movie clip instances.

Figure 3-45. Screenshot of DropShadowLight.fla casting realistic drop shadows with cursor on left

In Figure 3-46, you can see how the drop shadows are generated by assuming that the Mouse cursor is the light source, thus casting shadows in the opposite direction. This example runs in real time, as you can witness if you test the movie. Let's break down the code a little bit so you can see clearly how this filter effect is generated.

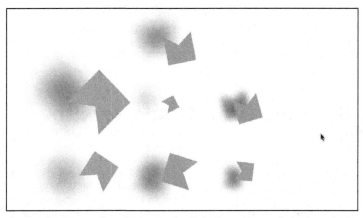

Figure 3-46. Screenshot of DropShadowLight.fla casting realistic drop shadows with cursor on right

The code for this example is placed inside of the movie clip on frame 1 of its timeline, so that multiple instances can be spawned and utilize the same base source code. If you take a look at the first part of the code, you will see there are an additional two lines used to import the classes used:

```
import flash.display.*; // Import all subclasses of the display
import flash.filters.*; // and filters classes.

var myDropShadow:DropShadowFilter = new DropShadowFilter();
```

```
// Assign the dropshadow to the targClip movie clip
var myFilterList:Array = new Array();
myFilterList.push(myDropShadow);
myFilterList[0].quality = 3;  // set default quality to 3
this.filters = myFilterList;
```

The first two lines are used to import the display and filters class into the movie clip so it can be used to create the filter effects. Once you import the classes, as you did in the last example, a variable is created and set to Type DropShadowFilter. Once created, it can be pushed into the myFilterList temporary array for applying properties.

Once the DropShadowFilter has been added to the movie clip's filter array, you can begin accessing and modifying it. The core code is placed inside an onMouseMove event handler. This means that the code in this function will be performed every time Flash detects mouse movement, which of course is exactly what we want to accomplish. Here's the code that generated the dynamic drop shadows, also found on frame 1 of the movie clip timeline, below the previous code:

```
this.onMouseMove = function(){

    // Measure how far the mouse (the lightsource) is from my center
    var offx:Number = this._xmouse;
    var offy:Number = this._ymouse;

    // Calculate distance to the light based on pythagorus.
    var dist:Number = Math.sqrt(offx * offx + offy * offy);
//Calculate the REVERSE angle from my cen ter to the mouse, Reverse is
//specified because the values of Math.atan2 are -offy and -offx
    // because the values of Math.atan2 are -offy and -offx
    var ang:Number = (Math.atan2(-offy, -offx) / Math.PI) * 180;

    var tempFilterList = this.filters;
    // Scale down distance a bit, because its too strong otherwise.
    tempFilterList[0].distance = dist / 6;
    tempFilterList[0].angle = ang;

    // Aribtrary - blur factor determines the size of the shadow.
    // Farther lights create a
    // more diffused, blurred shadow.
    tempFilterList[0].blurX = (dist / 10);
    tempFilterList[0].blurY = (dist / 10);
// Semitransparent shadow please. Note documentation says alpha is 0 to
// 100, but it's actually
    // 0 to 1, where .5 is 50%.
    tempFilterList[0].alpha = .5;

    this.filters = tempFilterList;
}
```

For this effect there are two main variables which are calculated: dist and ang.

The `dist` variable is calculated using the current mouse position. This variable is later used in two places, in order to generate the drop shadow. First it's used in setting the Drop Shadow distance property:

```
tempFilterList[0].distance = dist / 6;
```

and secondly when applying a `Blur X` and `Blur Y` value, it's used to create a realistic blur amount based on how far away from the movie clip it is:

```
tempFilterList[0].blurX = (dist / 10);
tempFilterList[0].blurY = (dist / 10);
```

In both these instances you will see that the `dist` variable is divided by another numeric value. Feel free to modify this value. It is used to create a more realistic level of drop shadow, based on this example.

As the name may imply, the `ang` variable is first used to calculate the reverse angle from the movie clip to the mouse cursor and then used directly in setting the Drop Shadow angle property:

```
tempFilterList[0].angle = ang;
```

By just using these two calculated variables, you have a purely dynamic drop shadow system, one which displays realistic shadows based on the position of the mouse, which acts as the light source. You don't have to understand how to calculate these variables, but with the knowledge of how to apply and set properties to newly created filters you can begin experimenting with interesting and different ways of altering the drop shadow of a movie clip, based on your own set of parameters and inputs. You could also experiment with the reverse and animate movie clips using a static value in place of the mouse cursor, in order to generate realistic lighting and shadow effects in an interactive environment.

Of course, by no means are you limited to only one filter! You can combine multiple filters to create more complex effects. Next you'll see how you can add a Bevel filter to the previous example to create an extra layer of filters.

You can see a list of the Drop Shadow filters in Table 3-2.

Table 3-2. Properties reference table for the Drop Shadow filter

Properties	Definitions
`alpha`: Number	The alpha percentage of the shadow color. Valid range is a normalized value from `0.0` to `1.0`. The default value is `1.0`.
`angle`: Number	The angle of the shadow. Valid values are from `0` to `360` degrees. The default is `45`.

Properties	Definitions
blurX: Number	The amount of horizontal blur, along the X axis, in pixels. Accepted values range from 0 to 255. The default value is 4.
blurY: Number	The amount of vertical blur, along the Y axis, in pixels. Valid values are from 0 to 255.0. The default is 4.
color: Number	The color of the shadow. Valid values are in the hexadecimal format 0x00RRGGBB. The default value is 0x000000.
distance: Number	The offset distance of the bevel in pixels. Valid values are -32 to 32. The default value is 4.
hideObject: Boolean	Hides the object when true, so that the movie clip is not rendered to the screen, but the shadow filter is. The default is false, which shows the object.
inner: Boolean	Determines whether the shadow is an inner shadow or outer. A true value creates an inner shadow. By default, the value is false, creating a regular outer shadow outside of the object's edges.
Knockout: Boolean	Produces a knockout effect true, which makes the object's fill .The default is false, producing no knockout.
quality: Number	The number of iterations the blur is performed. Valid numeric values are from 0 to 15, however it is recommended that you use Bitmap➡ Filter.Quality.LOW for best performance.
strength: Number	The punch strength of the drop shadow. Valid values are from 0 to 255.0. The default value is 1.

Casting dynamic drop shadows with bevels

In this example, only four additional lines of code are added to the DropShadowLight.fla, in order to generate the additional illusion of 3D. The same information used to calculate the distance and angle can be used here and applied to an additional Bevel filter.

Open the `DropShadowLightBevel.fla` and perform a test movie to see the finished result. Figures 3-47 and 3-48 are two more images which illustrate the addition of a bevel to the movie clip instances.

Figure 3-47. Screenshot of `DropShadowLightBevel.fla` casting realistic drop shadows with bevels

Figure 3-48. Screenshot of `DropShadowLightBevel.fla` casting realistic drop shadows with bevels

As illustrated in the previous Drop Shadow example, the mouse position dictates the type and level of effect that is applied to each and every instance of the movie clip. Here, the addition of a bevel using default colors is used. As you move your mouse closer to a movie clip, you will see in real time the Bevel filter's modification. This extra filter creates a further illusion of depth and gives the previously flat vector elements a more physical 3D appearance.

If you take a look at the code in any of the movie clips, there are two lines of code that are added first, which create the reference to the new Bevel filter and add it to the filter array of the movie clip:

```
var myBevel:BevelFilter = new BevelFilter();
....
myFilterList.push(myBevel);
```

Once these lines of code are added, you are ready to start adjusting values. Based on the previous code, there is an addition to the onMouseMove function with the following two lines of code around lines 40 and 44:

```
tempFilterList[1].angle = ang;
tempFilterList[1].strength = 100 / dist;
```

The Bevel filter is referenced as [1] because we still have the original Drop Shadow filter occupying the first slot [0] of the filter array. Each subsequent filter gets pushed to the array and the array element identifier is increased by one.

The only properties that are affected are the angle and strength. You can also modify the colors used, if you want to, by adding the following line of code immediately after the previous code, in order to modify the highlightColor of the bevel to a magenta:

```
tempFilterList[1].highlightColor = 0x00ff33ff;
```

You could also apply a knockout to the Bevel filter with the following code:

```
tempFilterList[1].knockout = true;
```

which creates the effect in Figure 3-49.

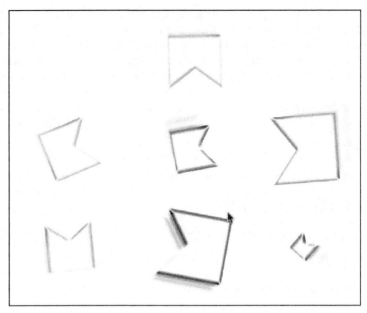

Figure 3-49. Bevel filter with knockout and `highlightColor` modifications

Notice that this `knockout` effect on the second filter overrides what was established with the original Drop Shadow filter, which had no knockout applied. Applying a `knockout` to an added filter will knock out the entire clip, regardless of the settings on previous filters. See Table 3-3 for Bevel filter properties.

Table 3-3. Properties reference for the Bevel filter

Property	Definitions
`angle`: Number	The angle of the bevel. Valid values are from 0 to 360 degrees. The default is 45.
`blurX`: Number	The amount of horizontal blur, along the X axis, in pixels. Accepted values range from 0 to 255. The default value is 4.
`blurY`: Number	The amount of vertical blur, along the Y axis, in pixels. Valid values are from 0 to 255.0. The default is 4.
`distance`: Number	The offset distance of the bevel in pixels. Valid values are -32 to 32. The default value is 4.
`highlightAlpha`: Number	Alpha value of the highlight color. Valid range is a normalized value from 0.0 to 1.0. The default value is 1.0.

Property	Definitions
highlightColor: Number	The highlight color of the bevel. Valid values are in the hexadecimal format, 0x00RRGGBB. The default value is 0x00FFFFFF.
knockout: Boolean	Produces a knockout effect (true), which makes the object's fill .The default is false, producing no knockout.
quality: Number	The number of iterations the blur is performed. Valid numeric values are from 0 to 15, However, it is recommended that you use BitmapFilter.Quality.LOW, for best performance.
shadowAlpha: Number	The alpha of the shadow color. Valid range is a normalized value from 0.0 to 1.0. The default value is 1.0.
shadowColor: Number	The shadow color of the bevel. Valid values are in the hexadecimal format, 0x00RRGGBB. The default value is 0x00000000.
strength: Number	The punch strength of the bevel. Valid values are from 0 to 255.0. The default value is 1.
type: String	The type of bevel to be applied. Valid values are: BitmapFilter.Type.INNER BitmapFilter.Type.OUTER BitmapFilter.Type.FULL

Displacement Map

The **Displacement Map** is one of the most visually stunning filters at our disposal. It is not available from the Flash IDE, like many of the filters covered earlier—to make use of it, we must use ActionScript.

At its core, the Displacement Map is a filter that essentially displaces selected pixels in an image and moves them to new positions, while leaving other pixels in the same image untouched. What does this mean exactly? Well, Displacement Maps are used to create morphing and warping effects, such as when an image is looked at through curved glass.

The Displacement filter uses something known as a map to tell Flash where to move specific pixels in the final image. A map is a bitmap image that is the same size as your source image, and therefore there is a 1:1 relationship between the pixels in the map and the source image.

In the map, the darker the color of the pixel, the more the corresponding pixel in the source image is displaced. A solid white map would have no effect on the source image, while a solid black map would shift all the pixels 100% of their predetermined maximums (which we'll get into in more detail soon).

Things get interesting, however, when you use a map that is a combination of lights and darks. Consider the displacement map in Figure 3-50, generated with `perlinNoise`:

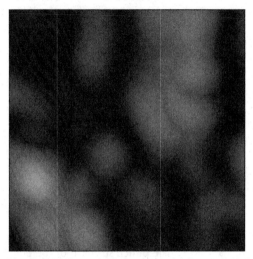

Figure 3-50. Example image created using perlinNoise

In the dark areas, the pixels on the corresponding source image would be displaced the most, while the lighter areas would have little displacement. The previous map, when applied to an image, creates the result shown in Figure 3-51.

Figure 3-51. An example image illustrating the effects of the previously mentioned displacement image

Notice near the right edge of Figure 3-51, there is a more dramatic displacement effect, and also notice that in the map itself there is a deep groove of black in the same position. The original image looks like Figure 3-52.

Figure 3-52. The original image, with no Displacement

We can make use of the displacement map for creating cool effects such as glass and water. Look at Figure 3-53 for an example.

Figure 3-53. Image with Displacement applied via ActionScript

We've recreated the classic Java water reflection effect, but this time in Flash! Ahhh, remember those days? It was the summer of 1997 when Java reflections were the "new black," but I digress. Of course, if you ran this movie, you would see that the water is actually animating and that the result is a really cool effect, all created with the `perlinNoise` bitmap effect.

So without further hesitation, let's build the water reflection effect!

1. Create a new Flash movie that is 512 × 400 in size, and set to 31 fps. If you want, you can see the final example from the code download in `displacementWater.fla`.

2. Import your favorite ocean front photograph to the stage (File ➤ Import ➤ Import to Stage).

3. Size it so that it fits horizontally on the stage.

4. Break it apart (CMD/CTRL+B) and cut it right where you want the reflection to begin.

5. Create a new layer below the first layer.

6. Copy the half-bitmap you have on the stage already, and paste it on the new layer.

7. Select the copied bitmap, and choose Modify ➤ Transform ➤ Flip Vertical.

8. With the flipped bitmap selected, press *F8* to convert to movie clip. Make sure that movie clip is selected, and name it targClip. Press OK.

9. Back at the main timeline, give the new movie clip the instance name `targClip`.

10. Position the `targClip` movie clip so that it is perfectly lined up with the original, unflipped bitmap half, and then move it up about 20 pixels, so the top bitmap overlaps it slightly.

11. From the properties panel, apply a slight tint to the `targClip` movie clip to make it look more like water. We applied color #99CCCC, at 28%.

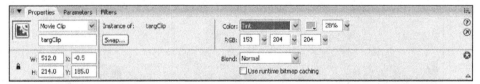

Figure 3-54. The Property Inspector displaying the color adjustment applied to the reflection

12. Create a new layer, call it code, and lock it by clicking on the small lock icon to the right of the word code in the layer.

13. Select Frame 1 of the new code layer, and press *F9* to open the Actions panel, if it is not already open.

14. Enter the following code:

```
import flash.display.*;
import flash.geom.* ;
import flash.filters.* ;

var myBitmap:BitmapData = new BitmapData(512, 214, false, 0);
```

The first thing you should do is to tell Flash to import all of the class headers for the display, geom, and filters classes. By doing this, we're telling Flash that we're going to be making use of the classes in each of these packages. When we specify the *, we're telling Flash to import all of the subclasses within the parent class. For example, we could say:

```
import flash.geom.Matrix;
import flash.geom.Point;
import flash.geom.Transform;
```

Matrix, Point and Transform are all classes in the flash.geom package. However, rather than having to say all that, if you use the *, you're simply telling Flash to import all of the classes in the flash.geom package, like so:

```
import flash.geom.*;
```

If we didn't do these imports, then when you tried to say:

```
var pt:Point = new Point(0, 0);
```

Flash would report an error such as "The class or interface 'Point' could not be loaded." in essence saying, "Hey, I've never heard of a Point, what's a Point?" Optionally, if you didn't want to import a whole package, you could create a quick and dirty single instance, and say:

```
var pt:flash.geom.Point = new flash.geom.Point(0, 0);
```

But, as you can see, that becomes very long and tedious to read and type. Now, of the three packages we did import, the first one we make use of is the flash.display package, because our next line of code was where we created the BitmapData object that will be our actual map. We'll be filling it with perlinNoise shortly. Continue by entering the following code below what you've already added:

```
var i:Number = 1;

var pt:Point = new Point(0, 0);
var myDispl:DisplacementMapFilter =
    new DisplacementMapFilter(myBitmap, mpoint, 1, 2, 10, 30);
```

Here we're creating a new instance of the DisplacementMapFilter. The first parameter is the displacement map itself, where you're passing in the myBitmap bitmap object. The second parameter is a point which refers to the "offset," where you want the displacement map to be overlaid on top of the target movie clip. You should specify 0,0 because you want the displacement map to be lined up with the upper left corner of the movie clip. The third and fourth parameters are componentX and componentY. These specify which color channel you want to use to displace along the x axis and which color channel we want to use to displace along the *y* axis. The values are 1, 2, and 3 for Red, Green, or Blue. We'll be using a grayscale `perlinNoise` rendering, which means that all the color channels will be identical—making these values somewhat arbitrary in this case.

The last two parameters are scaleX and scaleY. These refer to how strongly we want the displacement to occur along each axis. If scaleX and scaleY were both 0, then there would be no displacement visible at all. A scaleX of 10 would mean that we move image pixels that correspond to pure black in the map, exactly 10 pixels to the right. If scaleX was –10, then we would be saying move the pure black mapped pixels exactly 10 pixels to the left. Everything else is a percentage of that number. So, 50% gray would move 5 pixels, and of course, white would not move, no matter what the value of scaleX and scaleY.

Continue entering the following code:

```
targClip.myList = new Array();
targClip.myList.push(myDispl);
targClip.filters = targClip.myList;
```

As seen before, here we're applying the filter to the `targClip` movie clip.

```
_root.onEnterFrame = function()
{
    templist = targClip.filters;
    var offs:Array = new Array();
    offs[1] = new Object();
    offs[1].x = i;
    offs[1].y = i/2;

    myBitmap.perlinNoise(100, 10, 2, 523, true, false, 7, true, offs);
    templist.mapBitmap = myBitmap;
    i++;
    targClip.filters = templist;
}
```

This is where the magic happens. Here you fill the map, `myBitmap`, with pixels using `perlinNoise`. In this case, you're specifying `perlinNoise`, which is vertically narrow, but horizontally wide, to create the effect of water waves that are moving away from you. We're also using the offset features of `perlinNoise` to make our noise animated, and therefore give our waves some life. For more on `perlinNoise`, refer to Chapter 8.

Once you've updated your noise, you then place the results in the `mapBitmap` property of the `DisplacementMapFilter`, and update the filter. With that, our scene comes to life, just like in Figure 3-53. Table 3-4 has a list of `DisplacementMapFilter` properties.

```
import flash.display.*;
import flash.geom.* ;
import flash.filters.* ;

var myBitmap:BitmapData = new BitmapData(512, 214, false, 0);

var i:Number = 1;

var pt:Point = new Point(0, 0);
var myDispl:DisplacementMapFilter =
    new DisplacementMapFilter(myBitmap, mpoint, 1, 2, 10, 30);

targClip.myList = new Array();
targClip.myList.push(myDispl);
targClip.filters = targClip.myList;

_root.onEnterFrame = function()
{
    templist = targClip.filters;
    var offs:Array = new Array();
    offs[1] = new Object();
    offs[1].x = i;
    offs[1].y = i/2;

    myBitmap.perlinNoise(100, 10, 2, 523, true, false, 7, true, offs);
    templist.mapBitmap = myBitmap;
    i++;
    targClip.filters = templist;
}
```

Table 3-4. Properties reference for the DisplacementMapFilter

Property	Definition
alpha: Number	Specifies what alpha to use for out-of-bounds displacements.
color: Number	Specifies what color to use for out-of-bounds displacements.
componentX: Number	Describes which color channel to use in the map image to displace the x result.
componentY: Number	Describes which color channel to use in the map image to displace the y result.
mapBitmap: flash.display.BitmapData	A BitmapFilter object containing the displacement map data.

Continued

Table 3-4. Properties reference for the DisplacementMapFilter *(Continued)*

Property	Definition
`mapPoint`: flash.geom.Point	A `flash.geom.Point` value that contains the offset of the upper left corner of the target movie clip to the upper left corner of the map image.
`mode`: String	The mode for the filter. This is a string that can be either `wrap`, `clamp`, `ignore`, or `color`. This determines the way that pixels near the edge are displaced.
`scaleX`: Number	Multiplier to use to scale the x displacement result from the map calculation.
`scaleY`: Number	Multiplier to use to scale the y displacement result from the map calculation.

The ColorMatrixFilter

The **ColorMatrixFilter** is a very powerful filter that allows us to create a large number of color effects with code. Things like converting images to black and white, mixing color channels, and creating cool psychedelic effects are all possible with the ColorMatrixFilter.

The ColorMatrixFilter uses one parameter: a 20 element array. Each element in that array corresponds to the amount of color from each channel, to place in every other channel, calculated on a per-pixel basis. Imagine an array a. When used in a ColorMatrixFilter, each element in the array is used in the following way:

```
redResult   = a[0]  * srcR + a[1]  * srcG + a[2]  * srcB + a[3] ➥
* srcA + a[4]
greenResult = a[5]  * srcR + a[6]  * srcG + a[7]  * srcB + a[8] ➥
* srcA + a[9]
blueResult  = a[10] * srcR + a[11] * srcG + a[12] * srcB + a[13] ➥
* srcA + a[14]
alphaResult = a[15] * srcR + a[16] * srcG + a[17] * srcB + a[18] ➥
* srcA + a[19]
```

So, if you wanted an untouched image, you would place 1 in a[0], a[6], a[12], and a[18], and 0 in every other position in the array, creating the following situation:

```
redResult   = 1 * srcR + 0 * srcG + 0 * srcB + 0 * srcA + 0
greenResult = 0 * srcR + 1 * srcG + 0 * srcB + 0 * srcA + 0
blueResult  = 0 * srcR + 0 * srcG + 1 * srcB + 0 * srcA + 0
alphaResult = 0 * srcR + 0 * srcG + 0 * srcB + 1 * srcA + 0
```

This is known as the identity matrix. If we simplify that by removing all the elements multiplied by zero, we get:

```
redResult   = 1 * srcR
greenResult = 1 * srcG
blueResult  = 1 * srcB
alphaResult = 1 * srcA
```

Which equals:

```
redResult   = srcR
greenResult = srcG
blueResult  = srcB
alphaResult = srcA
```

So the red channel of the filtered movie clip, is exactly equal to the red channel of the source movie clip. The same applies to the green, blue, and alpha channel. What this means is, the image is untouched. If we were to place a 1 in a[5] instead of a[6], we would end up with:

```
redResult   = 1 * srcR + 0 * srcG + 0 * srcB + 0 * srcA + 0
greenResult = 1 * srcR + 0 * srcG + 0 * srcB + 0 * srcA + 0
blueResult  = 0 * srcR + 0 * srcG + 1 * srcB + 0 * srcA + 0
alphaResult = 0 * srcR + 0 * srcG + 0 * srcB + 1 * srcA + 0
```

Which reduces to

```
redResult   = srcR
greenResult = srcR
blueResult  = srcB
alphaResult = srcA
```

Notice that this means the source red channel is used to determine both the destination red channel and the destination green channel. Things like this make the image begin to take on a unique and different look.

The black and white icon rollover

One of the coolest and most practical navigational effects we can do with the ColorMatrixFilter is to have a series of navigational elements that are black and white until rolled over, at which point they smoothly transition to full color. See Figure 3-55 for more information.

Figure 3-55. Color Matrix applied to MovieClips setting color values to black and white

Here we have four different items, all of them ready to be rolled over. When we do roll over them, we get the results shown in Figure 3-56.

Figure 3-56. RollOver effect using Color Matrix to color movie clip.

The rolled-over image smoothly transitions to full color. To do this, all we're ultimately doing is smoothly transitioning between two different matrixes; black and white, and the identity matrix. Let's create this effect. The final file can be found for your viewing pleasure in `colormatrix-BWIcons.fla`.

1. Open Flash and create a new movie 570 × 400 at 31 fps.

2. Import or draw four shapes, icons, images, etc. The choice is yours.

3. Convert each one to a movie clip, and give them the instance names `icon1`, `icon2`, `icon3`, and `icon4`.

4. Create a new layer and call it `code`.

5. Click on frame 1 of that layer, and in the actions window, enter the following code:

```
import flash.filters.* ;
```

You begin by importing the filters package, which you'll need to do to make use of the ColorMatrixFilter. Notice that you don't need to import that `flash.geom.Matrix` class because the matrix used in the ColorMatrixFilter is not technically a Flash matrix as defined by the `Matrix` class. The ColorMatrixFilter uses a special 20 element array as its matrix. Proceed with the following code:

```
var fullColor:Array = new Array(1, 0, 0, 0, 0,
                                0, 1, 0, 0, 0,
                                0, 0, 1, 0, 0,
                                0, 0, 0, 1, 0);

var blackAndWhite:Array = new Array(.3, .59, .11, 0, 0,
                                    .3, .59, .11, 0, 0,
                                    .3, .59, .11, 0, 0,
                                    0, 0, 0, 1, 0);
```

Here we defined our two matrix arrays. The first array is our identity matrix, which has the effect of not making any change to the colors. The second array is our black and white matrix array, and this will effectively combine all the channels into a uniform grayscale arrangement where each color channel in the filtered result is identical. Continue by entering the following code:

```
function initMe()
{
    var myColorMatrixFilter:ColorMatrixFilter = new
ColorMatrixFilter();

    this.myMatrix = new Array();
    var templist:Array = new Array();

    templist.push(myColorMatrixFilter);
    this.filters = templist;
    // Add the ColorMatrixFilter to "this"

    this.onEnterFrame = BWFadeIconEnterFrame;
```

```
                    // Initialize values so they're black and white at first
             this.perc = .99;
             this.destperc = 1;
             this.destalpha = 20;

             this.onRollOver = function()
             {
                 this.destperc = 0;
             }

             this.onRollOut = function()
             {
                 this.destperc = 1;
             }
         }
```

This is a general function that we'll be applying to each of our movie clips on stage. In it, we create an instance of the ColorMatrixFilter, an empty array `myMatrix`, and then create a new array `templist`, which is used to pass the new list of filters into the movie clip's filters. In this case, `templist` will only contain one ColorMatrixFilter object.

We then set the `onEnterFrame` function of the movie clip to be our general handler, `BWFadeIconEnterFrame` (defined shortly). We also set the value of three variables, `perc`, `destperc`, and `destalpha`. The first two variables will be used to determine where we are (by percentage) between our two matrixes. When perc is 0, the movie clip will have the `fullColor` matrix array applied to it. When perc is 1, then movie clip will have the `blackAndWhite` matrix array applied to it. Any value in between will be a combination, creating the smooth effect we're looking for. The `destalpha` variable is used additionally, for modifying the alpha level of the movie clip in order to accentuate the colorization effect.

Finally, we create `onRollOver` and `onRollOut` functions. In these, we set `destperc` to either 0 or 1. The variable `destperc` refers to "destination" percentage, and our movie clips will always be trying to move towards that number using a standard easing equation. Setting `destalpha` will modify the alpha value from between 20 when not rolled over and 100 when the user places the mouse over the movie clip. Continue entering the following code:

```
function BWFadeIconEnterFrame()
{
    // Are we at our color destination yet?
    if (this.destperc != this.perc)
    {
        // Ease perc 10% of the way towards destperc.
        this.perc += (this.destperc - this.perc) * .1;
        this._alpha += (this.destalpha - this._alpha) * .3;
        // If we're less than .01 away from destperc then
        // let's simply set this.perc to this.destperc
        if (Math.abs(this.destperc - this.perc) < .01)
            this.perc = this.destperc;
```

```
// Move each element in the color matrix arrays
// closer to its destination
for (var i:Number = 0; i < 20; i++)
{
    var pos = ((blackAndWhite[i] - fullColor[i]) *
            this.perc) + fullColor[i];
    this.myMatrix[i] = pos;
}

templist = this.filters;
templist[0].matrix = this.myMatrix;
this.filters = templist;
    }
}
```

This is the function that is applied to each movie clip's onEnterFrame event. First thing you should do is check to see if destperc and perc are equal. If they're not, then you know that you have some work to do to get perc where you want it to be. Apply an easing equation to increase perc by 10% of the difference between destperc and perc. This way, perc will slowly ease into destperc. This same equation is applied to the alpha value as well, increasing it by 30%.

Next there's an if statement. When the difference between destperc and perc is less than .01, then you should simply set perc to be equal to destperc. This ensures that all of this code will not be executed the next time, as the first if statement will register false.

Next, you'll have a loop from 0 to 19, where you can calculate the a value that is the perfect combination of the corresponding element in the blackAndWhite and fullColor arrays. You can calculate it by taking the difference between the two arrays at that element, multiplying that by perc, and then adding fullColor[i] back on. Then, take this result and put it in the correct place in myMatrix.

Finally, you should grab the filters array, put it in templist, and then replace the matrix in templist with the new myMatrix you just created. Once you re-set the filters object to be equal to templist, your newly calculated color matrix array will be applied to the movie clip. We will have used the value perc to determine how to color a movie clip by smoothly combining two color matrix arrays. This same effect can be used with *any* two color matrix arrays, in order to create some really cool ColorMatrixFilter effects! Last, enter the following code:

```
icon1.init = initMe;
icon2.init = initMe;
icon3.init = initMe;
icon4.init = initMe;

icon1.init();
icon2.init();
icon3.init();
icon4.init();
```

Here, you're simply setting the initMe function to a function on each movie clip called init, and then we're calling that function, thus bringing everything to life.

Property reference for the ColorMatrixFilter

The ColorMatrixFilter only takes one parameter; the Matrix array. If you do not specify one, then a basic identity matrix is used by default.

The matrix: array is a20-element array, representing a 5 wide by 4 high color matrix to be applied to the object being filtered.

Convolution filter

The Convolution filter is one of the most versatile, yet least understood filters in general computer graphics. The word "convolution" is derived from the word "convolve." According to the dictionary, "convolve" means to roll up, twist, wind, or curl together.

So what does that mean for the Convolution filter? It means, basically, that the Convolution filter can be thought of as a filter that does its magic by combining adjacent pixels together. What makes the Convolution different from the Blur filter is the fact that you can *define* how the pixels are joined together, according to a specific formula. Some cool examples of useful Convolution filters can be found at http://www.opengl.org/resources/tutorials/advanced/advanced97/notes/node152.html.

The Convolution filter performs its actions based upon a *matrix* of numerical values. The matrix determines how a given pixel of the input image is combined with its neighboring pixels to produce a resulting pixel value. The matrix can be any size, and the larger the matrix, the farther each pixel will reach out to its neighbors for influence. For example, imagine a 3 X 3 matrix:

a0	a1	a2
a3	a4	a5
a6	a7	a8

Your matrix array will be defined later with

```
var matrixArray:Array = new Array(a0, a1, a2, a3, a4, a5, a6, a7, a8);
```

Although it's probably easier to line it up like so:

```
var matrixArray:Array = new Array(a0, a1, a2,
                                  a3, a4, a5,
                                  a6, a7, a8);
```

The matrix is moved across the source image, and is then applied to each color channel in the following way, in order to produce the result:

```
dst (x, y) =  (src(x-1, y-1) * a0 +
               src(x,   y-1) * a1 +
               src(x+1, y-1) * a2 +
               src(x-1, y)   * a3 +
               src(x,   y)   * a4 +
               src(x+1, y)   * a5 +
               src(x-1, y+1) * a6 +
               src(x,   y+1) * a7 +
               src(x+1, y+1) * a8)
```

As you can see, a4 is the source pixel, and every other array index is a neighbor. So, if we wanted to make a convolution matrix that had no effect whatsoever (where the output and the input image are identical), we would make the following matrix:

0	0	0
0	1	0
0	0	0

This would be defined in code as

```
var matrixArray:Array = new Array(0, 0, 0,
                                  0, 1, 0,
                                  0, 0, 0);
```

If we replace the values in the formula, we get the following:

```
dst (x, y) =  (src(x-1, y-1) * 0 +
               src(x,   y-1) * 0 +
               src(x+1, y-1) * 0 +
               src(x-1, y)   * 0 +
               src(x,   y)   * 1 +
               src(x+1, y)   * 0 +
               src(x-1, y+1) * 0 +
               src(x,   y+1) * 0 +
               src(x+1, y+1) * 0)
```

Mathematically, any number multiplied by 0 is 0, and anything multiplied by 1 is unaltered, so applying that math, you would get the following:

```
dst (x, y) =  (0 +
               0 +
               0 +
               0 +
               src(x, y) +
               0 +
               0 +
               0 +
               0)
```

Or, if you remove all the zeros

```
dst (x, y) = (src(x, y))
```

An identical copy!

If you wanted to blur an image, you could make a matrix that was an even combination of all neighbors:

```
var blurMatrix:Array = new Array(.1, .1, .1,
                                 .1, .1, .1,
                                 .1, .1, .1);
```

You can make your matrix any size, like 5 × 5, 7 × 7, etc., but for simplicity we will be making our example with a simple 3 × 3 matrix.

Embossing example

In this example, you're going to create a Convolution filter that embosses an image. With embossing, edges are highlighted and shaded in such a way that the image takes on a 3D textured effect. This is can be found in the file convolutionEmboss.fla.

1. Create a new movie in Flash and set the size to 512 × 400.

2. Use File ➤ Import ➤ Import to Stage to import an image to the stage. Any image will do (preferably a photograph).

3. Resize the image so that it fits perfectly on the stage, by either scaling or cropping it.

Figure 3-57. Default image imported to apply Convolution Filter to.

4. With the image selected, press *F8* to convert to a movie clip. In the dialog box that appears make sure that its behavior is set to movie clip.

5. On the stage, select the new movie clip and give it the instance name `targClip`

6. Create a new layer, lock it, and call it code.

7. Select the first frame of the code layer, and open the Actions Panel (F9).

Enter the following code:

```
import flash.filters.* ;

var myConvolution:ConvolutionFilter = new ConvolutionFilter(3, 3);
```

Here you're importing all the classes in the `flash.filters` package, and then you're creating a new instance of the `ConvolutionFilter` called `myConvolution`. The two parameters you pass into the constructor are the width and height of the Convolution filter matrix. In this case, you're specifying 3 X 3. Continue entering the code below:

```
targClip.myList = new Array();
targClip.myList.push(myConvolution);
targClip.filters = targClip.myList;
```

Here, you're assigning the filter, `myConvolution`, to the filters list of the `targClip` movie clip. Continue entering the following code:

```
var matrix1:Array = new Array(4, 1, 0,
                              1, 1, -1,
                              0, -1, -4);
```

That is the nine-element matrix that does the embossing action. It has the effect of increasing a pixel's intensity by the value of its upper-left neighbor, but decreasing it by its lower-right neighbor. This does the embossing. Continue entering the following code:

```
templist = targClip.filters;

templist[0].divisor = 1;
templist[0].bias = 0;

templist[0].matrix = matrix1;
targClip.filters = templist;
```

Here you're setting the divisor to 1 and the bias to 0. We'll explain those in a moment. Then, you should set the `matrix` property of the `ConvolutionFilter` to `matrix1`, and then apply these changes to the filter. Now you're done. Save and test this movie by pressing *CTRL/CMD+ENTER*, and you should see your image embossed like Figure 3-58.

Figure 3-58. Original imported image with applied Emboss effect using Convolution filter. Notice the 3D-type effect.

There are two properties we mentioned a few moments ago, called `divisor` and `bias`. The function of the divisor is to take the result, and divide it by a number before applying it to the destination pixel. For example, consider the following matrix:

1	1	1
1	1	1
1	1	1

Seems harmless enough, and it looks almost like a blur. In fact it *is* a blur, but the results will be unusable, because consider the formula:

```
dst (x, y) =  (src(x-1, y-1) * 1 +
               src(x,   y-1) * 1 +
               src(x+1, y-1) * 1 +
               src(x-1, y)   * 1 +
               src(x,   y)   * 1 +
               src(x+1, y)   * 1 +
               src(x-1, y+1) * 1 +
               src(x,   y+1) * 1 +
               src(x+1, y+1) * 1)
```

Which would translate to

```
dst (x, y) =  src(x-1, y-1) + src(x,   y-1) + src(x+1, y-1) +
              src(x-1, y) + src(x,   y) + src(x+1, y) +
              src(x-1, y+1) + src(x,   y+1) + src(x+1, y+1))
```

In other words, the output would almost certainly be blown out white, because adding all those numbers together would almost always create something that was far above 255 (full white). So what you should do is make use of the divisor, which takes the final result, and divides it by a certain number, before applying it to the final image. So, in the previous example, if we used a divisor of 9, then the export would look like a normally blurred image. This is because the previous matrix would result in the adding of nine pixels together, so if you use a divisor of 9, you would then divide the result by 9, bringing the pixel back into the "useful" or "visible" range.

The bias is simply the amount to add or subtract to the final result before applying it to the destination image. So our overall formula can be looked at like so:

destination pixel = ((matrix multiplication) / divisor) + bias

Table 3-5. Property reference for the ConvolutionFilter

Property	Definition
`matrixX`: Number	The X dimension of the matrix.
`matrixY`: Number	The Y dimension of the matrix.
`matrix`: Array	An array of values used for matrix transformation.
`divisor`: Number	The divisor used during matrix transformation.
`bias`: Number	Bias to add to result of matrix transformation.
`preserveAlpha`: Boolean	Indicates to what the convolution applies. Specifying true means the Convolution filter only applies to the color channels, whereas false means that the convolution is applied to the alpha channel as well.
`clamp`: Boolean	Whether the image should be clamped. This means that if the Convolution filter reaches the edge of the image that it should reuse the edge pixels, as it cannot reach off the image to neighbors that don't exist. If clamp is false, then we're telling the filter to use a different color for these edge pixels.
`color`: Number	The hexadecimal color to substitute for pixels off the source image.
`alpha`: Number	The alpha of the substitute color.

Summary

As you can see, there is an incredible wealth of possibilities with the new filters added in Flash 8. From Dynamic Motion blurs and Drop Shadows to transforming color and displacing pixels with Displacement, the array of options available is impressive. Of course, the examples you've just discovered are fairly basic examples of single filters. True power comes with the intelligent integration of multiple filters to create custom effects that can be applied dynamically, based on any number of dynamic input date. You can now create realistic environments with lighting and shadows or create weird and wonderful image transitions using some of the more complex filters. Don't forget blending modes from the previous chapter either! With the combination of blends and filters you should be able to keep yourself busy for days experimenting and exploring unique visual effects!

4 DRAWING AND GRAPHIC IMPROVEMENTS

by Todd Yard

Flash 8 introduces a number of welcome enhancements to its drawing capabilities—features that are accessible both through the IDE and through ActionScript. These changes give the developer, designer, or animator more control over how vectors are drawn within the IDE and how Flash will display strokes and fills for these vector shapes. Although the fill and stroke changes might be viewed as small additions to an application with such a wealth of new tools, these enhancements are quite significant to the level of control now offered to the user when using Flash's native vectors. As for the addition of Object Drawing, this enhancement can quite simply change the way you draw and work in Flash. Now that's significant (and so I guess a good place to start)!

Object drawing when drawing objects

Any user who has come to Flash after using another vector drawing program such as Illustrator, FreeHand, CorelDRAW, or Canvas has been immediately taken aback by its different method of manipulating vectors within the IDE. (OK, that's a blanket assumption, but I would almost bet money on it.) Some have loved the difference, some still can't get used to it. This difference lies mainly in the fact that in those other applications, vector shapes are drawn and exist as distinct objects that don't interact with the other shapes. If one object is drawn right on top of another, the first object still retains all of its vector information and is unaltered by the shape above. Not so in Flash.

Previous versions of Flash have always used a "cookie-cutter" approach with the drawing tools—now dubbed the Merge Drawing model. If one symbol was drawn on top of another, the top shape would delete the portion of the lower shape that it overlapped, as illustrated in Figure 4-1. This was a powerful tool, but sometimes frustrating for users used to other vector drawing programs. The only way to simulate the methods of these other applications and avoid the cookie-cutter drawing was to group all individual drawing objects or make everything into a symbol.

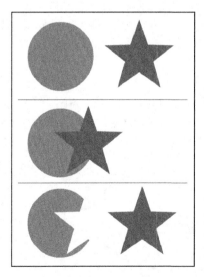

Figure 4-1.
An example of Flash's Merge Drawing model

With the latest version, Flash has introduced the Object Drawing model, offering another way of drawing vector shapes in Flash—and one that's much closer to the object model of other vector programs. Essentially, the **Object Drawing mode**, which can be toggled on or off for every shape as it's initially drawn (this is a shape-by-shape tool, not a document-wide feature), marks a shape as a unique entity that can't be altered by its interaction with other shapes. Using Object Drawing, a user can stack multiple shapes without the top shapes cutting into the shapes below, as illustrated in Figure 4-2.

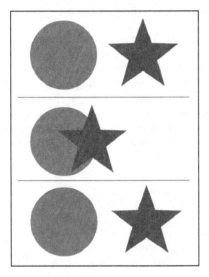

Figure 4-2.
Shapes drawn with Object Drawing toggled on will not interact with and alter other shapes.

This feature is accessed in the IDE through the Options section of the Tools bar when a drawing tool is selected (Rectangle, Oval, PolyStar, Pencil, or Paintbrush), as shown in Figure 4-3. In addition, the *J* key may be used to toggle the feature on or off. When it's toggled on, Object Drawing mode is enabled for the next shape drawn. When it's toggled off, Flash will draw the object as it has in past versions using Merge Drawing. It's important to note that when using the Paintbrush tool with Object Drawing, the Brush Mode feature, though active, has no effect since the drawn shape isn't set to interact with other shapes.

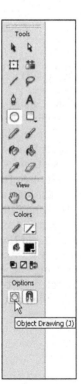

Figure 4-3.
The button to enable Object Drawing is located in the Tools bar under Options.

Once an object has been drawn with Object Drawing, it may be modified in the same way as a shape drawn without Object Drawing—namely, through manipulation with the Selection, Subselection, and Free Transform tools. You can use the same push and pull methods to distort the shape, the same distort and envelope transform options, and the same fields in the Transform or Properties panels. Even after you've used any of these transform methods, the shape still maintains its Drawing Object status. The only way to change a shape from Object Drawing mode to Merge Drawing is to break it apart with Modify ➤ Break Apart. To switch a shape from the Merge Drawing model to the Object Drawing model, you use Modify ➤ Combine Objects ➤ Union, described in the next section.

Don't be daunted by this new method of drawing. If you're used to another vector application, then you'll immediately take to this model, but if you're used to previous versions of Flash, you may find this approach strange. What's important to understand is that, essentially, using Object Drawing works in much the same way as using Merge Drawing, except that shapes don't cut into each other. You can bend and reshape them with the same tools, you can animate them with the same shape tweens and add the same shape hints, and you can alter their color and size using the same methods. These aren't "automatic groups," but simply shapes that don't interact with each other. Plus, you get a few extras! (How's that for a segue?)

> One subtle but useful feature of the Object Drawing model is that you can at any time assign a stroke to an Object Drawing shape without having to use the Ink Bottle tool. All you have to do is select the shape and assign a stroke color in the Properties panel, the Color Mixer panel, or the Tools bar, and a stroke will be automatically added to your shape.

Combining objects

At first glance, Object Drawing might seem similar to drawing a shape in past versions and immediately grouping it, except for the fact that you can directly edit and manipulate the path of an Object Drawing shape without having to double-click it on the stage. However, Object Drawing has a few more tricks up its sleeve that make it more than a shortcut. These tricks can be found in the Modify menu under Combine Objects, as shown in Figure 4-4. The menu options available here—Union, Intersect, Punch, and Crop—are Boolean operations that should be familiar to users of other vector drawing applications (think the Pathfinder palette in Illustrator). Each describes a way for two or more objects to interact to produce a single, modified shape (though in Flash, the Boolean operations Punch and Crop don't actually combine shapes into a single entity as in other programs). It goes without saying then that these options aren't useful unless two or more Object Drawing shapes are selected. In fact, if only one shape is selected, these options are disabled—except for Union, which will in this case unify a shape with itself (accomplishing absolutely nothing).

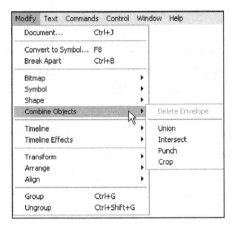

Figure 4-4.
The Combine Objects menu for Object
Drawing shapes

To illustrate the four Boolean operations, we'll use the same three shapes—a circle, square, and pentagon—all drawn with Object Drawing toggled on and positioned in the same way (shown in Figure 4-5 in both solid and outline mode). Look closely at the outline version and compare it with the results of the Boolean operations.

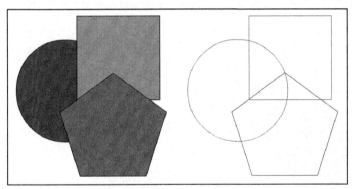

Figure 4-5. The three shapes used to demonstrate the Combine Objects operations, in both solid and outline view

Union

When two or more shapes are combined using the Union method, the result is a single Object Drawing shape made up of all the portions visible on the shapes before they were unified. The invisible, overlapping portions of the shapes are deleted in the same way they would be if the shapes had been drawn using the old Merge Drawing model. An illustration of this is shown in Figure 4-6.

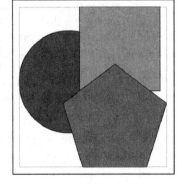

Figure 4-6.
Combining objects using Union

Intersect

When two or more shapes are combined using the Intersect method, the result is a single Object Drawing shape made up of the overlapping portions of all the combined shapes. Any part of any shape that doesn't overlap with all other shapes is deleted. The resulting shape takes the fill and stroke of the top-level shape in the stack. An illustration of this is shown in Figure 4-7.

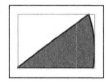

Figure 4-7.
Combining objects using Intersect

Punch

When the Punch method is used on two or more Drawing Object shapes, the top-level shape in the stack acts as a cookie cutter on all shapes below it in the operation. Any part of a shape that overlaps with this top-level shape is deleted (and the top-level shape is deleted in its entirety). The resulting shapes all remain separate objects and don't actually combine into a single object as in the Union or Intersect operations. An illustration of this is shown in Figure 4-8.

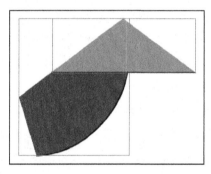

Figure 4-8.
Combining objects using Punch

Crop

The Crop method acts in a similar way to the Punch method, except the top-level object acts as the region with which to crop all underlying shapes in the operation. Any part of an underlying shape that overlaps with the top-level shape will remain, while all other portions of the underlying shapes will be deleted (and the top-level shape will be deleted in its entirety). The resulting shapes all remain separate objects and don't actually combine into a single object as in the Union or Intersect operations. A illustration of this is shown in Figure 4-9.

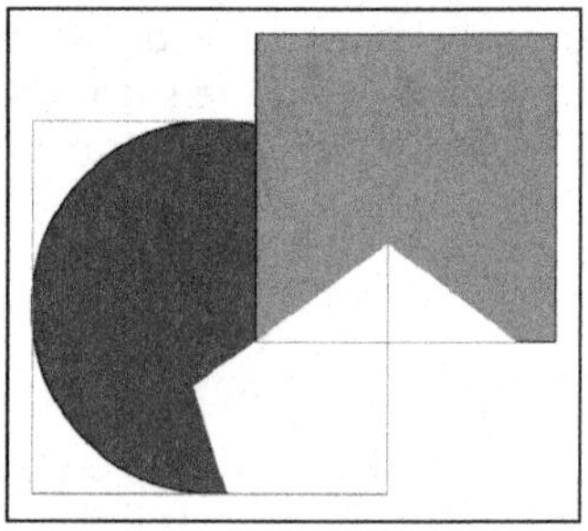

Figure 4-9.
Combining objects using Crop

Envelopes and object drawing

One especially nice feature supported and actually enhanced by Object Drawing is **envelope transformation**. Envelope transformations are transformations of a shape using the Envelope option of the Free Transform tool, or the menu command Modify ➤ Transform ➤ Envelope. If you draw a shape with Merge Drawing enabled, these envelope transformations are destructive, in that they irreversibly (apart from Undo) apply their transformations to the shape. Not so with Object Drawing shapes—when an envelope transformation is applied to an Object Drawing shape, it can at any time be removed with the menu option Modify ➤ Combine Objects ➤ Delete Envelope. Let's take a closer look at how this works.

1. Create a new Flash document and select the Text tool. Choose a thick font, a large text size, and a dark, distinguishing color. Add a field to the stage and enter the text ENVELOPE.

Figure 4-10. A text field is added to the stage.

2. Break the text apart twice (press *CTRL+B* or select Modify ➤ Break Apart twice). This will turn the text into a Merge Drawing shape.

3. Change the text into an Object Drawing shape by selecting the Modify ➤ Combine Objects ➤ Union menu option.

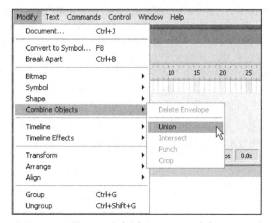

Figure 4-11. The text is broken apart and then turned into an Object Drawing shape using Union.

4. Now that the text is an Object Drawing shape, apply an envelope using Modify ➤ Transform ➤ Envelope. A number of anchors and control points appear around the text.

Figure 4-12. An envelope is added to the shape.

5. Drag the two anchor points in the center of the shape up to create a wave in the text. This effect is easy to achieve with an envelope and extremely difficult to achieve otherwise.

Figure 4-13. The shape is transformed using an envelope.

6. Select the Free Transform tool and rotate the text to the right by 30 degrees or so.

7. Select the Skew option of the Free Transform tool to skew the text to the left.

Figure 4-14. The shape is skewed and rotated with the Free Transform tool.

8. Now, if you decide at this point that you no longer want the wave in the text, you can remove the envelope, but retain the rotation and skew. Do this by selecting the menu option Modify ➤ Combine Objects ➤ Delete Envelope. Your envelope transformation is removed (even though you performed additional transformations after making it), and you're left with a skewed and rotated shape. *Take that*, Merge Drawing!

Figure 4-15. Removing the envelope removes the envelope transformation but retains all other transformations.

Greater image-loading support

Here's an enhancement that will only take a paragraph or two to explain in full. However, don't let such a simple explanation mask the power provided by this new feature. Previously, if a developer wished to load a bitmap at runtime, their only option with Flash was to load a non-progressive JPG file. One file format was better than none, and we in the Flash community ate it up. Now, however, Flash additionally supports the loading of progressive JPGs, non-animated GIFs, and the coup de grace, PNGs. This final format is arguably the most exciting, in that since PNGs offer 8-bit transparency, developers can dynamically load bitmaps of varying opacity at runtime.

How is this new enhancement implemented? That's the beauty of this feature—it's implemented exactly as it was in MX 2004 when loading non-progressive JPGs: by using the `MovieClip` object's `loadMovie()`. Here's a simple example:

```
_root.createEmptyMovieClip("background", 0);
_root.background.loadMovie("assets/images/wallpaper.png");
```

It doesn't get much simpler than that!

Filling shapes with bitmaps

Flash has always given users the ability to fill shapes with bitmap images imported into the IDE, but it has never offered a way to fill shapes with bitmaps using ActionScript—at least not until `beginBitmapFill()`. This is an amazingly powerful new feature that requires knowledge of the new `BitmapData` object, which we're reserving for a full chapter in itself. As such, let's hold off discussing it until that point (although take a look at Figure 4-16 to see what's in store).

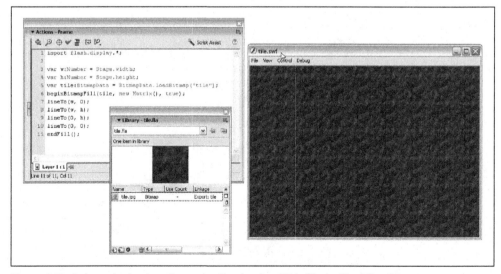

Figure 4-16. A shape drawn at runtime using the drawing API is filled with a tiling bitmap.

Enhancements to gradients

Gradient fills have also seen a bit of an overhaul with Flash 8, with more options being added to both the IDE and ActionScript. These new features give users more control over how gradients display when drawn, including how many color stops may be added to the Color Mixer, what interpolation mode is used to grade the colors, where a radial gradient's focal point lies, and my personal favorite, how a gradient is drawn out of bounds.

Color stops

Here's one of those simple but extremely nice improvements. In previous versions of Flash, users were limited to adding 8 color stops to the gradient color well in the Color Mixer panel. Now you can add up to 16, as shown in Figure 4-17. Have fun and go wild.

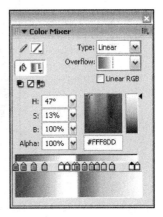

Figure 4-17.
Up to 16 color stops can be added to a gradient.

Interpolation mode

When a gradient fill is selected in the Color Mixer panel, an option for Linear RGB becomes visible. This is the mathematical method used to calculate the intermediate colors between color stops in the gradient. This was added for better compatibility with SVG, which uses this interpolation method. If you don't select this option, Flash will use the RGB interpolation used in previous versions. Generally, you can toggle this on or off to see which method works best for what you're trying to accomplish.

This option is available through ActionScript and if in MovieClip's beginGradientFill() method, discussed in the ActionScript section that follows.

Radial focal point

Flash 8 now offers the ability to set the focal point for a radial gradient somewhere other than its center (or the center of its transform)—in past versions, a central focal point was the only option. Access to this feature in the IDE is provided only through the Fill Transform tool. Once you've selected a shape filled with a radial gradient with this tool, the gizmo used to transform the gradient appears with an extra handle. This handle (a triangle) lies along a straight line drawn through the gradient and can be dragged anywhere along this line. One use for offsetting the focal point is to achieve a more realistic 3D effect when using a radial gradient on a circle to emulate a sphere.

This option is available for radial gradients through ActionScript as well in MovieClip's beginGradientFill() method, discussed in the ActionScript section that follows. Let's first test it out in the IDE.

1. Create a new Flash document and use the Oval tool to draw a perfect circle on the stage.

2. Use the Color Swatches or Color Mixer to apply the default white-to-black radial gradient.

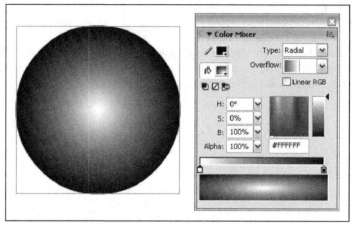

Figure 4-18. An oval with a gradient is drawn on the stage.

3. Change the black stop to a very light gray and drag the white stop to about 80% on the gradient well. Add a new black stop at the far left.

4. Add two green stops to the right of the black stop and drag them to about 40% and 60% on the gradient well. Add another black stop to the left of these so there's a harder line between the green and black.

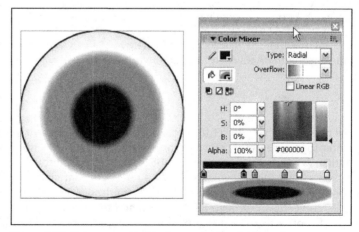

Figure 4-19. Colors are added to the gradient and adjusted.

5. Add a yellow stop between the green and black stops, and add a white stop to the left of the black stop on the very left (you'll have to drag the black stop to the right to about 5% on the color well to do this). Adjust to your taste and add more stops to control the color flow if you like—but this should leave you with a fairly decent eyeball gradient.

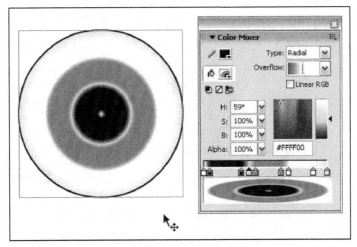

Figure 4-20. Final colors are added for a gradient eyeball effect.

6. To change the direction of the eye, use the Fill Transform tool to horizontally scale the gradient (the box on the right of the transform gizmo). Drag the center of the gradient to the right (the center circle on the transform gizmo). As you can see, this doesn't leave a particularly nice effect.

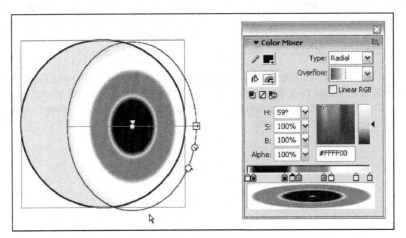

Figure 4-21. The gradient is transformed, but the effect isn't realistic.

7. To fix this, use the Fill Transform tool to drag the upside-down arrow that lies on the line bisecting the transform gizmo. This controls the radial focal point. Drag it slightly to the right to change how the gradient lies. This should give a much more realistic effect.

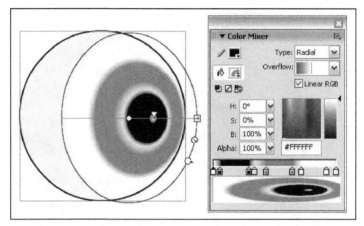

Figure 4-22. By offsetting the focal point of a radial gradient, the effect is complete.

Spread modes

The most obvious improvement to gradients in Flash also opens the door to the most possibilities. In past versions, when a gradient was transformed to be smaller than the shape it filled, the final colors in the gradient simply extended to the edges of the shape. If a user used a yellow-to-blue linear gradient on a square and scaled the gradient horizontally, yellow would extend to the edge on one side of the square while blue would extend to the other side, as demonstrated in Figure 4-23. This effect is now called Pad spread mode, and is selected as the default Overflow option in the Color Mixer.

In Flash 8, users are offered two additional modes to define how a gradient will be drawn past its limits. These two new methods, Reflect and Repeat, can be found along with Pad in the Overflow drop-down menu in the top-right corner of Color Mixer panel, under the gradient Type drop-down menu.

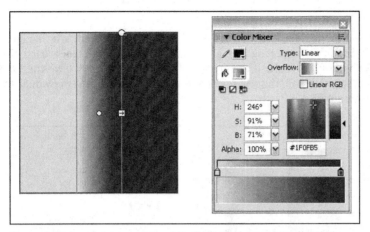

Figure 4-23. In previous versions of Flash, the Pad spread mode was the only option available for a gradient.

Reflect

Reflect spread mode draws the gradient in the opposite direction once its limit is reached, and continues reversing the gradient colors repeatedly until the edge of the shape is reached. This means that a yellow-to-blue gradient, when past its limit, will continue on as a blue-to-yellow gradient for an equivalent distance, and then will be drawn as yellow-to-blue again, etc., until the edge of the shape is reached. This effect offers a smooth transition between all gradients drawn. An example is shown in Figure 4-24.

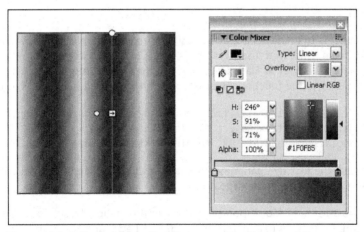

Figure 4-24. Reflect mode continually reverses the direction of the gradient in the area beyond its limit.

Repeat

Repeat spread mode does just what it says: it repeats the gradient after its limit has been reached. It continues repeating the gradient for the same distance each time until it reaches the end of the shape. If the gradient being drawn doesn't have the same color at both ends of its color well, this will result in hard lines between the individual gradients, as shown in Figure 4-25.

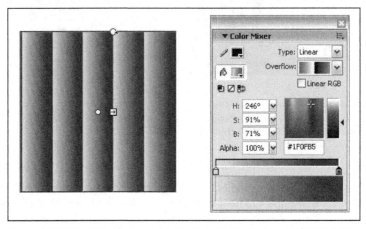

Figure 4-25. Repeat mode draws identical gradients in the area beyond the gradient's limit.

ActionScript with beginGradientFill()

The enhancements to gradients are all accessible through ActionScript, as well as the one drawing API command that uses gradients: `beginGradientFill()`. The method works the same as it does in Flash MX 2004, but the new features are set by additional parameters passed to the function. The method, with the added parameters, is defined as

```
public beginGradientFill(fillType:String, colors:Array, alphas:Array,➥
ratios:Array, matrix:Object, spreadMethod:String,➥
interpolationMethod:String, focalPointRatio:Number) : Void
```

As you can see, the first five parameters remain unchanged. The last three, which are all optional, apply to the new gradient features.

- `spreadMethod`: Corresponds to the overflow types described in the previous section. Acceptable parameters are `pad`, `reflect`, and `repeat`.

- `interpolationMethod`: Specifies the color interpolation method of the gradient to be drawn. Acceptable parameters are either `RGB` or `linearRGB`.

- `focalPointRatio`: Defines the gradient's focal point. This is a number between −1 and 1, with 0 being the center of the gradient transform and −1 and 1 lying on the gradient borders.

For example, the following code on your main timeline would produce the output displayed in Figure 4-26.

```
var type:String = "radial";
var spreadMethod:String = "reflect";
var interpolationMethod:String = "RGB";
var focalPointRatio:Number = 0.7;

var colors:Array = [0x00FFFF, 0xFF00FF, 0x0000FF];
var ratios:Array = [0, 200, 255];
var alphas:Array = [100, 100, 100];
var matrix:Object = {matrixType:"box", x:150, y:150, w:200, h:100,➥
r:Math.PI};

with (createEmptyMovieClip("clip", 0)) {
     _x = 125;
     _y = 50;
     lineStyle(0, 0, 100);
     beginGradientFill(
             type,
             colors,
             alphas,
             ratios,
             matrix,
             spreadMethod,
             interpolationMethod,
             focalPointRatio
     );
     lineTo(300, 0);
     lineTo(300, 300);
     lineTo(0, 300);
     endFill();
}
```

Figure 4-26.
Using `focalPointOffset` and the spread modes, interesting effects can be achieved through ActionScript as well.

Strokes of genius

Even more so than with gradients, Flash 8 boasts a wealth of enhancements to its vector strokes, including multiple types of caps and joins (which can be set in the Properties panel, as shown in Figure 4-27), stroke hinting, scale options, and the powerful ability to fill a stroke with gradient colors or bitmaps. All of these translate into finer control for the user over the visuals in Flash.

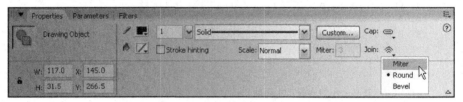

Figure 4-27. The Cap and Join options in the Properties panel

Caps

The Cap options describe the way strokes end on open lines. (Caps can't be seen on closed shapes.) The default in previous versions of Flash was Round, which draws a perfect half-circle past the endpoint of the line, with the width of the line defining the half-circle's diameter, as shown in Figure 4-28. Although this is a perfectly fine way to draw a line, it made it impossible to draw lines with straight ends. (A common workaround was to draw small rectangles with no strokes instead, which offered sharp corners.) It also caused irregularities when importing vectors from other programs that used cap types other than round caps. Luckily, Flash 8 now offers two other cap options in addition to Round, None, and Square, which are all available from the Properties panel when a stroke or drawing tool is selected.

Figure 4-28.
The Round cap option draws a half-circle just beyond the endpoint of the line.

The None cap option does just what it says—it doesn't draw any cap past the endpoint of a line. The result is a straight edge that runs right through the endpoint, as shown in Figure 4-29.

Figure 4-29.
The None cap option doesn't draw a cap at the end of a line, but ends the line in a straight edge through the endpoint.

Just like the None option, Square draws a straight edge, but draws it as a cap that extends past the endpoint of the line by half of the line's thickness, as shown in Figure 4-30.

Figure 4-30.
The Square option draws a straight-edged cap that extends past the endpoint of a line by half of the line's thickness.

Joins

Joins work in a very similar way to caps, but whereas caps define how a stroke ends, joins define the shape at which two strokes meet (e.g., a corner). As with caps, the default in past versions of Flash is Round. The additional joins now offered are Bevel and Miter, both available along with Round and located to the right of all the options in the Properties panel when a stroke or drawing tool is selected. An example of a round join is shown in Figure 4-31.

Figure 4-31.
The Round join option creates a smooth curve from one stroke into the next.

The Bevel join option squares off the edge where two strokes meet. The length and angle of the bevel depends on the angle at which the two strokes meet. A sharp angle will produce a longer bevel, while a wide angle will produce a smaller bevel. The result of the bevel join can be seen in Figure 4-32.

Figure 4-32.
The Bevel join option squares off the edge where two strokes meet.

The Miter join option continues the two joining edges up to a sharp point, as shown in Figure 4-33. This is the option to use if you want to create sharp corners on a shape.

Figure 4-33.
The Miter join option creates a sharp point where two strokes meet.

However, there does come a point at which a miter join doesn't produce welcome results—when the angle is too sharp between strokes. In this case, the miter limit option, an input field in the Properties panel, is available to set the length at which a miter can be drawn. The value specified serves as a multiple of the stroke width (e.g., a value of 2 sets the miter limit to twice the thickness of the stroke). Any join that produces a miter that is longer than the value specified will be drawn with the Bevel option instead. An example of this can be seen in Figure 4-34, in which a shape with a thickness of 40 and a miter limit of 3 has its sharp-angled join beveled. Increasing the miter limit to 7 allows the miter to be drawn, as shown in Figure 4-35.

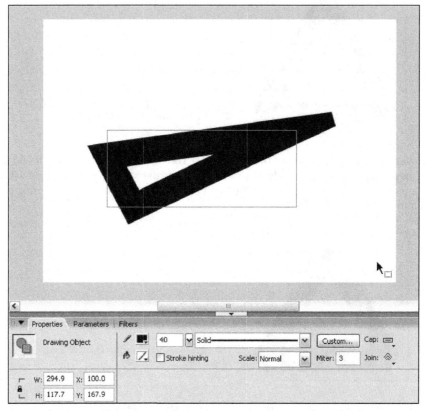

Figure 4-34. A miter limit of 3 on this shape causes the sharp-angled join to be beveled.

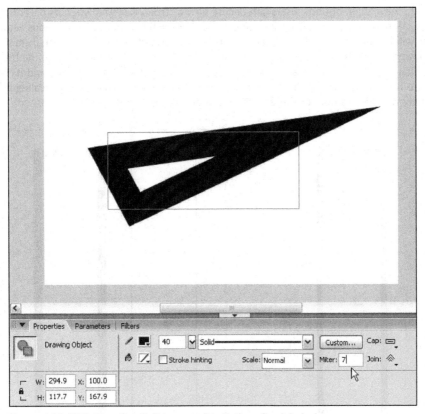

Figure 4-35. With the miter limit increased to 7, the miter join is drawn.

Stroke hinting

Stroke hinting is a new option available as a check box in the Properties panel when a stroke or drawing tool is selected. With this option enabled, stroke endpoints are drawn on their closest full-pixel values, even though they might have been off the pixel in the IDE. This helps to prevent anti-aliasing or blurring of lines at runtime, if this is what you're trying to achieve. For those users who want to produce pixel-perfect pages and applications, this is a welcome addition.

Scale options

Here's a quirky but handy new feature for strokes, found in the Scale drop-down menu in the Properties panel when a stroke or drawing tool is selected. In past versions of Flash, stroke thickness was scaled as its stroke was scaled—so although a user might specify a stroke with a 1-pixel thickness, if the stroke was scaled inside a movie clip to 500%, the stroke thickness would appear to be 5 pixels. Needless to say, this was not always the desired behavior.

With the new Scale options, users can decide how a stroke is scaled when its parent clip is scaled. Normal is the default setting, and works the way it has worked in previous versions. None will retain the stroke's thickness no matter the parent clip's scale, so a 1-pixel stroke will always remain a 1-pixel stroke. Horizontal and Vertical are options that define the axis on which a stroke may be scaled. For instance, if a box has a 10-pixel stroke and its Scale is set to Horizontal, scaling the box vertically won't affect the stroke, though scaling it horizontally will. An example of these options can be seen in Figure 4-36.

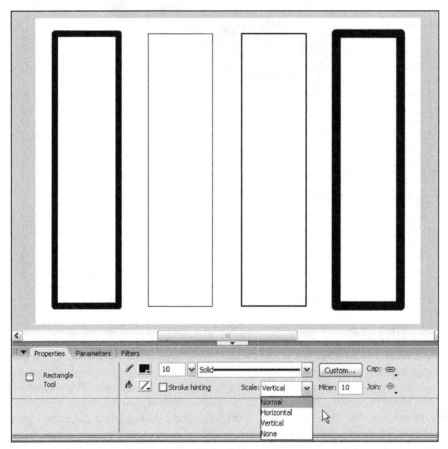

Figure 4-36. A square scaled vertically with its Scale mode set to Normal, None, Horizontal, and Vertical, respectively

Changes to lineStyle()

Settings for a solid stroke's options still rely on a single ActionScript command: MovieClip's lineStyle(), the definition of which now looks like this:

```
public lineStyle(thickness:Number, rgb:Number, alpha:Number,➡
pixelHinting:Boolean, noScale:String, capsStyle:String,➡
jointStyle:String, miterLimit:Number) : Void
```

The first three parameters are the same as in Flash MX 2004. The additional parameters are all optional and include the following:

- `pixelHinting`: Parameters are `true` or `false`; corresponds with stroke hinting in the IDE, and specifies whether horizontal or vertical strokes are drawn on exact pixels to prevent anti-aliasing.

- `noScale`: Parameters are `"none"`, `"normal"`, `"horizontal"`, or `"vertical"`; specifies how a stroke scales within a parent clip.

- `capsStyle`: Parameters are `"round"`, `"square"`, or `"none"`; specifies the style for the endpoints of a line.

- `jointStyle`: Parameters are `"round"`, `"miter"`, or `"none"`; specifies the style for the corner points of a line.

- `miterLimit`: Parameters are a number from 0 to 255; is only valid if `jointStyle` is set to `"miter"`.

The polygon in Figure 4-37 is drawn using the following ActionScript:

```
lineStyle(40, 0x0000FF, 100, false, "none", "square", "miter", 2);
moveTo(100, 220);
lineTo(400, 90);
lineTo(200, 340);
lineTo(100, 220);
```

Figure 4-37. A stroke produced with the drawing API and the new `lineStyle()` parameters

Gradient strokes

The last new feature you'll explore in depth in this chapter is also one of the most powerful, with numerous applications. Users are no longer limited to using a solid color for strokes. Just as with fills, users can specify whether a stroke has a solid or gradient fill. There's not much to explain with this one, as setting up a gradient for a stroke is the same as for a fill—Flash just no longer prevents you from applying the gradient to a stroke as in the past. Examples of unique gradient strokes are shown in Figure 4-38.

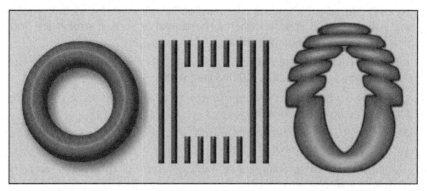

Figure 4-38. A circle, square, and oval with no fills, but gradient strokes and filters applied

The true power of this comes when combining the new gradient stroke options with the new spread modes. Using these two new features together, users can cause colors to repeat or reflect along the length of the entire stroke. It's never been easier to construct a new type of dotted line using a gradient stroke and 0% opacity. An example of this is demonstrated next.

1. Create a new Flash document and use the Line tool to draw a horizontal line the width of the stage. Give the line a solid black 40-point stroke and round caps.

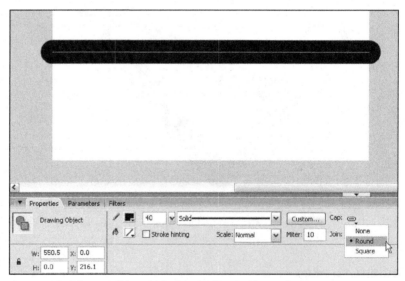

Figure 4-39. A large, solid stroke is drawn using the Line tool.

2. In the Properties panel, click the Custom button next to the line styles. In the Stroke Style pop-up menu, set the type to Dashed, the stroke length to 1 (the first field next to the Dash: label), and the gap length to 60 (the field in front of the pts label). This will give a rounded dotted stroke to your line.

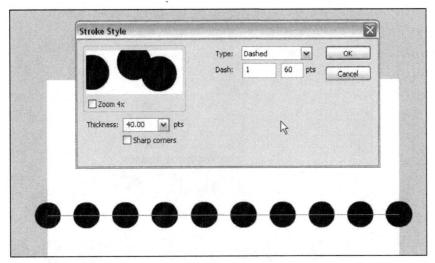

Figure 4-40. The stroke is given a custom dotted style.

3. Use the Color Mixer panel to assign a horizontal linear gradient to the stroke. Do this by selecting and opening the stroke swatch and assigning the default white-to-black gradient from the swatches. Now alter the gradient in the Color Mixer by setting the white swatch to red and the black swatch to blue.

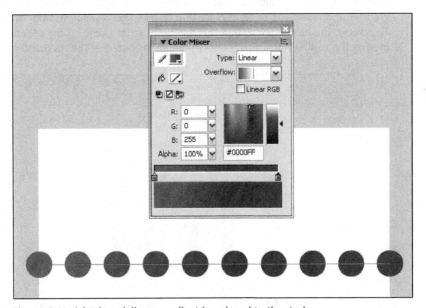

Figure 4-41. A horizonal, linear gradient is assigned to the stroke.

4. Add another red swatch at around 33%, two green swatches at around 34% and 66%, and another blue swatch at around 67%. This will create a gradient that moves from red to green to blue with little transition between colors.

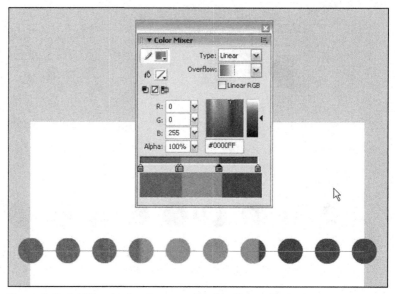

Figure 4-42. Additional color stops are added to the gradient.

5. Set the Overflow method in the Color Mixer to Repeat, and then select the Fill Transform tool and scale the gradient down horizontally. This should give you repeating red/green/blue patterns. Experiment with how far you need to scale the gradient and where you need to place it in order to get a separate color on each dot. To achieve the effect, try setting the gradient center point on the second dot and moving the scaling transform gizmo so that it lies between the third and fourth dot.

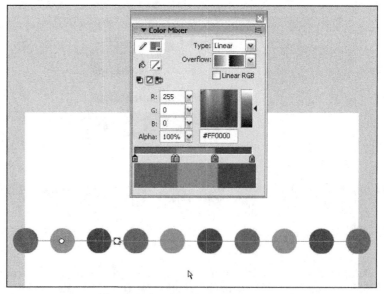

Figure 4-43. The gradient is scaled down horizontally with a Repeat overflow method, effectively assigning a different color per dot.

Introducing lineGradientStyle()

Because of the new addition of gradient strokes, ActionScript introduces a new command to handle this functionality, MovieClip's lineGradientStyle(). This method is exactly the same as beginGradientFill(), except it obviously applies to strokes and not fills. The definition looks like this:

```
public lineGradientStyle(fillType:String, colors:Array, alphas:Array,➥
ratios:Array, matrix:Object, spreadMethod:String,➥
interpolationMethod:String, focalPointRatio:Number) : Void
```

Since the new method works exactly the same as as beginGradientFill(), with its new parameters explained previously in this chapter and its old parameters working as they did in previous versions, you can skip right to implementing it with some code. One powerful aspect of this new command is that you can call the method any number of times while drawing a line, and change the style or direction of the gradient whenever necessary. For instance, if you created a gradient that went from blue at 100% opacity, to blue at 0% opacity, to red at 100% opacity, to red at 0% opacity, creating a two-color dashed line, the results in the IDE would look like Figure 4-44 since the direction of the gradient would be set for the entire stroke.

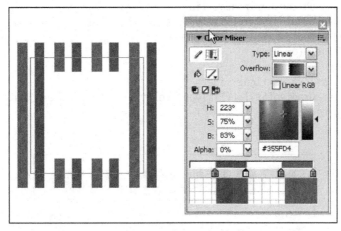

Figure 4-44. A unique gradient stroke created in the IDE

However, with ActionScript, a gradient can be set to change direction as the shape is drawn. The following code, which you can add to your main timeline in a new Flash document, produces Figure 4-45. Notice that lineStyle() needs to be called before line➥GradientStyle() in order to set the stroke thickness.

```
var fillType:String = "linear";
var colors:Array = [0x0000FF, 0x0000FF, 0x0000FF, 0x0000FF, 0xFF0000,➥
0xFF0000];
var alphas:Array = [0, 100, 100, 0, 0, 100];
var ratios:Array = [64, 64, 127, 127, 191, 191];
var spreadMethod:String = "repeat";
// the matrix to draw horizontal dashed lines
```

```
var matrixH:Object = {matrixType:"box", x:-2, y:0, w:41, h:0, r:0};
// the matrix to draw vertical dashed lines
var matrixV:Object = {matrixType:"box", x:0, y:-2, w:20, h:40,➡
r:Math.PI/2};

createEmptyMovieClip("clip", 0);
clip._x = 100;
clip._y = 100;
clip.lineStyle(40);

// draws top horizontal line
clip.lineGradientStyle(fillType, colors, alphas, ratios, matrixH,➡
spreadMethod);
clip.lineTo(350, 0);

// draws right vertical line
clip.lineGradientStyle(fillType, colors, alphas, ratios, matrixV,➡
spreadMethod);
clip.lineTo(350, 200);

// draws bottom horizontal line
clip.lineGradientStyle(fillType, colors, alphas, ratios, matrixH,➡
spreadMethod);
clip.lineTo(0, 200);

// draws left vertical line
clip.lineGradientStyle(fillType, colors, alphas, ratios, matrixV,➡
spreadMethod);
clip.lineTo(0, 0);
```

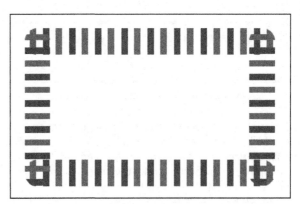

Figure 4-45. The direction and settings for a gradient stroke
can be changed as a stroke is drawn using ActionScript.

Bitmap strokes

One final feature to point out is that in addition to allowing gradients to fill strokes, Flash 8 now provides the facility to fill a stroke with a bitmap. This works exactly as it has in previous versions when filling shapes with bitmaps, except now strokes can accept bitmaps as well. So import those tileable bitmaps into the IDE and apply them to your strokes to get effects like those found in Figure 4-46, which you can find in the file `picture.fla`. So many possibilities . . .

Figure 4-46. A tileable bitmap of a wood texture is applied to a stroke to create a wooden frame effect.

Summary

It's nice that after so many developer-centric features appeared in Flash MX 2004, Flash 8 is offering so many new and powerful tools to help developers, designers, and animators together. The new drawing improvements, both in the IDE and through ActionScript, enable a multitude of creative and extremely beneficial uses and are a welcome addition to the tool set. I have a feeling these improvements to strokes and gradient fills, not to mention the introduction of the Object Drawing model, are the sorts of improvements that, a year from now, we'll all be wondering how on Earth we ever lived without!

5 VIDEO: ALPHA CHANNELS AND OTHER IMPROVEMENTS

by Glen Rhodes and Craig Swann

Video has been an integral part of the Web for years, most often in an attempt to make the Internet more like television—sit back technology. However, what has made Flash so popular, ubiquitous, and loved is the ability to be truly interactive with it. Using video in Flash is no different. It allows us to create lean-forward content that can bring users in and encourage them to interact and make the experience their own.

Ever since Flash MX, video has been a large component of the Flash toolset. Developers across the world have been integrating video into their projects to create compelling content. However, although video is a much desired aspect of interactive development, it has largely remained little used due to bandwidth constraints. Video not only requires a large amount of bandwidth to stream at decent qualities, but it also requires CPU usage on the client machine to process and play back.

Flash MX brought on the wonderful world of video when it incorporated the Sorenson Spark codec. At the time, this was an excellent choice in codec and allowed for more interesting uses of video in Flash projects due to its ease of integration and compression capabilities. However, with Flash 8, Macromedia has taken on a new codec—the On2 VP6. Coupled with the amazing new video features, the On2 VP6 has opened the doors for even more compelling content creation.

Overview of new video features

With Flash 8, there has been a dedicated move into the world of *expressiveness*. This is the idea of creating and offering tools such as the new image API, blends, filters, and video to create amazing new possibilities for developers and designers to express themselves interactively. Video was one of the main areas of focus in this release, and it shows. Before going deeper, let's summarize everything new this version has to offer in the realm of video development.

The new ON2 VP6 codec

Moving on from the Sorenson Spark codec, which has been integrated into the last two iterations of Flash, Macromedia has moved to a new, more advanced codec with the On2 VP6. With the wide range of current online video codecs available, including Sorenson, Windows Media, Real Networks 9, and H.264, this decision required some serious research. Many factors other than video quality were involved, including portability, code increase to the player, hardware support, stability, performance, encoding, and possible costs to Flash users. With the On2 VP6, Flash developers have access to a far more advanced codec that provides superior quality and a much smaller file size than the previous Sorenson codec.

Advanced video encoding options

The process of importing video into Flash has also advanced through a more powerful and robust Import Video wizard. The wizard can handle all sorts of options for importing, allowing for editing, resizing, cropping, and modifying of video prior to importing. This allows for quick, easy video integration without the need for external video editing applications to prepare video before it can be used directly within the Flash environment.

Not only can video be imported within the Flash IDE, but there are also options for creating Flash video (FLV) files with plug-ins to professional video editing applications and the new stand-alone encoder, allowing for greater flexibility in handling video.

New stand-alone video encoder

Flash 8 Professional comes bundled with a new stand-alone video encoder that allows for advanced encoding options. The greatest aspect of this encoder is the ability to batch process video files for easily encoding multiple video files at once. Gone are the days of staring at a progress bar waiting for a single video clip to import! You can now set it up to encode using a number of options, including both the previous Sorenson Spark codec (for use in pre-Flash 8 players) and the new Flash 8 On2 codec. You'll take a look at this encoder later, in the section on importing.

Video alpha channel support

That's right—full video alpha channel support is now available! This feature alone is going to allow for some very creative interactive possibilities in the coming years. If you're unsure of what benefits this feature brings, it basically allows for true runtime video compositing in real time. The ability to import video with alpha channel information (similar to that used in transparent GIFs and alpha PNG graphic files) means that a video can be overlaid on other Flash assets to create a more seamless experience—no more masking or square video experiences. Rendered effects from 3D and special effects programs, such as After Effects, mean that transparent and semitransparent effects such as smoke, water, and fire can be used. Imagine the possibilities for the next generation of Flash games! As well, with the recent move toward personal experiences using video and narration, actors can now be "blue screened" so that content can easily be composited seamlessly.

Embedded cue points

Another powerful new feature is the ability to add cue points directly into an FLV file during the importing/encoding process. These cue points can then either be used during playback as navigational cue points that can be controlled through an interface, or used dynamically to trigger events as the video is played back. You can think of these cue points as a similar yet special set of frame labels for video. These cue points provide an excellent way to control additional information to support video; they can be easily linked and synched to trigger when the video reaches them in the timeline. No longer do you need to create sophisticated timing and tracking procedures to link content. Simply adding a cue point allows for simple linking of video, interface, and content.

New FLV component with skinning options

The new powerful FLV component allows for instant video use, as well as easily customizing and changing the look and feel of the player without bloating the file size of your project. With integrated options such as progressive download and streaming, as well as a number of skinning options and the ability to design your own custom players, it's never been easier or quicker to get your video content into Flash and out to the world.

Importing video

Now that you have an idea of all the wonderful new things that can be done with video, let's take a look at the first and most crucial step to working with video: importing it.

You're going to take a look at two methods of getting video into the Flash environment. First, we'll cover the steps and options involved in importing video directly into the Flash authoring environment, and then we'll discuss the wonderful new batching options available in the stand-alone encoder.

Importing video using the Embed option

This example covers the steps involved in embedding video into Flash. This option is used if you need to edit or modify the original video file. Once you see how easy it is to modify and edit video, feel free to try it with your own video clips.

From the File menu, select Import Video, as shown in Figure 5-1.

Figure 5-1. Menu selection for Import Video

This will prompt the Import Video dialog box (Figure 5-2), which offers several initial options.

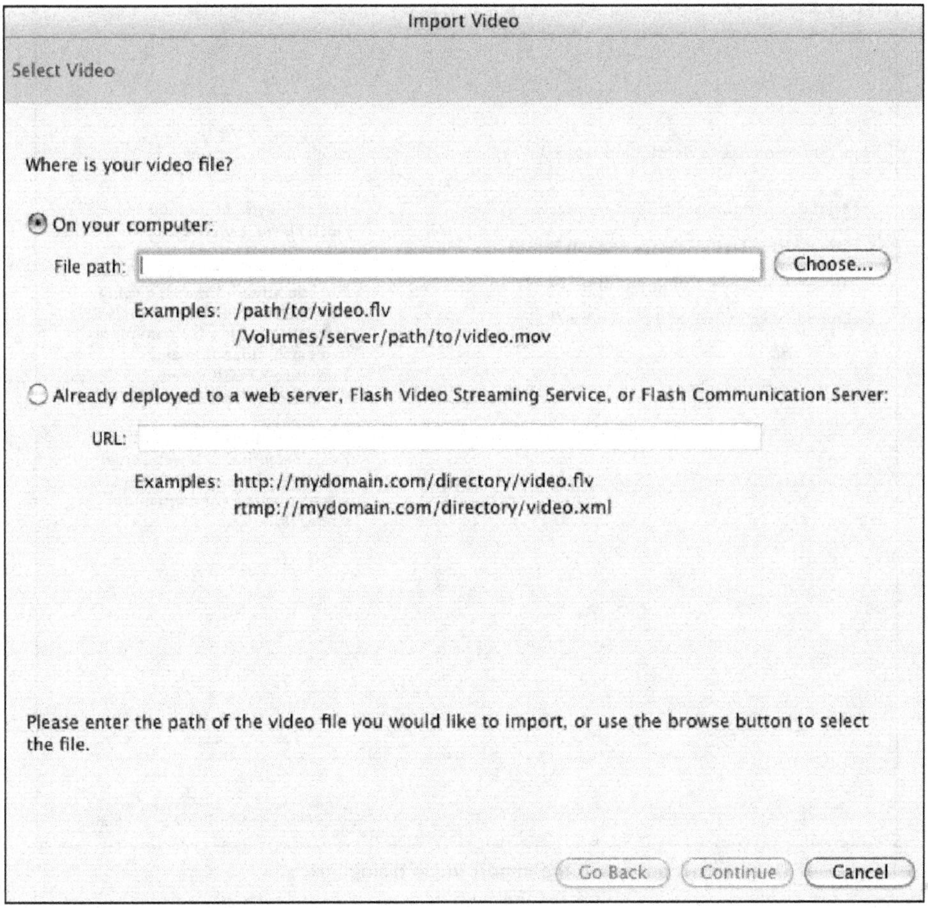

Figure 5-2. Import Video dialog box

Here, you can select the video location from a file on your computer, or select a previously deployed file online that can be linked to a player. For this example, you'll import a local file to cover the editing options available. You'll be using the exampleVideo.avi file, which can be found in the code download at www.friendsofed.com.

Select the On your computer: option, click Choose, browse to the exampleVideo.avi video file that you've downloaded, and then select Continue.

Next, you're shown the deployment options for how you would like to integrate this video (shown in Figure 5-3).

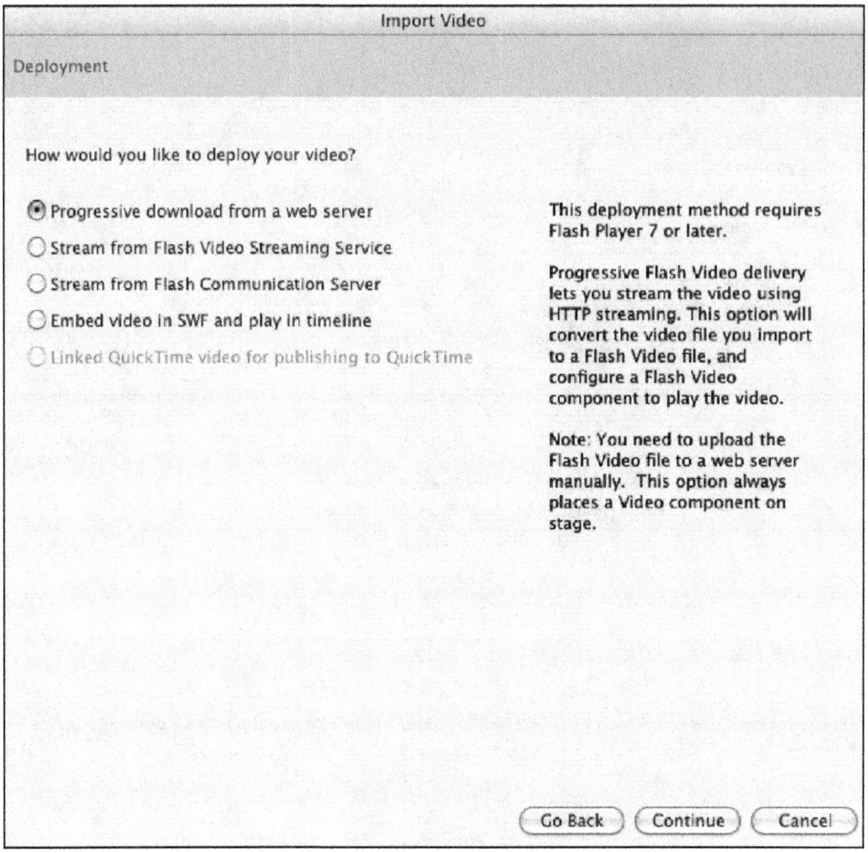

Figure 5-3. Deployment options in the Import Video dialog box

The options available are as follows:

■ Progressive download from a web server *(Flash Player 7 or later)*: This option allows for streaming via HTTP. It converts the video file to the FLV format and automatically configures a Flash video component to play the video. The component will link to the external FLV file, which must be uploaded separately from the generated SWF file containing the playback component.

■ Stream from Flash Video Streaming Service *(Flash Player 7 or later)*: This option lets you upload a video to a Flash Communication Server hosted by a service provider (account required). Like the previous option, this option will configure a component and convert the video file to the FLV format.

■ Stream from Flash Communication Server *(Flash Player 7 or later)*: This is identical to the previous option, except that it's used when you're hosting your own Flash Communication Server.

■ Embed video in SWF and play in timeline: This option embeds a video directly in the SWF file, allowing for direct and visual integration with other elements in the Flash movie. This deployment option is less stable when it comes to synchronization issues, and isn't suggested for long clips containing audio.

■ Linked QuickTime video for publishing to QuickTime *(Flash Player 3, 4, and 5 only)*: This deployment method is used with older versions of Flash, and can only be used with QuickTime files. It's used to link to a reference QuickTime file so that interactive elements can be added to the file, output, and viewed with the QuickTime 4 plug-in.

In this example, you'll be selecting the Embed video in SWF and play in timeline option to explore some of the editing capabilities that exist.

After selecting the Embed option, select Continue.

You can choose the Symbol Type (options are Embedded video, Movie clip, and graphic), as well as whether you want the audio track to be integrated or separate. Further, you can choose whether to place the instance directly on the stage or in the library. Finally, you're given the options to embed the entire video or edit it first, as shown in Figure 5-4. To view the editing options, select Edit the video first and click Continue.

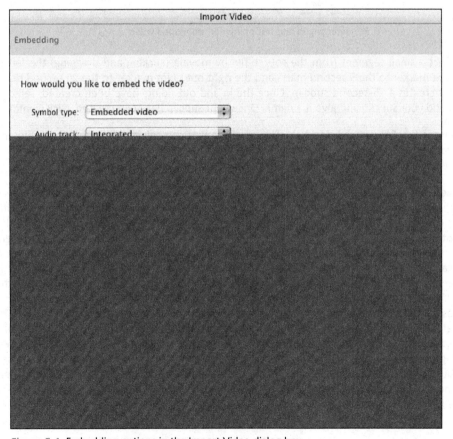

Figure 5-4. Embedding options in the Import Video dialog box

Here, there are several options available for fine-tuning the embedding process. The first option allows you to create in and out points by selecting the segment or segments that you would like to import. You can create multiple small clips from your source video and import them as separate elements. The screenshot in Figure 5-5 illustrates the selecting of in and out points.

Figure 5-5. Selecting in and out points for embedded video

Select a small segment from the source file by moving (clicking and dragging) the left in point marker to the 5 second mark, and the right out point marker to the 20 second mark. This creates a 15-second subclip. Once the in and out points have been created, select + to add your subclip and give it a name. Once your subclip has been created, click Continue.

Next is the Encoding dialog box. This is where you can select the encoding profile and codec you would like to use from the defaults, or select Advanced Settings to tweak it specifically for this import. Figure 5-6 illustrates all of the options.

There are a number of default options available in the drop-down menu at the top, which are generally more than adequate; however, there may be times when you have specific video content that can be best optimized by tweaking the available parameters. Also notice the new Cue Points option in the Advanced Settings section. Since the current example is an embedded video, this option isn't available, but we'll cover that in the next example. There are a number of possible options for selecting a good compression setting for your video. If your piece is largely what's called "talking head" footage, with very little difference from frame to frame, you can afford to lower the settings; whereas footage that has a lot of cuts will require a higher setting to retain quality through these transitions. The default settings available are often more than adequate to use, with Medium quality being an excellent compromise between file size and quality. It's always best to try different settings and review the video to select what's right for your content. Once you've chosen your compression selections, click Continue, and you'll be taken to a confirmation dialog. Once there, select Finish, and your video will be imported into the Flash environment.

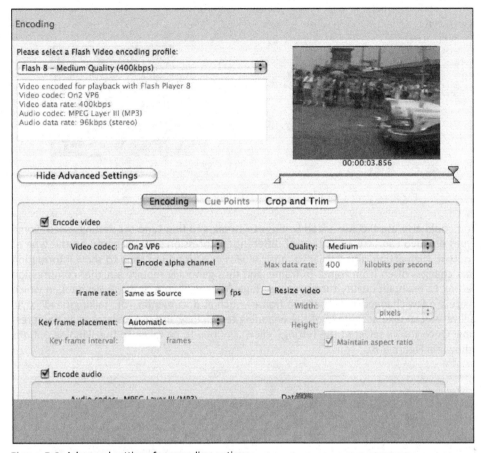

Figure 5-6. Advanced settings for encoding options

This method of embedding is the same as in previous versions of Flash, and it can be quite useful when you're required to modify or edit larger clips for use inside the Flash environment. However, many times you'll be handed finalized video files that have already been edited and modified—in such cases, it's best to select the Progressive option, which you'll look at now.

Encoding video using progressive download and adding player skin

This example demonstrates the importing of a video using the new On2 codec and adding a skin for playback. Again, you'll use exampleVideo.avi from the code download.

As with the previous import example, exampleVideo.avi is selected locally from the computer and imported using the Progressive download from a web server option. Figure 5-7 shows a screenshot of the Encoding screen. For this example, the default encoding profile of Flash 8 – Medium Quality (400kbps) is used to import the video.

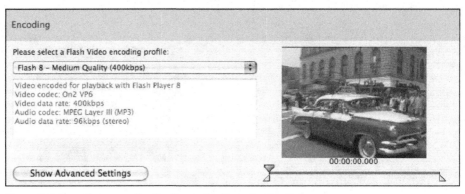

Figure 5-7. Encoding screen for the Progessive Download option

You could also use the Advanced Settings to tweak and fine-tune the settings used. Some types of video can take advantage of different compression settings based on the type of content. High action clips similar to music videos or action films tend to show information that changes often from frame to frame, and thus generally require a higher compression setting to maintain quality through these high-frequency cuts. Static video data, in which there are few changes from frame to frame—such as documentary or "talking-head"-style delivery—can take advantage of the encoding technology and use lower-quality compression. Once you've selected the settings, click Continue to be taken to the skinning options (shown in Figure 5-8).

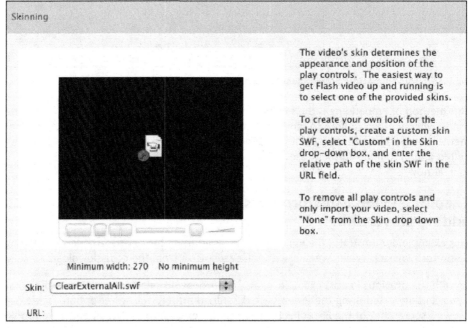

Figure 5-8. FLV component skinning options

This step in the importing process is new as of Flash 8, and allows for the selection of a skin, which is applied to the FLVPlayback component. There are a number of provided skins available, which you can see in the list provided in the Skin drop-down menu (see Figure 5-9).

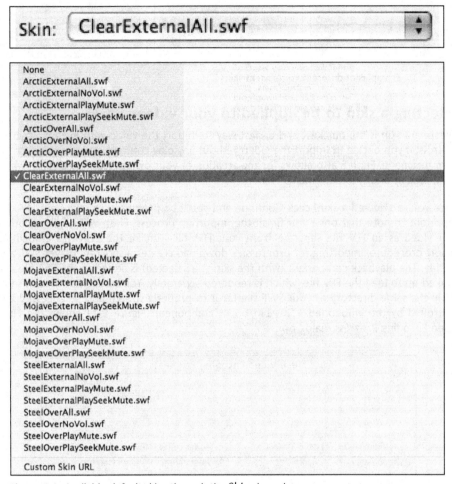

Figure 5-9. Available default skins through the Skin drop-down menu

Figure 5-10 shows a few examples of the different component skins you can choose from.

Figure 5-10. Examples of different component skins

Selecting a skin to be applied to your video

Selecting a skin is the quickest and easiest way to import the video with instant playback controls. If you decide to import the video without any play controls, you can select None from this menu. Flash 8 also allows for the creation of your own personalized skins, which you'll look at briefly in a moment.

Once you've selected a skin, click Continue and you'll be prompted to save your FLA. It's important to note that once you finish the importing process, Flash will begin encoding your video as an FLV file separate from your FLA file—unlike the previous embedded import procedure, importing for progressive download creates a separate player SWF and FLV file. The playback component (with the skin you selected) is added to the FLA file and hooked up to load the FLV file, which is rendered separately. You'll need to place this FLV file in the same directory as your SWF file for it to properly stream and be accessed and controlled by the embedded FLVPlayback component. Figure 5-11 shows the Flash Video Encoding Progress dialog box.

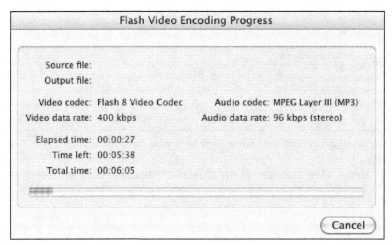

Figure 5-11. Encoding progress dialog box

Once the import process is complete, you should see the playback component of the newly created FLA file on the stage (as shown in Figure 5-12). This component is wired to load the video file that was encoded.

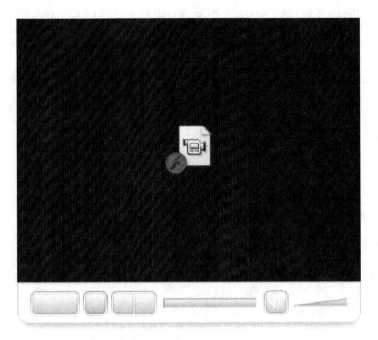

Figure 5-12. Default playback component on the stage

If you click the component and check the parameters, you'll see that it's already configured to load the FLV that was created (see Figure 5-13).

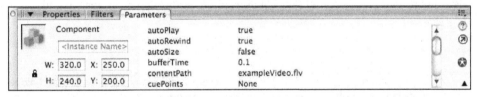

Figure 5-13. Playback component parameters for setting the content path of the FLV file

Test or publish the movie to see it run. Flash automatically places the encoded FLV file in
the same directory that the FLA is saved to. You'll now have an FLA, a SWF, and an FLV file
located in the same directory with a functioning video player based on your player skin.
You can also download the finished example from www.friendsofed.com.

Creating customized skins

Although there are a number of great looking skins that you can instantly use, sometimes
you need a level of design and customization that these don't offer. For this reason, it's
possible to create your very own skins. To do this, all that's required is to load one of the
existing skins (they're stored in FLA files) and modify the movie clips in that file as you
would modify any other movie clip.

The FLA for the skins can be found in the Configuration ➤ SkinFLA directory, which is inside the Macromedia Flash 8 folder on your machine. Figure 5-14 shows an example of the layout and design of the component when you open it in the Flash authoring environment.

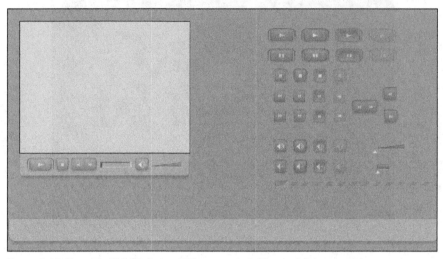

Figure 5-14. Template FLA file for an FLV component skin; used for customizing

All the interface elements are created as movie clips and can be edited in the same way you would modify your own clips. Once you've modified the elements to your design, you simply need to export a SWF of the file into the Macromedia Flash 8 ➤ Configuration ➤ Skin directory. Once this is done, the next time you go through the import process and select a skin, your newly created skin will be available in the Skin drop-down menu.

The stand-alone Flash 8 Video Encoder

One of the great new additions to Flash 8 Professional is the inclusion of a separate stand-alone application called the Flash 8 Video Encoder. (This is found in the Flash 8 VideoEncoder folder, installed alongside the Macromedia Flash 8 folder on your machine.) This application is very similar to the import process within the Flash IDE—however, it has the much-requested addition of batch processing. With the Video Encoder, you can select multiple files, choose custom compression settings for each video, and let it do its magic.

Unlike the regular import process, there's no automatic creation of FLVPlayback components—only the strict creation of FLV files, which can be loaded and accessed by either custom video controls or components in your Flash files.

Let's start by looking at an example in which you'll encode a file to be used later on in the chapter, in the "Cue point functionality" section. The movie, entitled chromeballs.mov, was created in a 3D application and contains alpha channel data. It's available for download at www.friendsofed.com. In addition, cue points will be added for further manipulation in the upcoming example.

Encoding video using the Flash 8 Video Encoder

When first launching the Video Encoder, you're presented with the screen shown in Figure 5-15.

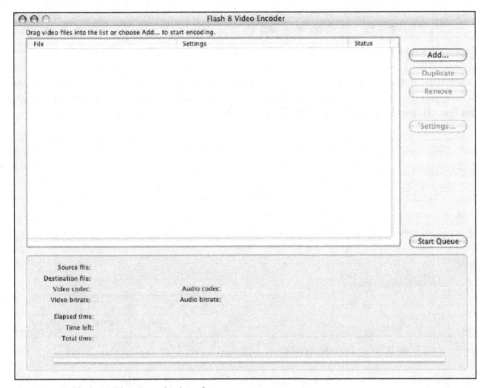

Figure 5-15. Flash 8 Video Encoder interface

The main benefit of using the Video Encoder is the ability to add multiple files and batch process them. Since the encoding process can be quite time consuming, using the Video Encoder allows you to specify multiple files to encode sequentially; and more importantly, it frees up Flash as an application. This means that you can be importing multiple files while retaining the ability to work with Flash, as the encoding is run in the background by a separate application.

Although the Video Encoder can encode multiple files (you'll have to trust us and Macromedia on that!), in this example you'll be using just one file. You'll look at the encoding process as well as the ability to embed cue points.

To add files to be encoded, you simply drag them into the list window or choose Add to select them from a file chooser window. Once a file has been selected, it will appear in the list along with the option of editing settings (see Figure 5-16). Add the `chromeballs.mov` file now.

File	Settings	Status
/Users/craig/Desktop/chromeballs.mov	Flash 8 – Medium Quality (400kbps)	Waiting

Figure 5-16. Adding a video file to the queue for encoding

The status of the file is set to Waiting until you select Start Queue to begin encoding. Before you do that, you'll adjust some properties by selecting the Settings button, which will launch the Flash Video Encoding Settings window shown in Figure 5-17.

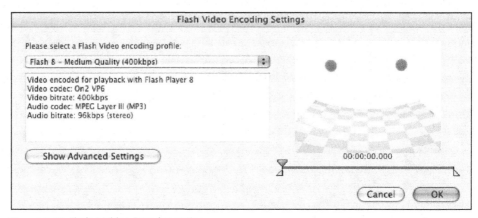

Figure 5-17. Flash 8 Video Encoder settings

As you may notice, this window is identical to the encoding window for importing video directly into Flash. You're going to leave the actual encoding profile at the default, Flash 8 – Medium Quality (400kbps). Now select the Show Advanced Settings button—this will expand the window and display the advanced settings. These are the same advanced settings that you saw in the previous example when importing video into the Flash environment. Clicking Cue Points will allow you to set points that can later be manipulated in Flash.

Adding cue points in the encoding process

There are two types of cue points that can be added to an FLV file: event and navigation. You can add up to 16 cue points per video file. The key difference between the two types is that event cue points can be listened for in Flash and used to trigger events, and navigation cue points set keyframes that can be used to control playback. For instance, if your video has several chapters or scenes in it, you may want to add navigation cue points so that users can click an interface to jump to a specific point—such as a video menu selection.

In this example, you're going to add event cue points. These are used so that they're triggered during playback and handled by a listener created in Flash, which can then perform an action or function based on hitting this cue point event. You're going to add an event cue point at the beginning, middle, and end of this video clip, to be used in a later example.

Clicking the + button will add a cue point based on the current time of the video shown in the preview window. Moving the playhead scrubber in the preview window to the middle of the video clip and clicking + will add a cue point at that location, as shown in Figure 5-18.

1. Move the scrubber to the beginning of the clip and click the + button to add a cue point. Set the type to Event, and in the Name field, type Start.

2. Move the playhead to the point at which the two spheres collide, and click the + button to add another cue point. Set the type to Event, and type Smash in the Name field.

3. Move the playhead to the very end of the clip, click the + button, set the type to Event, and type End in the Name field.

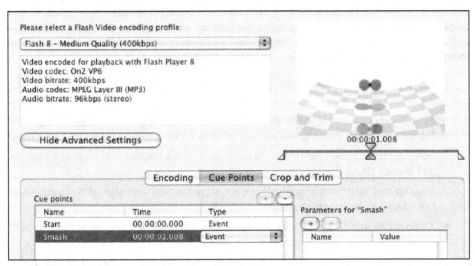

Figure 5-18. Adding cue points to FLV encoding

Once your three cue points are added, click OK to exit the Settings screen, and then click Start Queue to begin encoding all the videos in the file list. One of the nice features of the Video Encoder (which doesn't exist in the built-in Flash encoding process) is the live preview of the process. Figure 5-19 shows an example of the Video Encoder as it encodes the video.

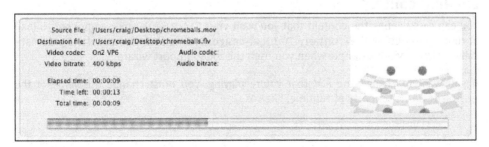

Figure 5-19. Flash 8 Video Encoder live preview progress dialog box

Not only is there a progress bar, but there's also a live preview window showing the frame that's currently processing.

Coding the FLVPlayback component

So far, you've looked at importing video into Flash using both the built-in video encoder and the stand-alone Flash 8 Video Encoder. You've also seen how the `FLVPlayback` component can be used in your Flash movies to automate the playback of FLV files at runtime and allow users to control the playback of your videos. Now that you understand how that all works, you're going to take a closer look at the `FLVPlayback` component and what you can do with it from an ActionScript perspective.

The main ActionScript methods and properties

The ActionScript methods, properties, and events of the `FLVPlayback` component are numerous. There are far too many, in fact, to cover everything within the scope of this chapter. For that reason, you're going to be looking at the main—or most important—methods, properties, and events of the `FLVPlayback` component. They can be broken down into the following main areas:

- *Loading content*: Specifies the ability to determine the content to load using the `contentPath` property
- *Basic playback control*: Includes necessities like play, stop, rewind, and seek, using the `play`, `stop`, `pause`, and `seek` methods and the events associated with them
- *General information and status*: Includes information about the playhead position and the length of the movie
- *Position and size*: Simply controls the physical position and size of the instance of the `FLVPlayback` component
- *Audio functionality*: Focuses mainly on the ability to get and set the volume level of the playing video and detect when the user changes it
- *Cue point functionality*: You can harness the new cue point functionality to trigger events at specific points in an FLV's playback

Let's look at the different areas now. In all of the example code that follows, it's assumed that you have an instance of the `FLVPlayback` component on the stage, and that you've given it the instance name `myFLVPlayback`.

Loading content

You can easily define the content that you want your `FLVPlayback` component to load at runtime by setting the `contentPath` at design time. In fact, this was done automatically in the previous example when you used the Video Import wizard.

If you want to change the FLV that you're playing, you must change the value of the `contentPath` property at runtime, like so:

```
myFLVPlayback.contentPath = "mynewmovie.flv";
```

or

```
myFLVPlayback.contentPath = "http://somesite.com/mynewmovie.flv";
```

When this is set or changed, the component knows to automatically close the current FLV (if `contentPath` was previously set), and then it immediately begins loading the new content. Depending upon the value of the `autoPlay` property, the content will either load and wait, or load and begin playing automatically.

The `contentPath` can either point directly to an FLV file (an HTTP connection), or it can be a connection to an RTMP video stream, like so:

```
myFLVPlayback.contentPath = "rtmp://something/somethingelse.flv";
```

If you use a streaming server, like Flash Communication Server or the Flash Video Streaming Service, then you must set the value of the `isLive` property to `true`, like so:

```
myFLVPlayback.isLive = true;
myFLVPlayback.contentPath = "rtmp://something/somethingelse.flv";
```

Basic playback control

One of the most fundamental aspects to the `FLVPlayback` component is that everything the user can do with the user interface, you can also trigger with code. This means you have the ability to play, stop, rewind, and seek with ActionScript code.

First, let's look at the main methods, each of which is followed by a code example and description.

FLVPlayback.play()

Example:

```
myFLVPlayback.play();
```

This starts the playback of the current video. If the component is in a paused state, then it continues from the paused position; otherwise it starts playing from the beginning.

FLVPlayback.play(contentPath)

Example:

```
myFLVPlayback.play("newmovie.flv");
```

This loads and then plays the content passed in as the first parameter. You can pass in a local or HTTP FLV, or an RTMP URL.

FLVPlayback.play(contentPath, totalTime, isLive)

Example:

```
myFLVPlayback.play("rtmp://something/newmovie.flv", 10, true);
```

This connects to a streaming server with the RTMP protocol, and tells the `FLVPlayback` component that the video is 10 seconds long and that it's a live stream.

Of the previous three uses of the play method, the one that will be used most often is the first, which just tells the component to play what it currently has loaded.

FLVPlayback.stop()

Example:

```
myFLVPlayback.stop();
```

This stops playing the current video. If the autoRewind property is set to true, it rewinds the playhead to the beginning of the video.

FLVPlayback.pause()

Example:

```
myFLVPlayback.pause();
```

This pauses the playback of the current video. The main difference between this and the stop method is that this method will not automatically rewind the video, and any subsequent calls to the play method will continue from the point at which it was paused.

FLVPlayback.seek() (method), FLVPlayback.seekSeconds(), FLVPlayback.seekPercent()

Example:

```
myFLVPlayback.seek(4.2);
```

Example:

```
myFLVPlayback.seekSeconds(4.2);
```

Example:

```
myFLVPlayback.seekPercent(83);
```

The first two examples cause the playhead to move to the time, in seconds, passed in to the seek or seekSeconds function. The third example moves the playhead to a position corresponding to the percentage of total elapsed time passed in to seekPercent. The seekSeconds function exists in order to tally with the seekPercent function, but seekSeconds and seek are in fact identical. It seems trivial, but the apparent redundancy of these methods is for those who can't remember whether seek refers to percent or seconds—you can just use seekSeconds or seekPercent instead.

FLVPlayback.autoPlay (property)

Example:

```
myFLVPlayback.autoPlay = false;
myFLVPlayback.seek(3);
myFLVPlayback.play();
```

The value of the autoPlay property determines whether the seek activity will automatically begin playing at the new position or wait for play to be triggered manually. The preceding example causes the movie to seek to the 3-second mark, and then play from there. Notice that autoPlay is set to false so that the video will not begin playing after the seek.

Now that you've looked at the main control methods, let's look at the most important properties.

FLVPlayback.playing (property)

Example:

```
if (myFLVPlayback.playing)
{
  // do something
}
```

This is a read-only value that's `true` if the video is currently playing; otherwise it's `false`.

FLVPlayback.paused (property)

Example:

```
if (myFLVPlayback.paused)
{
    // do something
}
```

This is a read-only value that's `true` if the video is in a paused state; otherwise it's `false`.

FLVPlayback.stopped (property)

Example:

```
if (myFLVPlayback.stopped)
{
  // do something
}
```

This is a read-only value that's `true` if the video is stopped; otherwise it's `false`.

FLVPlayback.state

Example:

```
var currentState:String = myFLVPlayback.state;
```

This property is a string that specifies the current state of the component, as determined by other influences such as calls to play, stop, or the video ending. The expected values are as follows:

- `buffering`
- `connectionError`
- `disconnected`
- `loading`
- `paused`
- `playing`
- `rewinding`
- `seeking`
- `stopped`

FLVPlayback.autoPlay

Example:

```
myFLVPlayback.autoPlay = true;
```

This is a Boolean value that, if set to `true`, causes the FLV to play immediately when `contentPath` is set. If `autoPlay` is set to `false`, the component waits for the `play` method to be called or the Play button to be clicked. This component always loads the content immediately, even if `autoPlay` is set to `false`. The default value for a new component placed on the stage is `true`.

FLVPlayback.autoRewind

Example:

```
myFLVPlayback.autoRewind = true;
```

This is a Boolean value that, if set to `true`, causes the FLV to rewind to the first frame when playback stops. Playback will stop either because the player reaches the end of the stream or the `stop()` method is called. The default value is `true` for new instances of the component. This property is ignored for live streams.

Finally, you have some events that are critical to the basic control of the `FLVPlayback` component. These are events that are triggered when the basic playback control events occur.

FLVPlayback.playing (event)

Example:

```
var listenerObject:Object = new Object();
listenerObject.playing = function(eventObject:Object):Void
{
    playlight_mc._visible = true;
}
myFLVPlayback.addEventListener("playing", listenerObject);
```

The playing event is triggered by the `FLVPlayback` component when the component *enters* the playing state. You could use this to do something simple like turn on a green light to indicate that the component is playing.

FLVPlayback.paused (event)

Example:

```
var listenerObject:Object = new Object();
listenerObject.paused = function(eventObject:Object):Void
{
  yellowlight_mc._visible = true;
}
myFLVPlayback.addEventListener("paused", listenerObject);
```

The paused event is triggered by the `FLVPlayback` component when the component enters the paused state. As in the previous example, you could use this to do something simple like turn on a yellow light to indicate that the component is paused.

FLVPlayback.stopped (event)
Example:

```
var listenerObject:Object = new Object();
listenerObject.stopped = function(eventObject:Object):Void
{
  redlight_mc._visible = true;
}
myFLVPlayback.addEventListener("stopped", listenerObject);
```

The `stopped` event is triggered by the `FLVPlayback` component when the component enters the stopped state. Again, as in the previous two examples, you could use this to do something simple like turn on a red light to indicate that the component is stopped.

FLVPlayback.seek (event)
Example:

```
var listenerObject:Object = new Object();
listenerObject.seek = function(eventObject:Object):Void
{
  trace("Moved to:" + myFLVPlayback.playheadTime);
}
myFLVPlayback.addEventListener("seek", listenerObject);
```

The `seek` event is triggered by the `FLVPlayback` component when the location of the playhead is changed by a call to `seek`, `seekSeconds`, or `seekPercent`.

FLVPlayback.fastForward (event), FLVPlayback.rewind (event)
Example:

```
var listenerObject:Object = new Object();
listenerObject.fastForward = function(eventObject:Object):Void
{
  trace("Moved forward to:" + myFLVPlayback.playheadTime);
}
myFLVPlayback.addEventListener("fastForward", listenerObject);
```

Example:

```
var listenerObject:Object = new Object();
listenerObject.rewind = function(eventObject:Object):Void
{
  trace("Moved back to:" + myFLVPlayback.playheadTime);
}
myFLVPlayback.addEventListener("rewind", listenerObject);
```

These two events are triggered, in addition to the `seek` event, depending upon whether the seek position is ahead of or behind the current position.

FLVPlayback.stateChange (event)

Example:

```
var listenerObject:Object = new Object();
listenerObject.stateChange = function(eventObject:Object):Void
{
  trace(eventObject.state);
}
myFLVPlayback.addEventListener("stateChange", listenerObject);
```

This is a general state change event. The `stateChange` event is dispatched when playback state changes. The `Object` event that's passed in has properties of `state` and `playheadTime`. This event is a nice catchall, and can be used to determine exactly what a movie is doing at any time—whether it's stuck loading, buffering, or has stopped and is waiting.

Running the preceding code on an `FLVPlayback` component and then doing lots of stopping and starting will produce output that looks something like the following:

- loading
- buffering
- playing
- rewinding
- stopped
- buffering
- playing
- rewinding

General information and status

The `FLVPlayback` component is able to tell you the current position of the playhead and the current length of the movie; that's how the playhead movie clip on the component determines its position.

You'll notice, however, that there's no timer display anywhere on the component. Nowhere do you see the actual "time" that the playhead is at.

Therefore, what better way to get to understand the status and playhead position methods than to write a small application that displays the playhead time, thereby enhancing the functionality of the `FLVPlayback` component?

The completed example can be found in the file `flvwithtimer.fla`.

1. Create a new default Flash movie.
2. Open the Components panel (*CTRL/CMD+F7*) and drag an instance of the `FLVPlayback` component onto the stage.

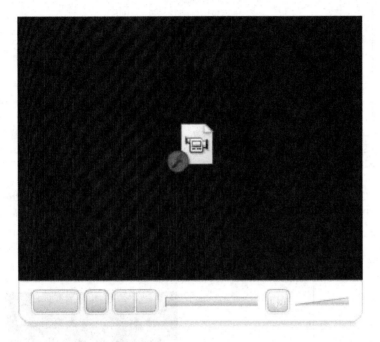

Figure 5-20. Default `FLVPlayback` component on the stage

3. Give it the instance name `myFLVPlayback`.

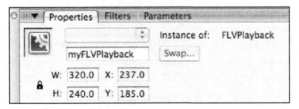

Figure 5-21. Setting the instance name of `FLVPlayback` component

4. Open the Properties panel (*CTRL/CMD+F3*).
5. Click the Parameters tab to view the component parameters.

6. Click in the contentPath field, and in the box that pops up, type myVideo.flv and then click OK. (Note that you can use any FLV video you want.)

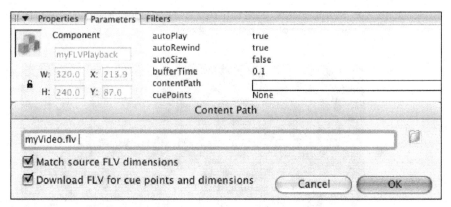

Figure 5-22. Setting the content path for the FLVPlayback component

7. Click the Skin parameter and choose MojaveExternalAll.swf from the drop-down menu. Click OK.

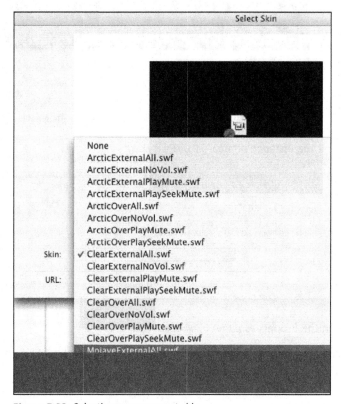

Figure 5-23. Selecting a component skin

8. Save the movie to the same location as the FLV video you selected in step 6, and call it `flvwithtimer.fla`.

9. Press *CTRL/CMD+ENTER* to test your movie.

   You should see the `FLVPlayback` component on the stage, and it should have the Mojave skin buttons beneath it. The video should automatically begin playing.

   Now you can add the code and text field to make the timer.

10. Close the running movie.

11. Just above the `FLVPlayback` component, create a new text field.

12. Set the text size to 10 point, the font to Arial, the color to #000000, the type to Dynamic Text, and the instance name to timer_txt.

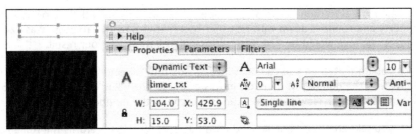

Figure 5-24. Setting the timer display text field

13. Create a new layer at the top of the current timeline, and name it Code.

14. Click frame 1 of the new layer.

15. Open the Actions panel (*F9*).

16. Begin by entering the following code:

```
import mx.video.*;
var listenerObject:Object = new Object();
listenerObject.playheadUpdate = function(eventObject:Object):Void
{
```

The preceding code tells Flash to import the `mx.video` class and all its subclasses. You then create a new object called `listenerObject`, and create a function on it called `playheadUpdate`. This is the function that will be called at a set interval while the video is playing. The timeframe of that interval will be specified later.

17. Continue by entering the following:

```
// Get the seconds
var sec:Number = Math.floor(eventObject.playheadTime);

// Calculate minutes
var min:Number = Math.floor(sec / 60);

// Strip out minutes from the second value
sec = sec % 60;
```

```
// Pad the zero if needed so 5 becomes 05, etc.
if (sec < 10)
  var secString:String = "0" + sec.toString();
    else
  var secString:String = sec.toString();

// get a nice round number for milliseconds, will be a number
// from 0 to 999
var ms:Number = Math.floor(eventObject.playheadTime * 1000) % 1000;
```

In the preceding code, the number of minutes, seconds, and milliseconds is determined from the `playheadTime` property. The `playheadTime` property is a number that contains the current position of the playhead, in seconds.

The first thing is to round down the number of seconds, so you take the `playheadTime` property and round it down with `Math.floor`. So if `playheadTime` was 124.22, then the `sec` variable would be 124. The `sec` variable now stores your result.

Once you do that, then you can take `sec`, divide it by 60, and then round down the result to give you the number of minutes. In this example, the value is 2 (124/60 is 2.067, which rounds down to 2). Now your `min` variable contains the number 2.

Next, you take the `sec` variable, and modulus it by 60, which returns the remainder after dividing by 60. If you do that, you get 4. So now, `min` is 2 and `sec` is 4.

Next, you must pad `sec` with a 0 if it's less than 10. If you don't do that, you'll end up with a time that looks like 2:4, when you really want to see 2:04. The result of the padded string is stored in `secString`.

Finally, you take the original `playheadTime`, multiply it by 1000, and then modulus that result by 1000. This will return to you a number between 0 and 999, which will represent the number of milliseconds that the `playheadTime` is at.

18. Continue by entering the following code below what you've already added:

```
// display the total constructed time in the on-screen text field
timer_txt.text = min + ":" + secString + ":" + ms;
}

// Force the time to update every 20 milliseconds so it's nice and
// fast. Default is 250 ms.
myFLVPlayback.playheadUpdateInterval = 20;
myFLVPlayback.addEventListener("playheadUpdate", listenerObject);
```

Here, you're setting the text of the `timer_txt` text field to the constructed string of *min:sec:millisec*—so you would get 2:04:0.

That's the end of the function. The second to last line of code updates the playhead interval—so the `playheadUpdate` function is called more frequently. The default is 250 milliseconds, which would result in a timer update four times per second. This would actually appear to be a very choppy timer, so you change the update interval to 20 milliseconds, which is more than 10 times as fast and will result in a nice, smooth timer display.

The last line of code simply assigns the `playheadUpdate` event to the `myFLVPlayback` component by adding an event listener to call the `playheadUpdate` function located on the `listenerObject`.

19. Run this example again, and you'll see the timer at the top, dutifully showing you the time that you're looking at in the video.

Figure 5-25. The `FLVPlayback` component with new dynamic time display

That's all there is to it. That's how you get the playhead time, and how you use the `playheadUpdate` event as well as change the frequency with which it's updated. The `playheadUpdate` event is a nice way to do lots of code at a regular interval, somewhat like a traditional `onEnterFrame` function.

Position and size

Setting the position and size of an `FLVPlayback` component is easy and trivial, and if you're familiar with setting the size and position of movie clips, then you're 90% of the way there.

The only difference is that instead of _width, _height, _x, _y, and _visible, you use `width`, `height`, `x`, `y`, and `visible`. In other words, you remove the underscore. This is because you're setting internal properties that automatically call methods to resize and reposition the buttons and other elements of the user interface associated with the component. If you were to simply use the _width and _height parameters, for example, everything would be stretched or squashed, rather than resized and reorganized visually.

So let's try an example. Drag an instance of the FLVPlayback component to the stage, give it the instance name myFLVPlayback, and put the following code on frame 1 of the main timeline:

```
myFLVPlayback.autoSize = false;
myFLVPlayback.maintainAspectRatio = false;
myFLVPlayback.width = 400;
myFLVPlayback.height = 350;
myFLVPlayback.x = 0;
myFLVPlayback.y = 0;
```

If you run this movie, you'll notice that the component moves to the upper-left corner, and is resized to 400 × 350.

Figure 5-26. Dynamic sizing and positioning of the FLVPlayback component

Notice the settings of autoSize and maintainAspectRatio. By setting these both to false, you ensure that your width and height code is properly applied.

If you set autoSize to true, then calls to width and height are ignored completely; but if you make autoSize false, and set maintainAspectRatio to true, then you'll be able to resize the component, but it will always maintain the aspect ratio of the FLV you're displaying. In other words, if the width and height you specify don't match the FLV's width and height, then the larger of the width or height will be used, and the smaller will be adjusted to the correct relative size.

There's an event you can make use of, too: the `resize` event, which is triggered whenever the component is moved or resized. The format of the code looks like the following:

```
var listenerObject:Object = new Object();
listenerObject.resize = function(eventObject:Object):Void
{
  trace ("Resized");
}
myFLVPlayback.addEventListener("resize", listenerObject);
```

Using the preceding movement and resize methods, the `autoSize` and `maintain➡AspectRatio` properties, and the `resize` event, it's possible to create an application that supports a wide variety of FLV sizes and positions.

Audio functionality

The `FLVPlayback` component has a few simple methods and properties, and an event to support the update and modification of the volume level of the playing FLV. You have the ability to change the volume and also detect when the volume is changed by the user sliding the volume knob in the user interface.

Perhaps the simplest aspect of the audio functionality is the way the volume is set with code. You simply set the volume property to a number between 0 and 100, and that's it.

```
myFLVPlayback.volume = 100; // full volume
myFLVPlayback.volume = 0; // silent
myFLVPlayback.volume = 50 // 50% volume
```

Once this property is set, the audio output level from the speakers will change accordingly. It's that simple.

You can also read the volume property, like so:

```
trace ("The volume is " + myFLVPlayback.volume);
```

You also have the ability to detect a change in volume as performed by the user. When the user slides the volume control of an `FLVPlayback` component skin, the component will dispatch a call to the `volumeUpdate` event, if it has been defined, which is done like so:

```
var listenerObject:Object = new Object();
listenerObject.volumeUpdate = function(eventObject:Object):Void
{
  trace ("The new volume is " + myFLVPlayback.volume);
}
myFLVPlayback.addEventListener("volumeUpdate", listenerObject);
```

The `volumeUpdate` function is triggered when the user changes the volume by a certain percentage, which is defined by the `volumeBarScrubTolerance` property. This property can be set, and the value it represents is the percentage the bar can be moved before the volume increase is audible. (When this is the case, the `volumeUpdate` event is fired as well.) For example:

```
myFLVPlayback.volumeBarScrubTolerance = 10;
```

This indicates that you want any motion of the volume bar scrubber greater than 10% to trigger the volume to change. The default value is 5.

Let's say you were to rapidly slide the volume scrubber left and right for several seconds—the frequency with which the volume is actually changed is defined by the `volume`➡ `BarInterval` property. This property basically defines how often the `FLVPlayback` component checks to see what the new volume is when scrubbing (it only performs this check when scrubbing is taking place). The default value for this is 250, which equates to 250 milliseconds, or 1/4 of a second.

```
myFLVPlayback.volumeBarInterval = 100; // update volume every 100 ms
```

If you want more detailed control of the sound and the ability to set the volume and pan of the video, you must make use of the `transform` property, which is a standard `Sound` class sound transform object. The property must be set to an instance of an object that you create. Here's an example:

```
myTransform = new Object();
myTransform.ll = 100; // 100% of the left channel in the left speaker
myTransform.lr = 100; // 100% of the left channel in the right speaker
myTransform.rr = 0; // none of the right channel in the right speaker
myTransform.rl = 0; // none of the right channel in the left speaker
myFLVPlayback.transform = myTransform;
```

The preceding code would cause the audio from the left channel in your FLV to be played out of both speakers, while the right channel would not be used at all. In essence, the transform object allows you to perform both pan and volume changes at once. The properties of the transform are as follows:

- `ll`: The amount of audio from the left source channel to play in the left speaker. Valid values are from 0 to 100.

- `lr`: The amount of audio from the left source channel to play in the right speaker. Valid values are from 0 to 100.

- `rr`: The amount of audio from the right source channel to play in the right speaker. Valid values are from 0 to 100.

- `rl`: The amount of audio from the right source channel to play in the left speaker. Valid values are from 0 to 100.

So, to completely flip the channels, you would do something like this:

```
myTransform = new Object();
myTransform.ll = 0; // none of the left channel in the left speaker
myTransform.lr = 100; // 100% of the left channel in the right speaker
myTransform.rr = 0; // none of the right channel in the right speaker
myTransform.rl = 100; // 100% of the right channel in the left speaker
myFLVPlayback.transform = myTransform;
```

That's all there is to the sound control in the `FLVPlayback` component.

Cue point functionality

Earlier in the chapter, you looked at adding cue points to an FLV file, made from the `chromeballs.mov` video file. Now you're going to take a look at doing something useful with those cue points.

In this example, there's a pair of chrome spheres that are swinging down toward each other. When they collide, you're going to make them trigger some on-screen text to change; this text will appear behind the spot at which the two spheres collide, because the video has an alpha channel.

Take a look at the sequence that follows to see how the spheres swing down and collide.

Figure 5-27. Frames from the `chromeballs.mov` video file

The white area behind the spheres is actually transparent, and anything that appears behind it on the stage will be seen. This is a great new feature of the On2 codec. (You'll be looking more at creative uses of the alpha channel later on.)

This example requires the file `chromespheres2.flv` from the code download files (or you can use the FLV you created earlier in the "Adding cue points in the encoding process" section). As you saw earlier, the FLV file has been created to have three event cue points in it: one at the beginning called `Start`, one at the point of impact called `Smash`, and one at the end called `End`.

The entire finished example can be found in `cuepoints1.fla`, but let's go through and build it up from scratch.

1. Start a new movie.
2. Set its dimensions to 640 × 480, with a frame rate of 31 fps and a background color of #FFFFFF.
3. From the Components panel (*CTRL/CMD+F7*), drag an instance of the `FLVPlayback` component onto the stage and give it the instance name `myFLVPlayback`.
4. Move it to the position x: 0 and y: 0, and set its size to 640 × 480 using the Properties panel (*CTRL/CMD+F3*).
5. Label the layer flv.
6. Save the file to the same location as the `chromespheres2.flv` file, and call it `cuepoints1.fla`.

7. Select the component, and in the Parameters tab of the Properties panel, set the value of contentPath to chromespheres2.flv. After you click OK, the cuePoints should automatically be filled in, as shown in Figure 5-28.

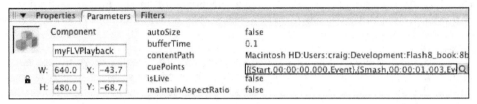

Figure 5-28. Embedded cue points in the `chromespheres2.flv` file

8. Create a new layer *below* the layer that contains the FLVPlayback component and label it text.

9. Hide the layer containing the component.

10. On the new layer, draw a 143 × 34 text field at the position x: 245, y: 250.

11. Set the type to Dynamic Text, the alignment to center, and the font to 21-point Arial Black.

12. Set the instance name of the text field to `label_txt`, click the Embed button, and select Basic Latin as the text to embed.

13. Create a new layer at the top of the timeline and label it code.

14. Open the Actions panel (*F9*).

15. Click frame 1 of this layer, and begin by entering the following code into the Actions panel:

```
var messages:Array = new Array("Hello", "there.", "how", "are",
"you?");
var currentMessage:Number = 0;
```

The `messages` array contains the text you're going to be displaying each time the spheres collide. Each collision will cause the next word in the `messages` array to be drawn in the text field. The `currentMessage` variable is used to keep track of which word is currently showing. Now, continue by entering the following code:

```
var listenerObject:Object = new Object();
listenerObject.cuePoint = function(eventObject:Object):Void
{
    var which:String = eventObject.info.name;
```

Here you're creating a new `listenerObject`, and the type of the function is a `cuePoint` event. This event will be triggered every time the `FLVPlayback` component encounters a cue point that you've previously defined.

The `cuePoint` event is triggered, and then you set the value of a string named `which` to the name of the `cuePoint`. The value of this string will be either `Start`, `Smash`, or `End`. Continue building the example by adding the following code:

```
    if (which == "End")
    {
      myFLVPlayback.stop();
      myFLVPlayback.play();
    }
    else if (which == "Smash")
    {
      label_txt.text = messages[currentMessage];
      currentMessage++;
      currentMessage %= messages.length;
    }
  }
}
```

This is where you decide what to do with your cue points. If the End cue point is encountered, then you want the video to play over again. This is basically how you loop the video. You want the spheres to collide over and over again.

The second case in the if statement is what you do when the Smash cue point is encountered. In this case, you set the value of the label_txt text field to the message you want to display, which is the message at the index of currentMessage. You then increment currentMessage and perform a modulus on it based on the length of the messages array. This will cause currentMessage to wrap back around to 0 once it has displayed the final word in the messages array. So, currentMessage will be 0, 1, 2, 3, 4, 0, 1, 2, 3, 4, 0, 1, 2, 3, 4, etc.

Now you just need to enter the last line of code:

```
myFLVPlayback.addEventListener("cuePoint", listenerObject);
```

Here, you're simply tying the event to the component. With that, the example is done. Press CTRL/CMD+ENTER to test the movie. You'll see the spheres continually colliding, and the text will appear behind them, updating on each collision.

Just like that, you've been able to connect a moment in the video with an event on your movie. The potential applications are huge. You could use these event cue points to trigger menus, other animations, characters, sounds, effects—you name it. Entire sites could be built out of videos that build the page layout and then populate the screen with dynamic pieces. The only limit is creativity. Following is the entire code listing for the previous example:

```
var messages:Array = new Array("Hello", "there.", "how", "are",
"you?");
var currentMessage:Number = 0;

var listenerObject:Object = new Object();
listenerObject.cuePoint = function(eventObject:Object):Void
{
  var which:String = eventObject.info.name;
```

```
      if (which == "End")
      {
        myFLVPlayback.stop();
        myFLVPlayback.play();
      }
      else if (which == "Smash")
      {
        label_txt.text = messages[currentMessage];
        currentMessage++;
        currentMessage %= messages.length;
      }
    }
    myFLVPlayback.addEventListener("cuePoint", listenerObject);
```

ActionScript cue points

It's also possible to add cue points to a video at design time without having them initially placed during the encoding process. This allows you to add a whole new layer of functionality because you can cause your videos to trigger events that might be user-defined, or dynamic in some sense. So what you're going to do now is make a small change to the previous example, which will add a cue point to the video every time a key is pressed on the keyboard. When these cue points are then encountered during playback, the text field is changed as previously shown. This new version can be found in the code download file cuepoints2.fla.

First, find the following line of code:

```
      else if (which == "Smash")
```

and change it to the following:

```
      else if (which == "Smash" || which == "ActionScripted")
```

The new cue points you're going to be adding at runtime will all have the name ActionScripted. Next, add the following code to the *end* of the previous example code, after the addEventListener line:

```
    var keyObject:Object = new Object();
    keyObject.onKeyUp = function(eventObject:Object):Void
    {
      myFLVPlayback.addASCuePoint(myFLVPlayback.playheadTime,
    "ActionScripted");
    }
    Key.addListener(keyObject);
```

It's deceptively simple—every time a key is released, you add an ActionScript cue point using the addASCuePoint method. The addASCuePoint method takes two parameters: time and name. You simply use the value of playheadTime, and the name is always ActionScripted.

Save your work as cuepoints2.fla and test this new movie. Now when you press and release a key, a cue point is remembered. Next time the video crosses that frame, you'll notice that the text changes. Here's the entire code for this example:

```
var messages:Array = new Array("Hello", "there.", "how", "are",
"you?");
var currentMessage:Number = 0;

var listenerObject:Object = new Object();
listenerObject.cuePoint = function(eventObject:Object):Void
{
  var which:String = eventObject.info.name;

  if (which == "End")
  {
    myFLVPlayback.stop();
    myFLVPlayback.play();
  }
  else if (which == "Smash" || which == "ActionScripted")
  {
    label_txt.text = messages[currentMessage];
    currentMessage++;
    currentMessage %= messages.length;
  }
}
myFLVPlayback.addEventListener("cuePoint", listenerObject);

var keyObject:Object = new Object();
keyObject.onKeyUp = function(eventObject:Object):Void
{
  myFLVPlayback.addASCuePoint(myFLVPlayback.playheadTime,
                             "ActionScripted");
}
Key.addListener(keyObject);
```

How Flash handles multiple video clips in one video player

When you have an FLVPlayback component on the stage, you can tell it to automatically begin playing a specific FLV video by setting its contentPath at design time. This is the most common use of the FLVPlayback component, and it's what you've done earlier in this chapter.

When the FLVPlayback component runs, the first thing it does is create an instance of a video player object, and then opens a NetConnection to the FLV that was specified.

A similar process occurs when you want to use the `FLVPlayback` component to play multiple FLV files. You can tell the component to create a series of video objects, and then specify which of those video objects will be played. Flash will then open a `NetConnection` object to the active video player, starting the video stream. Meanwhile, any other video player is waiting and ready to go, yet you only need to have one `FLVPlayback` component.

Playing multiple video clips in one video player

One of the greatest things about the new `FLVPlayback` component is its ability for one `FLVPlayback` component to handle multiple FLV video streams. This means that you can create a single `FLVPlayback` component on-screen, but you can preload any number of videos into it, and then watch them play back in any order, switching between them as desired.

Since you only need one instance of the component on-screen, you keep your system resource usage down, and also it makes things simpler because you're able to take advantage of the built-in indexing system included in the `FLVPlayback` component.

When specifying which internal player you're talking to, in the `FLVPlayback` component, you use the `activeVideoPlayerIndex` and the `visibleVideoPlayerIndex` properties, like so:

```
myFLVPlayback.activeVideoPlayerIndex = 2;
myFLVPlayback.visibleVideoPlayerIndex = 2;
myFLVPlayback.play();
```

When you do this, you're telling Flash that you would like to see and hear the video player at index 2. By specifying a value for `visibleVideoPlayerIndex`, you're not just specifying which video player is seen, but also which video player is heard. When you set `activeVideoPlayerIndex` to any value greater than 0 for the first time, the `FLVPlayback` component then creates an instance of a video player object within the component at that index. Any other subsequent reference to that index will refer to the video player previously created.

So remember, the `FLVPlayback` component can in itself contain a number of video player objects. By default, when you use an `FLVPlayback` component to play only one video, you're referring to the internal video player at index 0. This is how most people, when simply dragging the `FLVPlayback` component onto the stage and specifying a content path, will be using the component.

If you want, you can get a direct reference to any of the video players within the `FLVPlayback` component by using the `getVideoPlayer` method, like so:

```
myFLVPlayback.getVideoPlayer(2);
```

This would return a direct reference to the video player object at index 2.

If at any time you want to delete an internal video player object, you can make a call to `closeVideoPlayer`, which takes an index value. This will close the `NetStream` connection and delete the video player.

```
myFLVPlayback.closeVideoPlayer(2);
```

An example including multiple videos

Let's make an example that takes advantage of the multiple–video player system—you'll create a file that loads and plays a series of FLV files whose file names are specified in an array. This example can be found as `multiplay.fla` in the code download. What you want to do is specify a list of file names, and have the first FLV play; then on completion, the second FLV will play, and so on. The idea is, while you're watching the first FLV file, the `FLVPlayback` component is busily loading the next FLV, and the next, and the next. This will create a smooth and somewhat transparent video-viewing experience for the user.

1. Create a new movie in Flash 8.

2. Set the frame rate to something higher than your FLV videos.

3. Open the components library with *CTRL/CMD+F7*.

4. Drag an instance of the `FLVPlayback` component onto the stage.

5. Give the new instance the instance name `vidPlayer`.

6. Set the parameters for the `FLVPlayback` component in the Parameters tab of the Component Inspector (Window ➤ Component Inspector) to match Figure 5-29.

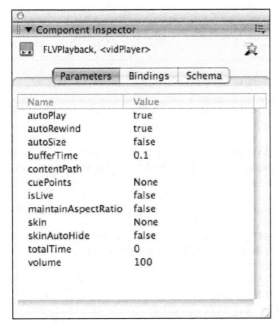

Figure 5-29.
`FLVPlayback` component parameters for the multiple–video player example

Note that `contentPath` must be set to nothing (blank).

7. Click frame 1 of the main timeline, open the Actions panel (*F9*), and enter the following code:

```
var flv_array:Array = new Array("crashflex_Medium.flv", "flux24.flv");

var loadingVideoNum:Number = 0;
var playingVideoNum:Number = 0;
var totalFLVs:Number = flv_array.length;
vidPlayer.contentPath = flv_array[playingVideoNum];

function finishedLoading(vid:Object):Void
{
  if (loadingVideoNum < totalFLVs)
  {
    loadingVideoNum++;
    vidPlayer.activeVideoPlayerIndex = loadingVideoNum;
    vidPlayer.load(flv_array[loadingVideoNum]);
  }
}
vidPlayer.addEventListener("ready", finishedLoading);

function finishedPlaying(vid:Object):Void
{
  playingVideoNum ++;
  playingVideoNum %= totalFLVs;

  vidPlayer.activeVideoPlayerIndex = playingVideoNum;
  vidPlayer.visibleVideoPlayerIndex = playingVideoNum;
  vidPlayer.play();
}
vidPlayer.addEventListener("complete", finishedPlaying);
```

8. Now save the movie in a location relative to your video files, and test it by pressing *CTRL+ENTER*.

So what happened? The videos in your array will play, one after the other, until all are finished playing, at which point they'll loop back to the first video and repeat. Let's look at the code.

```
var flv_array:Array = new Array("crashflex_Medium.flv", "flux24.flv");
```

First of all, you're setting the list of FLVs that you want to iterate through (modified to match FLV files you've created). Then you're initializing a few variables.

```
var loadingVideoNum:Number = 0;
var playingVideoNum:Number = 0;
var totalFLVs:Number = flv_array.length;
```

The `loadingVideoNum` variable specifies which video is currently loading in the background. The `playingVideoNum` variable specifies which video is currently being viewed in the `FLVPlayback` component, and the `totalFLVs` variable simply contains the total number of videos you want to load, taken from the length of the `flv_array` array.

Next, you kickstart the whole process by setting the `contentPath` of the component to your first video.

```
vidPlayer.contentPath = flv_array[playingVideoNum];
```

This begins the loading and playing process.

Next, you create a function that's called every time a video has finished loading. All events are passed up to the `FLVPlayback` component; even the events that are technically events of the video players within.

```
function finishedLoading(vid:Object):Void
{
  if (loadingVideoNum < totalFLVs)
  {
    loadingVideoNum++;
    vidPlayer.activeVideoPlayerIndex = loadingVideoNum;
    vidPlayer.load(flv_array[loadingVideoNum]);
  }
}
vidPlayer.addEventListener("ready", finishedLoading);
```

In this function, the first thing you do is check to make sure the next video to load isn't past the last video. If it is, then you know all videos are loaded; otherwise, you increment the `loadingVideoNum` variable and then set the `activeVideoPlayerIndex` to that value. You need to do this so that, when you then call the load method, the component knows that you would like to load the video into that particular video player index. You then load the FLV specified by the file name in `flv_array` at the `loadingVideoNum` index.

Finally, you tell `vidPlayer` to direct all calls to the `ready` event to the `finished➡ Loading` function. The `ready` event is dispatched every time the `FLVPlayback` component has finished loading a video.

Next, you have a function to handle the progression from one video to the next.

```
function finishedPlaying(vid:Object):Void
{
  playingVideoNum ++;
  playingVideoNum %= totalFLVs;

  vidPlayer.activeVideoPlayerIndex = playingVideoNum;
  vidPlayer.visibleVideoPlayerIndex = playingVideoNum;
  vidPlayer.play();
}
vidPlayer.addEventListener("complete", finishedPlaying);
```

The `finishedPlaying` function will be triggered every time the currently playing video has finished playing and has reached its final frame. You then increment the `playingVideoNum` variable to increase the index of the video you're currently playing. You then also perform a modulus function: `playingVideoNum %= totalFLVs`. In a nutshell, this will make `playingVideoNum` loop back to 0 when it has played the last video in the list, ensuring that your video list plays forever.

You then set the value of `activeVideoPlayerIndex` and `visibleVideo➥ PlayerIndex` to `playingVideoNum`, telling the `FLVPlayback` component which internal video player you would like to switch to and make visible. Then, by saying `vidPlayer.play`, you're telling the component to play that internal video player.

Finally, you point the `complete` event to call the `finishedPlaying` function. Every time a video finishes playing, you'll step forward to the next video in the list and begin playing it. That's all the code required to make your video list loop and play over and over.

Transitioning between videos

If you have a series of video players ready within your `FLVPlayback` component, you can easily make use of the `TransitionManager` class to fade smoothly between them. You're not going to get into specifics on how the `TransitionManager` itself works as a whole, as it's not new to Flash 8, but you are going to look at a specific usage of it with respect to your videos.

You're going to make use of the several types of transitions to allow the user to transition smoothly between a series of three videos. The transitions you'll be using are as follows:

- *Fade*: One video crossfades (dissolves) into another. This is the most common type of transition.
- *Iris*: The video transitions through a circle that reveals a video behind, like the iris of a lens.
- *Blinds*: One video transitions to another as if through Venetian blinds.
- *Squeeze*: One video squeezes into the screen. The video expands in size.
- *Wipe*: One video wipes away diagonally to reveal the other.

The finished example for this can be found as `transitions.fla` in the code download files, and you can look at that now to play with it. You'll see that there are three buttons along the bottom, five buttons along the side, and a single instance of the `FLVPlayback` component on the stage. Let's build it now.

1. Start a new movie in Flash.
2. Set its width to 550, its height to 400, its background color to #000000, and its frame rate to 31 fps.
3. Draw a 34 $\times$ 34 square on the stage.
4. Select the square and press *F8* to convert it to a symbol. Give it the name vidButton, make sure its type is set to Button, and set its registration point to the upper-left corner of the nine boxes. Click OK.

5. Make copies of the button so that they match Figure 5-30, shown later in the example. The bottom video buttons are 34 × 34, but the transition-style buttons on the right side are 89 × 29, so you'll have to scale them a bit.

6. Give the buttons instance names. The three buttons along the bottom are named (from left to right) `vid1`, `vid2`, and `vid3`.

   The five buttons at the side are named (from top to bottom) `fadeButton`, `irisButton`, `blindsButton`, `squeezeButton`, and `wipeButton`.

7. From the Components panel (press *CTRL/CMD+F7* if it's not visible), locate the `FLVPlayback` component and drag an instance of it onto the stage.

8. Give it the instance name `vPlay`.

9. Name the layer Assets.

10. Create a new layer above the Assets layer.

11. Name the new layer Text.

12. Use your favorite text color and font to give the buttons labels that match the screenshot. They're all just text fields placed over the buttons. This example uses white, 21-point Arial, static text fields. Make sure they're static text fields so they'll be embedded properly and won't be selectable with the mouse at runtime.

13. Create a new layer and call it Code.

Now the stage is set up and ready for you to begin entering code. Click the first frame of the Code layer and open the Actions panel. Press *F9* if it isn't visible. Begin by entering the following code:

```
import mx.transitions.*;
var numReady:Number = 0;
var numVideos:Number = 3;
var vidList:Array = new Array("fx1.flv", "fx2.flv", "fx3.flv");
```

With the preceding code, you're telling Flash that you're going to be using the `Transitions` class by importing it and all of its subclasses. These include all of the different types of transitions and the different styles of easing. You also set two variables: `numReady` to 0 and `numVideos` to 3.

You'll be using the `numReady` variable to detect when all videos have completed loading. The details of this will be shown shortly. You're also creating an array of three video names. These are the videos you'll be loading and showing.

Continue by entering the following code:

```
irisTrans = new Object({type:Iris,
    direction:Transition.IN,
    duration:2,
    easing:Strong.easeOut,
    startPoint:5,
    shape:Iris.CIRCLE});
```

```
fadeTrans = new Object({type:Fade,
    direction:0,
    duration:0.5,
    easing:easing.None.easeNone,
    param1:empty,
    param2:empty});

blindsTrans = new Object({type:Blinds,
    direction:Transition.IN,
    duration:0.5,
    easing:None.easeNone,
    numStrips:10,
    dimension:0});

squeezeTrans = new Object({type:Squeeze,
    direction:Transition.IN,
    duration:1,
    easing:Elastic.easeOut,
    dimension:1});

wipeTrans = new Object({type:Wipe,
    direction:Transition.IN,
    duration:1,
    easing:None.easeNone,
    startPoint:1});

var activeTransition:Object = fadeTrans;
```

Here you've created five objects: `irisTrans`, `fadeTrans`, `blindsTrans`, `squeeze➡` `Trans`, and `wipeTrans`. They're simply objects that have been preinitialized with the required parameters to perform different types of transitions. The values shown in the previous code block are the exact values used in the example code included with the Flash help documentation. The only difference is that the duration has been changed to 1. For more information on the transition types, look for the "Transition-based classes" entry in the Flash help documentation.

You'll be using these objects later with the `TransitionManager.start` method. You're also setting a variable called `activeTransition` to `fadeTrans`. The `active➡` `Transition` variable will be used as your transition, so you initially set it to the fade transition.

Continue by entering this code:

```
for (var i:Number = 0; i < numVideos; i++)
{
  vPlay.activeVideoPlayerIndex = i;
  vPlay.load(vidList[i]);

  this["vid" + (i+1)].myNum = i;
  this["vid" + (i+1)].onPress = function()
```

```
    {
      doTransition(_level0.vPlay, this.myNum);
    }
  }
}
```

Here you're telling the FLVPlayback component to load each video by setting activeVideoPlayerIndex to 0, 1, and then 2; and then calling the load method with the corresponding value within the vidList array.

You're also setting the onPress code of each of the three buttons at the bottom of the screen, and telling them to call a function called doTransition, which you'll be seeing later. So, when each button is clicked, it will call the doTransition function, and will pass in a reference to the FLVPlayback component and the value of myNum, which is set to 0, 1, or 2, depending on the button.

Continue by entering the following code:

```
function amReady(e:Object)
{
  numReady++;

  if (numReady == numVideos)
  {
    for (var i:Number = 0; i < numVideos; i++)
    {
      e.target.activeVideoPlayerIndex = i;
      e.target.play();
    }
  }
}
vPlay.addEventListener("ready", amReady);
```

The amReady function is triggered each time a video has finished loading. This is where the numReady variable comes into play. Since numReady is incremented each time a video finishes loading, you therefore know that when numReady is equal to numVideos, all your videos will have finished loading. When this is the case, you step through each loaded video and tell it to begin playing. This way, all three of your videos will always be playing, and you can smoothly transition between them as if they were live feeds in a television studio.

Continue with this code:

```
function transDone(e:Object)
{
  vPlay.visibleVideoPlayerIndex = e.target.content._name;
}
```

The transDone function is called when a transition is complete. In this case, all you do is set the value of visibleVideoPlayerIndex to the value of the event target's content name. In the case of the FLVPlayback component, the _name of target.content will be either 0, 1, or 2. In other words, the internal video player's names correspond to the values that they possess in the internal video player array. This is a property of arrays; it will ensure that the sound from this video is heard, while the non-visible videos will be silent.

Now you need to enter the code for the doTransition function, as follows:

```
function doTransition(m:MovieClip, d:Number)
{
  if (d != m.visibleVideoPlayerIndex)
  {
    m.bringVideoPlayerToFront(d);
    var vp:MovieClip = m.getVideoPlayer(d);
    TransitionManager.start(vp, activeTransition);
    vp.__transitionManager.addEventListener("allTransitionsInDone",➡
transDone);
  }
}
```

This function is called when the user presses one of the three transition buttons at the bottom of the screen. You can see that this function takes two parameters: a reference to a movie clip, and a number, stored in a variable d. The d variable will be 0, 1, or 2, depending upon which button was pressed.

The first thing that you do is make sure that the user isn't trying to transition to the currently visible video. There's no point in doing a transition from one video to itself; nothing would appear to happen.

If, on the other hand, the user has selected a different video, you tell the FLVPlayback component (passed in via m) to bring the video player with the index of d to the front of the stack of video players.

You then grab a reference to that internal video player by calling getVideoPlayer and storing that reference in the vp variable. The internal video player is an instance of a video player object, which has all the properties of a movie clip, so you define it as such.

You then make a call to the TransitionManager class by calling the start method and passing in the movie clip you want to transition and the type of transition you want to perform. In this case, you're passing in the activeTransition variable, which you set earlier.

Next, you tell the transitionManager object (on the video player object, vp) that you would like it to call the transDone function when the transition is complete. If you recall, that will cause the FLVPlayback component to "activate" the video so that its audio is heard.

Continue by entering the code that follows:

```
function playComplete(e:Object)
{
  for (var i:Number = 0; i < numVideos; i++)
  {
    e.target.activeVideoPlayerIndex = i;
```

```
      if (e.target.stopped)
      e.target.play();
    }
  }
vPlay.addEventListener("complete", playComplete);
```

Here you've created an event handler called playComplete. This function is called when-ever the FLVPlayback component broadcasts a complete event. This event will be trig-gered when any of its playing videos reach the end and stop. The main purpose of this function is to cause any finished videos to loop back to their beginnings.

When the function is triggered, the program steps through each of the videos and checks to see if its stopped flag is set to true. If it is, it's told to play again, which will cause the video to start over from the beginning. This doesn't bring the video to the front or make it visible (if it's not visible)—it simply causes the video to keep playing as it was, but from the beginning.

Remember, by setting the value of activeVideoIndex, you're telling the FLVPlayback component that the stopped variable you're checking, or the play method you're potentially calling, both refer to the video at that index.

You then add an event listener to your vPlay FLVPlayback component, telling it to broadcast its "complete" events to the playComplete event handler.

Finally, enter the following five small functions:

```
fadeButton.onPress = function()
{
  activeTransition = fadeTrans;
}

irisButton.onPress = function()
{
  activeTransition = irisTrans;
}

blindsButton.onPress = function()
{
  activeTransition = blindsTrans;
}

squeezeButton.onPress = function()
{
  activeTransition = squeezeTrans;
}

wipeButton.onPress = function()
{
  activeTransition = wipeTrans;
}
```

Here you're simply setting the code of each of the right-hand five buttons. The idea is that you're setting the value of `activeTransition` to the corresponding transition object that you defined at the beginning of your code.

If you run this now, you should see the first video begin playing, and if you click the video 2 or 3 buttons, you'll see that video fade in. If you select a different type of transition, then any subsequent presses of the video buttons will cause them to transition in with the newly selected transition type.

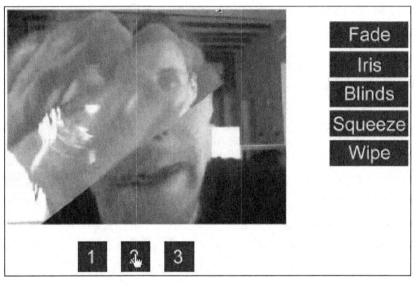

Figure 5-30. Example of transitioning FLV files

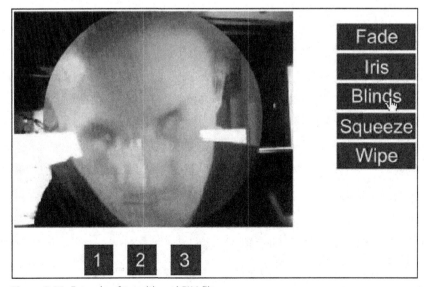

Figure 5-31. Example of transitioned FLV files

The complete code listing follows:

```
import mx.transitions.*;
var numReady:Number = 0;
var numVideos:Number = 3;

var vidList:Array = new Array("cadillacfairview.flv",
                             "crashflex_Medium.flv",
                             "betina.flv");;

irisTrans = new Object({type:Iris,
    direction:Transition.IN,
    duration:2,
    easing:Strong.easeOut,
    startPoint:5,
    shape:Iris.CIRCLE});

fadeTrans = new Object({type:Fade,
    direction:0,
    duration:0.5,
    easing:easing.None.easeNone,
    param1:empty,
    param2:empty});

blindsTrans = new Object({type:Blinds,
    direction:Transition.IN,
    duration:0.5,
    easing:None.easeNone,
    numStrips:10,
    dimension:0});

squeezeTrans = new Object({type:Squeeze,
    direction:Transition.IN,
    duration:1,
    easing:Elastic.easeOut,
    dimension:1});

wipeTrans = new Object({type:Wipe,
    direction:Transition.IN,
    duration:1,
    easing:None.easeNone,
    startPoint:1});

var activeTransition:Object = fadeTrans;
for (var i:Number = 0; i < numVideos; i++)
{
  vPlay.activeVideoPlayerIndex = i;
  vPlay.load(vidList[i]);
```

```
        this["vid" + (i+1)].myNum = i;
        this["vid" + (i+1)].onPress = function()
        {
          doTransition(_level0.vPlay, this.myNum);
        }
      }

      function amReady(e:Object)
      {
        numReady++;

        if (numReady == numVideos)
        {
          for (var i:Number = 0; i < numVideos; i++)
          {
            e.target.activeVideoPlayerIndex = i;
            e.target.play();
          }
        }
      }
      vPlay.addEventListener("ready", amReady);

      function transDone(e:Object)
      {
        vPlay.visibleVideoPlayerIndex = e.target.content._name;
      }

      function doTransition(m:MovieClip, d:Number)
      {
        if (d != m.visibleVideoPlayerIndex)
        {
          m.bringVideoPlayerToFront(d);
          var vp:MovieClip = m.getVideoPlayer(d);
          TransitionManager.start(vp, activeTransition);
          vp.__transitionManager.addEventListener("allTransitionsInDone",
                                                  transDone);
        }
      }

      function playComplete(e:Object)
      {
        for (var i:Number = 0; i < numVideos; i++)
        {
          e.target.activeVideoPlayerIndex = i;

          if (e.target.stopped)
            e.target.play();
        }
      }
```

```
vPlay.addEventListener("complete", playComplete);

fadeButton.onPress = function()
{
   activeTransition = fadeTrans;
}

irisButton.onPress = function()
{
   activeTransition = irisTrans;
}

blindsButton.onPress = function()
{
   activeTransition = blindsTrans;
}

squeezeButton.onPress = function()
{
   activeTransition = squeezeTrans;
}

wipeButton.onPress = function()
{
   activeTransition = wipeTrans;
}
```

Alpha in video

As previously discussed in this chapter, one of the best new developments on the Flash 8 video front is the addition of the alpha channel in video. This allows you to have completely and partially transparent areas in your videos, allowing you to create video masking effects, a semitransparent effect like glass or smoke.

When you have a video with an alpha channel and you apply effects to it, the effects will be applied to the actual alpha channels properly, rather than the overall square shape of the video. This means that if you have a video of a jagged asteroid spinning on the spot, you can apply the glow or drop shadow, and the effect will cleanly surround the asteroid *itself*—not just the rectangle of the video, as it would have in previous versions of Flash.

In Figure 5-32, the movie is actually a square-shaped video, but Flash now takes into account the alpha channel, correctly provides the glow, and makes the bottom drop shadow the proper shape.

Figure 5-32. Screenshot of alpha asteroid video file

One of the coolest examples we could think of to display this new functionality is through the creation of a game of some sort. Inspired by the asteroid idea, we've created the smash hit, hereafter known as "Asteroid Game"—a winning title indeed!

The game will consist of the following elements:

- A distant background of stars (a static image)
- The Earth (another static image)
- Asteroids (movies of spinning asteroids with alpha transparency around them)
- Explosions (movies that include alpha channels, and have semitransparency as well as full transparency)
- Text fields

To preview this game (shown in Figure 5-33), load `asteroidgame.swf` from the code download files.

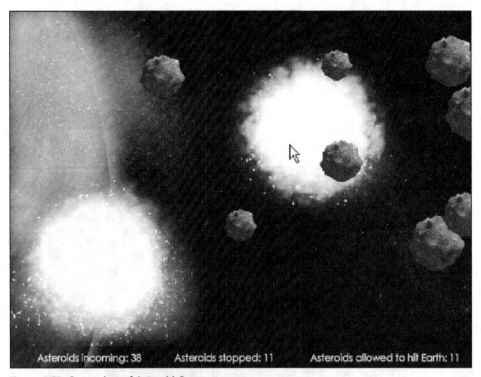

Figure 5-33. Screenshot of Asteroid Game

The premise is that there are asteroids zooming toward Earth, and you must aim your cannons by clicking on the asteroids to destroy them before they hit the surface of the planet. The entire game is finished and ready to view in `asteroidgame.fla`. Rather than go through a step-by-step creation of this game from the ground up, please load the FLA file and we'll explain all of it, one piece at a time.

First, look at the stage (see Figure 5-34).

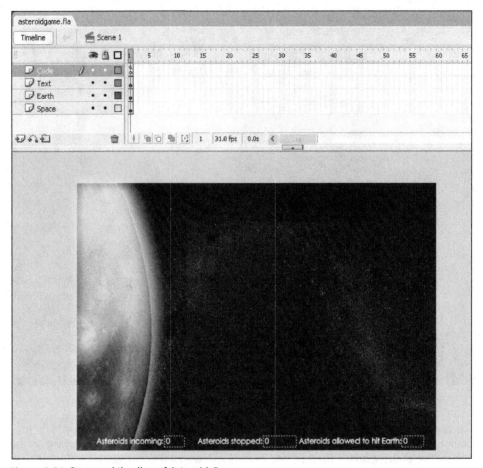

Figure 5-34. Stage and timeline of Asteroid Game

On the bottom layer, named Space, you can see that you have a distant background, which is a bitmap instance. The bitmap is a picture of deep space, with Earth at the far left side.

On the next layer up, you have an instance of a movie clip called Earth. This movie clip simply contains a bitmap image of half the Earth. This is overlaid on the background, and a glow effect is applied to it.

On the next layer up, Text, is a series of text fields, used to show game stats. They have the instance names `incoming_txt`, `stopped_txt`, and `hit_txt`.

On the top layer, Code, is the code that makes the game run.

Next, look at the library (shown in Figure 5-35), which you can open by pressing *CTRL/CMD+L*.

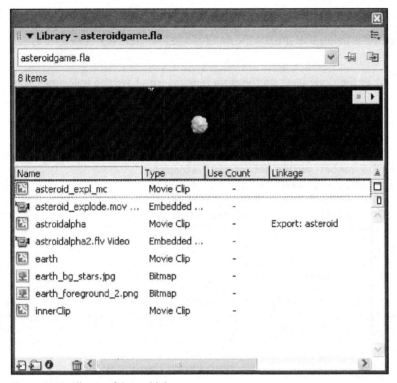

Figure 5-35. Library of Asteroid Game

You'll notice that you have a list of movie clips, as well as videos that have been imported directly into the library. Take a look at innerClip first, even though it's the last item in the library. Click innerClip, and press the small Play button in the library window. You'll see an asteroid that will explode.

Now, the first item in the library is a movie clip called asteroid_expl_mc, which contains an instance of innerClip. If you select it and press Play on the library preview window, you'll see a stationary asteroid that glows to white and then fades out to black. In the game, when this is played, the effect is that the explosion is played, changes to bright white, and then fades away. On the last frame of this movie clip is the code, which looks like so:

```
this._parent.removeMovieClip();
```

Below this movie clip is asteroid_explode.mov, an embedded video, which is the actual video data for the explosion.

Beneath that, you have another movie clip, called asteroidalpha, which has an embedded linkage ID of asteroid. This is a movie clip that's two frames long. On frame 1 is the embedded video of the rotating asteroid. On frame 2 is an instance of the asteroid_expl_mc movie clip. Functionally, at runtime, there will be many instances of asteroidalpha on the stage. When you want an asteroid to explode, you simply tell the instance of asteroidalpha to go to frame 2, and it will explode.

The video below that is the actual video of the asteroid spinning, unexploded.

The three items below that are the movie clips and bitmap that you've already seen on the stage.

On frame 1 of the Code layer on the main timeline, you have the following code:

```
// This movie clip will hold all the asteroids, rather than
// placing them on the _root timeline.
this.createEmptyMovieClip("asteroids", 1);

// The number you've successfully stopped
var numStopped:Number = 0;

// The number that have hit the earth
var numHit:Number = 0;

// The number still incoming
var incoming:Number = 0;
```

Here, the movie clip that will hold all the instances of your on-screen asteroids is created, and three variables are initialized: the number of asteroids stopped, the number that have hit Earth, and the number still incoming.

```
// Creates 60 asteroids.
for (var i = 0; i < 60; i++)
{
  incoming++;

  // Attach the "asteroid" linkage ID movie clip to the
  // asteroid holder clip
  var mc:MovieClip = asteroids.attachMovie("asteroid", "ast" + i, i);
  mc.cacheAsBitmap = true;

  // place them off screen, farther and farther out,
  // spaced 40 pixels apart, starting at
  // x = 650, 690, 730, 770, etc.
  mc._x = (i * 40) + 650;

  // Random y
  mc._y = Math.random() * 300;

  // A random scale / size between 20% and 40%
  mc._xscale = mc._yscale = Math.random() * 20 + 20;
```

The preceding code block begins the creation of 60 asteroids. These are all instances of the asteroidalpha movie clip, which has the linkage name asteroid. First, the cacheAsBitmap flag is set to true to help the performance (as you learned in Chapter 7, a game involving lots of moving movie clips that don't really change internally is an ideal situation to use bitmap caching for performance enhancements). Then, the asteroids are spaced offscreen to the right, 40 pixels apart, starting at position 650.

Their _y position is then set to a random value so that they appear at any position on-screen. Next, their size is set to a random value between 20 and 40.

```
// Stop them from playing. Frame 2 is the explosion. We don't want
//them to blow up yet
mc.stop();

// Decide on a horizontal speed - how fast they're flying in
// between -3 and -8.  -3 is slow, -8 is fast.  Negative number
// because they're moving left, not right.
mc.dx = (Math.random() * -5) - 3;
```

We don't want them to explode, which happens on frame 2, so they're told to stop on frame 1. Then, a variable called dx is created, which determines the speed at which the asteroid moves across the screen. This is set anywhere between –8 and –3, which means the motion will be toward the left (–8 is fast and –3 is slow).

```
// The onEnterFrame for the asteroid
mc.onEnterFrame = function()
{
  // Move it
  this._x += this.dx;

  // Has it hit the earth?
  if (this._x < 50)
  {
    // Increase numHits, and display it on screen.
    numHit++;
    hit_txt.text = numHit;

    // Decrease the number of incoming and display on screen.
    incoming--;
    incoming_txt.text = incoming;

    // Goto the explosion frame, and stop moving.
    this.gotoAndStop(2);
    delete this.onEnterFrame;
  }
}
```

The asteroids are then brought to life by the creation of onEnterFrame functions for each instance. First, they're moved by their dx, which means their _x position will decrease by the amount specified in dx. If their _x value happens to be less than 50, then the aster-oid has hit Earth. When this happens, the numHit variable is incremented, the text is updated on the screen, the number of incoming asteroids is decreased, and the asteroid is then caused to explode by being sent to frame 2. Its onEnterFrame function is also killed so it will stop moving; when it explodes, the explosion is stationary, not moving.

179

```
// clicked on the asteroid
mc.onPress = function()
{
  // Increase numStopped and display on screen
  numStopped++;
  stopped_txt.text = numStopped;

  // Decrease the number of incoming and display on screen.
  incoming--;
  incoming_txt.text = incoming;

  // Goto the explosion frame, and stop moving,
  // and make non-clickable
  this.gotoAndStop(2);
  delete this.onEnterFrame;
  delete this.onPress;
  }
}
```

The preceding code tells the asteroid instances to listen out for user clicks. You want it to explode when the player clicks an asteroid and a successful hit is counted. On click, the numStopped variable is first incremented and displayed on-screen; then the incoming variable is decremented (because one fewer asteroid is incoming), and the number is updated on-screen.

Next, the asteroid is told to explode by going to frame 2, and both the onEnterFrame and onPress events are deleted.

```
incoming_txt.text = incoming;
```

The last line of code sets the incoming_txt text field to the value of incoming, which was just determined when the asteroids were created. Here's the entire code:

```
this.createEmptyMovieClip("asteroids", 1);

// The number you've successully stopped
var numStopped:Number = 0;

// The number that have hit the earth
var numHit:Number = 0;

// The number still incoming
var incoming:Number = 0;

// Creates 60 asteroids.
for (var i = 0; i < 60; i++)
{
  incoming++;
```

```
// Attach the "asteroid" linkage ID
//movie clip to the asteroid holder clip
var mc:MovieClip = asteroids.attachMovie("asteroid", "ast" + i, i);
mc.cacheAsBitmap = true;

// place them off screen, farther and farther out,
// spaced 40 pixels apart, starting at
// x = 650, 690, 730, 770, etc.
mc._x = (i * 40) + 650;

// Random y
mc._y = Math.random() * 300;

// A random scale / size between 20% and 40%
mc._xscale = mc._yscale = Math.random() * 20 + 20;

// Stop them from playing. Frame 2 is the explosion.
// We don't want them to blow up yet
mc.stop();

// Decide on a horizontal speed - how fast they're flying in
// between -3 and -8.  -3 is slow, -8 is fast.  Negative number
// because they're moving left, not right.
mc.dx = (Math.random() * -5) - 3;

// The onEnterFrame for the asteroid
mc.onEnterFrame = function()
{
  // Move it
  this._x += this.dx;

  // Has it hit the earth?
  if (this._x < 50)
  {
    // Increase numHits, and display it on screen.
    numHit++;
    hit_txt.text = numHit;

    // Decrease the number of incoming and display on screen.
    incoming--;
    incoming_txt.text = incoming;

    // Goto the explosion frame, and stop moving.
    this.gotoAndStop(2);
    delete this.onEnterFrame;
  }
}
```

```
            // clicked on the asteroid
            mc.onPress = function()
            {
                // Increase numStopped and display on screen
                numStopped++;
                stopped_txt.text = numStopped;

                // Decrease the number of incoming and display on screen.
                incoming--;
                incoming_txt.text = incoming;

                // Goto the explosion frame, and stop moving,
                //  and make non-clickable
                this.gotoAndStop(2);
                delete this.onEnterFrame;
                delete this.onPress;
            }
        }

        incoming_txt.text = incoming;
```

That's it—that's all there is to it. Just like that, you have a cool game that makes terrific use of alpha video!

Summary

Now that you've looked at the new video functionality of Flash 8 in depth, it's up to you to decide where you would like to take it. This chapter was big, but it still only scratched the surface of all the things possible with Flash 8 video. To fully cover all of the video functionality and the creative possibilities, you would need an entire book—this is something in the works, so watch the friends of ED space in 2006!

You've learned that you can run things through the FLVPlayback component—this is good if you've got entire videos you want to show in a television-type format. You've also seen that video can be imported directly into the library and used in different situations, such as games—especially when the alpha channel is employed.

6 TEXTFIELD IMPROVEMENTS

by Matt Voerman

One of the issues with previous versions of Flash was its inability to clearly render text at small font sizes. Traditionally, small text (i.e., below 10 point) appeared blurred and fuzzy, which often made it unreadable. This was due to the built-in anti-aliasing feature of the Flash Player. Designers found a work-around to this issue by using pixel fonts for situations where small point-sized text was required. **Pixel fonts** are custom designed fonts that render at low point sizes, without anti-aliasing.

With the release of Flash 8, Macromedia has addressed these issues and made significant improvements to the text rendering—in both the Flash 8 authoring environment and the new Flash Player 8.

Saffron

The **Saffron Type System** is a new text-rendering technology that has been developed by Mitsubishi Electric Research Labs (MERL) and licensed to Macromedia for integration into Flash Player 8. Saffron is used for embedded font-rendering for static, dynamic, and input text fields.

Saffron works by taking the outline descriptions of a font and converting them to an internal **Adaptively-sampled Distance Field (ADF)** which is rendered in real time. ADFs allow glyphs to be anti-aliased to a far higher standard than current coverage/image-based rendering technologies.

ADF's are also used to output sub-pixel rendering on LCD displays. **Sub-pixel rendering** refers to the ability to "split" a standard pixel on an LCD display into its three separate "sub-pixels" (red, green, and blue) as illustrated in Figures 6-1 and 6-2. This technique of sub-pixel rendering effectively improves standard screen resolution by a power of three on the horizontal access. Microsoft uses a similar technique in their ClearType rendering technology.

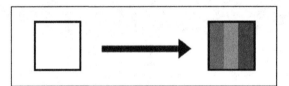

Figure 6-1. The square on the left is how the eye views a pixel. The image on the right is the same pixel magnified so that its sub-pixels (red, green, and blue) can be seen.

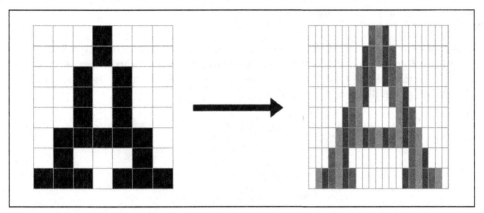

Figure 6-2. The capital A glyph on the left shows how a font is rendered using standard technology. The glyph on the right has three times the horizontal resolution, due to sub-pixel rendering using ADFs (like those in Saffron).

Saffron offers the following features:

- Highly legible type (even at very small font sizes)
- Text that can be scaled and rotated
- Comparable quality rendering to Microsoft's ClearType technology
- Unparalleled reproduction on LCD flat panel displays via sub-pixel rendering
- Supports thousands of existing OpenType, Type 1, and TrueType outline fonts
- Interactive fine-tuning for enhanced viewing via the unique Continuous Stroke Modulation (CSM) feature
- Auto-hinting ability to automatically align strong horizontal and vertical lines to the pixel grid
- Completely different technology to current coverage/image-based rendering technologies
- Text that can be rendered up to 255 points in size
- Sub-pixel rendering gives greater control over kerning (the space between characters)

One of the major advantages of using Saffron is that its rendering technique is computationally simple and doesn't use the TrueType or Type 1 hinting required by competing technologies. As such, fonts don't need to be special-cased.

A point worth watching out for when using the new font-rendering feature is that it causes an increase (approximately 1MB) in the Flash Player's memory usage with each additional font used. This additional memory usage can cause a slight delay when you're loading movies.

Text anti-aliasing

As was mentioned earlier, Mitsubishi Electric Research Lab's new Saffron Type System has given Flash 8 greatly improved font rasterization over its predecessors. These new features are only enabled when Flash Player 8 is selected as the Flash Player Version within the Publish Settings as illustrated in Figure 6-3.

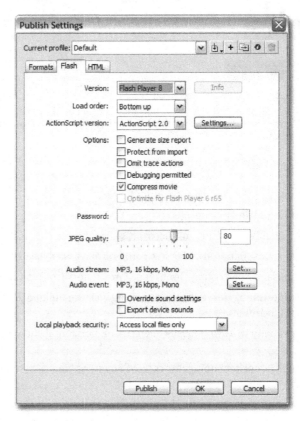

Figure 6-3. Publish settings with Flash Player 8 enabled

With that in mind, a potential trap for unsuspecting players is to open an FLA that was created using Flash 7 (or earlier) and attempt to update text blocks contained within it with the new anti-aliasing features. The Text Property Inspector will initially indicate that the selected text block is either No Anti-Alias for text with no anti-aliasing, or Standard for regular text. In order to display the new text anti-aliasing options, within the Text Property Inspector, you'll need to update the Flash Player Version, within the Publish Settings, to Flash Player 8.

The following anti-aliasing options are available to Flash 8 users from within the Text Property Inspector, and are illustrated in Figures 6-4, 6-5, 6-6, and 6-7 respectively.

Use device fonts

By enabling Use device fonts, SWF file sizes are reduced because no font outlines are embedded within the file. Device fonts rely on the default system fonts installed on the local computer, while the Flash Player selects the closest available font—and this can sometimes produce unexpected results. The three standard device fonts in Flash are sans serif, serif, or monospace fonts.

Lorem ipsum dolor

Figure 6-4. Font rendering with device font selected

Bitmap text (no anti-alias)

Compared to device fonts, bitmap text is larger in file size due to the requirement for font outlines to be embedded within the SWF. In addition to this, text is rendered with sharp jagged edges due to the lack of anti-aliasing.

Lorem ipsum dolor

Figure 6-5. Font rendering with Bitmap text selected

Anti-aliasing for readability

This option uses the new Saffron text-rendering technology to provide superior anti-aliasing and readability of fonts, particularly at small sizes. In order to use the advanced anti-alias setting, you must publish to Flash Player 8.

Lorem ipsum dolor

Figure 6-6. Font rendering with Anti-alias for readability selected

Anti-aliasing for animation

Also leveraging the Saffron technology, Anti-alias for animation ignores alignment and kerning information, and renders smaller fonts as smoothly as possible to create smoother animations. This option creates a slightly larger SWF file, because font outlines are embedded.

Lorem ipsum dolor

Figure 6-7. Font rendering with Anti-alias for animation selected

Custom anti-aliasing (Flash Professional 8 only)

Custom anti-aliasing lets you modify both the sharpness and thickness of the rendering of your fonts (as illustrated in Figure 6-8). The Sharpness option relates to the smoothness of the transition between the text edges and the background. While the Thickness option refers to the degree of blending that occurs between the text edges and the background.

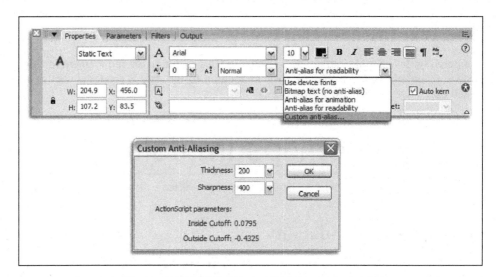

Lorem ipsum dolor

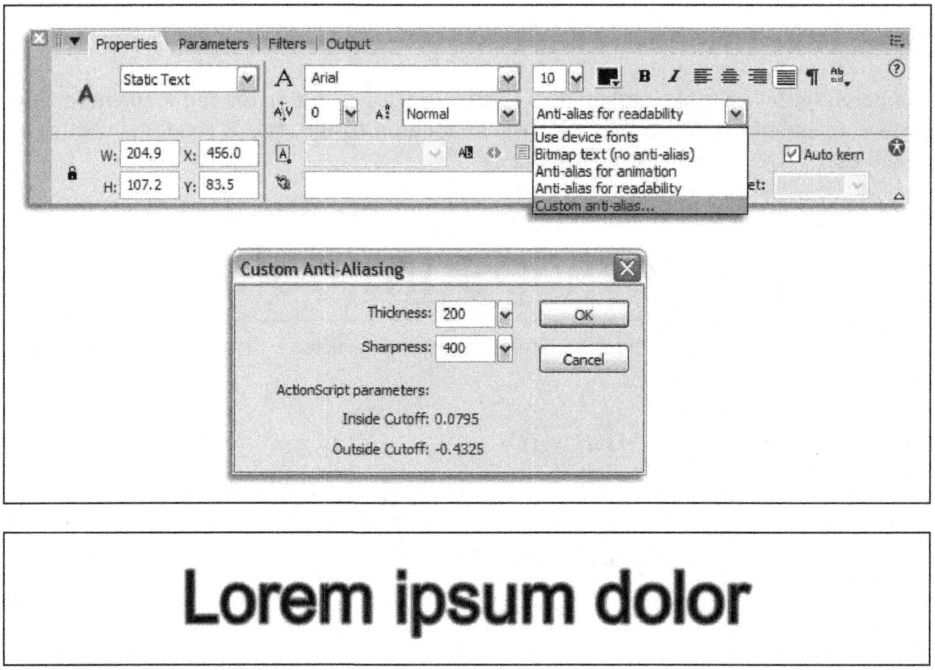

Figure 6-8. Font rendering with Custom anti-alias selected

ActionScript-based anti-aliasing

The text package contains classes for working with text fields, text formatting, text metrics, style sheets, and text layout. Within this package is a new class and several new properties that are specifically designed to take advantage of the advanced anti-aliasing features of Flash 8.

The new `TextRenderer` class allows designers to target the new anti-aliasing function-ality within Flash Player 8. The `TextFormat` class has received added support for *negative leading (i.e.,* a value of leading less than the point size). The `TextField` class has had the `sharpness` and `thickness` properties added.

The `Text` Object has also received an upgrade with three new properties; font➡️`RenderingMode`, `antialiasSharpness`, and `antialiasThickness`. All of these properties target the new text enhancements in Flash 8.

Text object enhancements

The new `antialiasSharpness` and `antialiasThickness` properties of the `text` object both accept float values that specify the anti-aliasing `sharpness` and `thickness` of text respectively. Both of these properties are only available if the font➡️`RenderingMode` property is set to `customThicknessSharpness`.

The `fontRenderingMode` property is a string that specifies the rendering mode for text displayed both on the stage and the Player. The `fontRenderingMode` property accepts one of five values; `advanced`, `bitmap`, `customThicknessSharpness`, `device`, or `standard`.

The following example demonstrates how to use the new `text` object properties, and specifically how the `customThicknessSharpness` value is used to specify the sharp-ness and thickness of the text:

```
fl.getDocumentDOM().setElementProperty("fontRenderingMode",
"customThicknessSharpness");
fl.getDocumentDOM().setElementProperty("antiAliasThickness", -185);
fl.getDocumentDOM().setElementProperty("antiAliasSharpness", 200);
```

TextRenderer class

The `TextRenderer` class provides the main, advanced Saffron-rendering functionality for embedded fonts within Flash Player 8. This superior anti-aliasing feature allows the very high-quality rendering of small sizes and is best used with large blocks of small text. This feature is not recommended for fonts larger than 48 points.

The `TextRenderer` class contains two properties; `antiAliasType` and `maxLevel`. `antiAliasType` specifies the type of anti-aliasing to be used in a movie. `maxLevel` specifies the Adaptively-sampled Distance Field (ADF) quality level for advanced anti-aliasing.

antiAliasType property As mentioned previously, the `antiAliasType` property spec-ifies the type of text anti-aliasing to be used on embedded fonts within a movie.

To enable advanced anti-aliasing on a text field, set the `antiAliasType` property of the text field instance to one of the `TextRenderer.AntiAliasType` constants.

The following example demonstrates how to specify either the normal or advanced anti-aliasing values of the `antiAliasType` property. In order for this example to display correctly, you need to ensure that you have a font symbol embedded within the library with a linkage identifier of `customArialFont`. If you're unsure how to embed a font within the library, simply follow these steps:

1. Open your library.
2. Click the Library Options menu in the upper right corner of the library.
3. Select New Font from the drop-down list.
4. Name the font customArialFont.
5. Select Arial from the font drop-down list.
6. Press the OK button.
7. Right-click on the newly created font and select Linkage.
8. Check the Export for ActionScript box.
9. Accept the default identifier customArialFont by pressing the OK button.

```
//create a new textFormat object and specify its attributes
var myTextFormatter:TextFormat = new TextFormat();
myTextFormatter.font = "CustomArialFont";
//create a textField to put some dummy text into
var myTextContainer:TextField = this.createTextField("myTextContainer",➡
this.getNextHighestDepth(), 10, 10, 300, 30);
myTextContainer.text = "This text uses advanced anti-aliasing.";

//set our anti-alias type to advanced
myTextContainer.antiAliasType = "advanced";
myTextContainer.border = true;
myTextContainer.embedFonts = true;

//apply our textFormat object to the textField
myTextContainer.setTextFormat(myTextFormatter);

//create a second textField to put some dummy text into
var mySecondTextContainer:TextField = this.createTextField
("mySecondTextContainer", this.getNextHighestDepth(), 10, 50, 300, 30);
mySecondTextContainer.text = "This text uses normal anti-aliasing."

//set our anti-alias type to normal
mySecondTextContainer.antiAliasType = "normal";
mySecondTextContainer.border = true;
mySecondTextContainer.embedFonts = true;

//apply our textFormat object to the textField
mySecondTextContainer.setTextFormat(myTextFormatter);
```

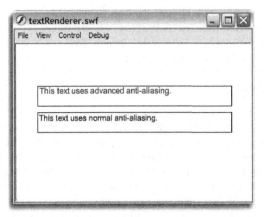

Figure 6-9. The normal and advanced anti-alias settings of the `antiAliasType` property

MaxLevel property `maxLevel` specifies the Adaptively-sampled Distance Field (ADF) quality level for advanced anti-aliasing. When using this property the only acceptable values are 3, 4, or 7.

As mentioned earlier, the Saffron Type System in Flash Player 8 works by using adaptively sampled distance fields (ADFs) to represent the outlines that determine a glyph. The higher the quality of the glyph, the more cache space is required for ADF structures. For example, a value of 3 takes the least amount of memory and provides the lowest quality. Larger fonts on the other hand require more cache space. At a font size of 64 pixels, the quality level increases from 3 to 4 or from 4 to 7 (unless of course the `maxLevel` value has been already set to 7).

The following example demonstrates how the maxLevel value for an SWF is specified, and then displays some dummy text within a text field. In order for this example to display correctly, you need to ensure that you have a font symbol available in the library with a linkage identifier of `customArialFont`:

```
//import the textRenderer class
import flash.text.TextRenderer;

//set the MaxLevel property to its highest level
TextRenderer.maxLevel = 7;

//create a new textFormat object and specify its attributes
var myTextFormatter:TextFormat = new TextFormat();
myTextFormatter.font = "CustomArialFont";
myTextFormatter.size = 64;

//create a textField to put some dummy text into
var myTextContainer:TextField = this.createTextField("myTextContainer",➡
this.getNextHighestDepth(), 10, 10, 700, 50);
```

```
//apply our textFormat object to the textField
myTextContainer.setNewTextFormat(myTextFormatter);
myTextContainer.text = "The quick brown fox";
myTextContainer.embedFonts = true;
```

TextFormat class

Tucked away within the `TextFormat` class lurks another couple of fresh text enhancements with the newly added **kerning** feature and much requested support for `Negative Leading` within Flash Player 8. Kerning refers to the amount of space between characters and directly affects readability. Leading has been a property of the `TextFormat` class since Flash Player 7 and refers to the height between the lines of text (line height). Flash Player 8 introduces `Negative Leading` which refers to instances where the amount of space between the lines is less than the text height. `Negative leading` is useful for rendering multiple lines of text very close together, such as in headings.

The following example dynamically creates a text field and uses the `TextFormat.leading` property to set the leading to 20:

```
//Create a new text format object to control the style of our text
var myTxtFormatter:TextFormat = new TextFormat();
with (myTxtFormatter) {
        font="Arial";
        color="0x000000";
        size=18;
        leading = 20;
        weight = bold;
}

//Create a blank textField and specify its attributes
this.createTextField("myTxtField_txt",1,125,100,300,100);
myTxtField_txt.wordWrap = true;
myTxtField_txt.multiline = true;
myTxtField_txt.border = true;

//Place some dummy text into our textField
myTxtField_txt.text = " The quick brown fox jumped over the lazy➡
sleeping dog";

//Apply our textFormat object to the textField
myTxtField_txt.setTextFormat(myTxtFormatter);
```

Figure 6-10. The new `TextFormat.leading` property in
Flash 8 set to 20

The following example is a repeat of the previous code, yet this time the `Text➡Format.leading` property is set to negative five to bring the second line of text closer to the top one:

```
//Create a new text format object to control the style of our text
var myTxtFormatter:TextFormat = new TextFormat();
with (myTxtFormatter) {
        font="Arial";
        color="0x000000";
        size=18;
        leading = -5;
        weight = bold;
}

//Create a blank textField and specify its attributes
this.createTextField("myTxtField_txt",1,125,100,300,100);
myTxtField_txt.wordWrap = true;
myTxtField_txt.multiline = true;
myTxtField_txt.border = true;

//Place some dummy text into our textField
myTxtField_txt.text = "The quick brown fox jumped over the lazy➡
sleeping dog";

//Apply our textFormat object to the textField
myTxtField_txt.setTextFormat(myTxtFormatter);
```

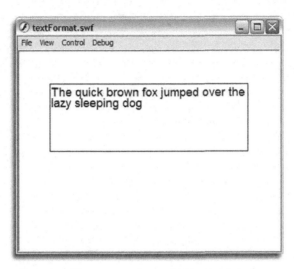

Figure 6-11. The new TextFormat.leading property in Flash 8 set to –5

TextField class

The `TextField` class is used to create text display and input fields. The `TextField` class contains several new properties that all target the advanced rendering features within Flash Player 8.

Sharpness This property relates to the sharpness of the glyph edges within a text field. This property is only available if the `antiAliasType` property of the text field is set to "advanced." The range value for sharpness is a number from –400 to 400. Setting the value outside that range results in the value defaulting to the nearest value in the range (either –400 or 400).

Thickness This property relates to the thickness of the glyph edges within a text field. Like the `Sharpness` property, this property is only available when `antiAliasType` is set to "advanced." The range value for thickness is a number from –200 to 200. Setting the value outside that range results in the value defaulting to the nearest value in the range (either –200 or 200).

GridFitType This is the type of grid fitting used for this `TextField` instance. This is available only if the `antiAliasType` property of the text field is set to "advanced."

For this property, use the following string values:

This example demonstrates all of the new `TextField` properties. It requires that you have a font embedded within the library with its Identifier name set to "Arial-12".

For those of you unfamiliar with how to embed a font within the library, simply follow the steps outlined next.

1. Open your Library.

2. Click the Library Options menu in the upper right corner of the library.

3. Select New Font from the drop-down list.

4. Name the font Arial-12.

5. Select Arial from the font drop-down list.

6. Press the OK button.

7. Right-click on the newly created font and select Linkage.

8. Check the Export for ActionScript box.

9. Accept the default identifier Arial-12 by pressing the OK button:

10. Add the following code to the Actions panel on the first frame of your default layer:

```
//Create a new text format object to control the style of our text
var myTxtFormatter:TextFormat = new TextFormat();
 myTxtFormatter.font = "Arial-12";

//Create a blank textField and specify its attributes
 this.createTextField("textFieldOne_txt", this.getNextHighestDepth(),➡
10, 10, 400, 100);
 textFieldOne_txt.text = "This text has sharpness set to 400 and➡
thickness set to 400"
 textFieldOne_txt.embedFonts = true;
 textFieldOne_txt.antiAliasType = "advanced";
 textFieldOne_txt.gridFitType = "none";
 textFieldOne_txt.sharpness = 400;
 textFieldOne_txt.thickness = 200;
 textFieldOne_txt.setTextFormat(myTxtFormatter);

//Create a blank textField and specify its attributes
 this.createTextField("textFieldTwo_txt", this.getNextHighestDepth(),➡
10, 40, 400, 100);
 textFieldTwo_txt.text = "This text has sharpness set to 0 and➡
thickness set to 0"
 textFieldTwo_txt.embedFonts = true;
 textFieldTwo_txt.antiAliasType = "advanced";
 textFieldTwo_txt.gridFitType = "pixel";
 textFieldTwo_txt.sharpness = 0;
 textFieldTwo_txt.thicknee = 0;
 textFieldTwo_txt.setTextFormat(myTxtFormatter);

//Create a blank textField and specify its attributes
 this.createTextField("textFieldThree_txt", this.getNextHighestDepth(),➡
10, 70, 400, 100);
 textFieldThree_txt.text = "This text has sharpness set to -400 and➡
thickness set to -200."
```

```
textFieldThree_txt.embedFonts = true;
textFieldThree_txt.antiAliasType = "advanced";
textFieldThree_txt.gridFitType = "subpixel";
textFieldThree_txt.sharpness = -400;
textFieldThree_txt.thickness = -200;
textFieldThree_txt.setTextFormat(myTxtFormatter);
```

When you test your movie, you should see the following:

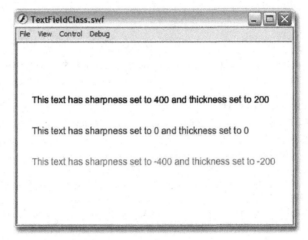

Figure 6-12. An example of the new `TextField` Class properties rendered to screen

TextField resizing

`TextFields` within the Flash 8 authoring environment can now be quickly and easily resized without distorting (scaling) the text contained within them as illustrated in Figure 6-13.

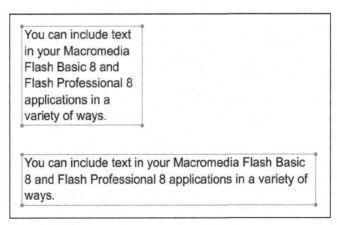

Figure 6-13. TextField resizing using handles makes text layout a breeze.

Text layout API

Flash Player 8 has two new text formatting properties that give designers greater control over the layout of text within their Flash files.

The first of these is support for full Justify text alignment. This includes:

- TextFormat. *TextFormat.align = "justify";*
- HTML tag. *<P align='justify'>*
- CSS Property. *bodyText { textAlign:justify}*

The following example (and Figure 6-14) demonstrates the new Justify text formatting property of the Text Layout API:

```
//Create a new text format object
var myTextFormatter:TextFormat = new TextFormat();

//Set the alignment to justify and the font to Arial
myTextFormatter.align = "justify";
myTextFormatter.font = "Arial";

//Create a new blank textField and specify its size and attributes
var myDynamicDemoTextField:TextField =
this.createTextField("myDynamicDemoTextField",
this.getNextHighestDepth(), 100, 100, 300, 100);
myDynamicDemoTextField.multiline = true;
myDynamicDemoTextField.wordWrap = true;
myDynamicDemoTextField.border = true;

//Add some content to our textField
myDynamicDemoTextField.text = "Flash 8's new Justify text property
allows "
    + "text to spread out and more evenly fill "
    + "the horizontal space for each line. This "
    + "is a great improvement over regular left-aligned "
    + " text that simply wraps and does little else.";

//Apply our text format object to our textField
myDynamicDemoTextField.setTextFormat(myTextFormatter);
```

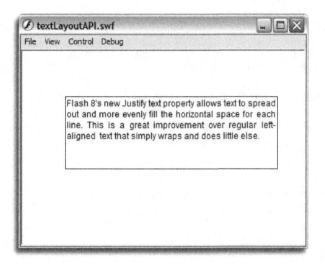

Figure 6-14. An example of the new `TextLayout.justify` property

The second is the support for Tracking (also known as character/letter spacing). This includes:

- TextFormat. *TextFormat.letterSpacing = 1;*
- HTML tag. *<font letterSpacing='1' face='Arial'>*
- CSS Property. *bodyText { letterSpacing:1}*

The following example (and Figure 6-15) demonstrates the new Tracking text formatting property of the Text Layout API:

```
//Create a new text format object
var myTextFormatter:TextFormat = new TextFormat();

//Set the letterSpacing to 10 and the font to Arial
myTextFormatter.letterSpacing = 10;
myTextFormatter.font = "Arial";

//Create a new blank textField and specify its size and attributes
var myDynamicDemoTextField:TextField =➡
this.createTextField("myDynamicDemoTextField",➡
this.getNextHighestDepth(), 100, 100, 300, 100);
myDynamicDemoTextField.multiline = true;
myDynamicDemoTextField.wordWrap = true;
myDynamicDemoTextField.border = true;
```

```
//Add some content to our textField
myDynamicDemoTextField.text = "Flash 8's new text Tracking property➡
allows you to control"
    + "the amount of space that is uniformly distributed between➡
characters ";
//Apply our text format object to our textField
myDynamicDemoTextField.setTextFormat(myTextFormatter);
```

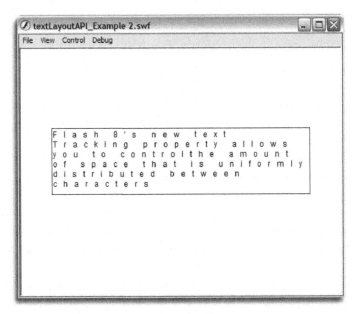

Figure 6-15. An example of the new TextLayout.letterSpacing property

Summary

Despite the minor file size and memory increase associated with the new text enhance-ments, the introduction of Saffron to Flash Player 8 has been a significant improvement for text rendering within Flash. Not only does it address the issue of small-sized text render-ing, features give designers greater control over how text is presented within the Flash Player.

7 SPEED IMPROVEMENTS

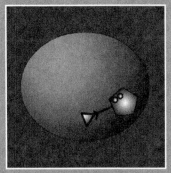

by Chris Mills

At its inception, Flash was a humble vector animation tool, and life was fairly easy for Flash Player in terms of what it was expected to handle by the SWFs fed to it. However, this is not so in modern times—these days, Flash is being used for rich Internet applications (RIAs) involving complex user interfaces and interactive ads, interactive streaming video, 3D games, and much more.

In short, Flash Player is now being pushed to its limits, and frame rates are beginning to choke. This tends to be most obvious when Flash Player is dealing with animations containing large numbers of objects. Up until now, every object on the stage needed to be redrawn with each passing frame, regardless of whether its state (position, color, size, whatever) had changed or not. It became apparent how memory intensive and unnecessary this was, so Flash 8 includes some new additions to significantly improve the performance of your movies. In this chapter, we'll look at these additions, including bitmap caching, `scrollRect`, and the Show Redraw Regions option.

Bitmap caching

As stated earlier, in previous versions of Flash Player, every object on the stage had to be redrawn with each passing frame, putting a lot of strain on the renderer (the part of Flash Player responsible for drawing all the visual elements of a Flash movie) when many objects were involved. Flash 8 addresses this issue with **bitmap caching**. This feature gives you the potential to greatly reduce the amount of work the renderer has to do when you're playing your Flash movies, making your movies faster and smoother.

Bitmap caching comes in the form of a new movie clip property. Using it is as easy as turning it on or off via the Property Inspector or programmatically using ActionScript. In the case of the former, the property is turned on and off using the Use runtime bitmap caching check box found in the lower-right corner of your movie clip's Property Inspector, as shown in Figure 7-1.

Figure 7-1. Here, bitmap caching is turned on for the selected movie clip.

In the case of the latter, bitmap caching is turned on dynamically at runtime by setting the movie clip's brand-new shiny `cacheAsBitmap` property to `true`, like this:

```
mc_myMovieClip.cacheAsBitmap=true;
```

So, as logic would suggest, turning off bitmap caching is a simple matter of setting this property back to `false`:

```
mc_myMovieClip.cacheAsBitmap=false;
```

In addition, you can determine whether a movie clip has bitmap caching turned on by grabbing the value of the cacheAsBitmap property, like so:

```
isCached=mc_myMovieClip.cacheAsBitmap;
```

So, now you know how to use bitmap caching, but you're probably still wondering, "How does it *actually* work?" When you run a Flash movie containing movie clips that have bitmap caching turned on, Flash Player converts the visual contents of those movie clips into bitmaps, and these bitmaps are stored in memory alongside their vector counterparts. Then—and this is the important bit—this content is displayed using a copy of the bitmap equivalent (which has had to be loaded only once and is now resident in memory) for each frame, rather than having to re-render the vector content with each passing frame. This happens until the movie clip changes and the bitmap has to be redrawn. The process can then start again.

As you can imagine, bitmap caching makes things *a lot* easier for the renderer, and this bonus comes at little or no cost to the quality of the visual output—certainly in my experiments, I haven't been able to notice any overly negative effect. It also works fine with nested movie clips. "Wow!" I hear you say. "That's the coolest thing since sliced bread!" It is, when used in the right circumstances.

"Use your gift wisely, young Jedi"

This sounds like a wonderful new dawn in the era of Flash development, but before you go gallivanting off, setting all your movie clips to use bitmap caching in the belief that it will solve your performance problems (well, in the context of Flash movies, anyhow), stay back a while longer and heed these words of warning.

If used correctly, bitmap caching can speed up your movies dramatically. However, if used in completely the wrong circumstances, bitmap caching could also seriously reduce the performance of your movies, so you need to use it wisely.

As I've said before, bitmap caching works best on movie clips that don't change much in terms of visual appearance throughout the course of a movie, especially if they involve lots of complex vector shapes including many lines, curves, and linear or radial fills. It's a lot quicker to simply display these as a single bitmap from memory, rather than expecting the poor renderer to slave away, redrawing them all onto the stage with every passing frame.

However, every time a movie clip changes—for example, if it's scaled or rotated—the bitmap has to be completely redrawn (simply changing its position doesn't matter, as the bitmap can simply be moved), which creates extra overhead. If this extra overhead comes only every so often, then there will be an overall **decrease** in the processing required of Flash Player. But if you've applied bitmap caching to a movie clip that's constantly changing, the bitmap will need to keep being redrawn, which will lead to a net **increase** in the processing required of Flash Player.

Some good scenarios in which bitmap caching could prove invaluable are as follows:

- A user interface featuring lots of draggable components such as information windows, items for purchase, or dynamic menus, all contained in movie clips. These items will be moved around the screen, but won't change internally, so the bitmaps won't need to be redrawn very often, leading to a smoother user experience.

- A cartoon featuring a chase scene through a haunted forest, with lots of trees that are contained in movie clips, so some of them can be animated. The vast majority of them will not change, so bitmap caching will again result in a much smoother end product.

- A simple 1980s arcade space invaders/defender/galaxians–style game, with moving enemy ships and missile sprites roaming around everywhere. The sprite movie clips could all have bitmap caching applied to them to increase the speed and smoothness of the game. (Of course, you could argue that, for that traditional 1980s experience, you'd want your graphics to be on the jerky side, but that's not the point of this discussion!)

I think you get the idea by now. Let's move on to look at some further points to be aware of when manipulating movie clips that have bitmap caching turned on.

Properties and circumstances that cause bitmap regeneration

From the previous discussion, you'll likely already be able to hazard a guess at these. In a movie clip with bitmap caching enabled, changing the following properties will cause Flash Player to redraw the cached bitmap, resulting in extra performance hits. Therefore, you should try to change them as little as possible when using bitmap caching.

- `_alpha`
- `_height`
- `_rotation`
- `_width`
- `_xscale`
- `_yscale`
- `blendMode`
- `filters`
- `opaqueBackground`
- `transform`

In addition, there are logically also various circumstances that will cause the bitmap to be redrawn, including the playhead or outer boundaries of the movie clip (or any of its child movie clips) changing position, images or symbols being attached inside the movie clip (or child movie clips) from the library, anything being drawn inside the movie clip (or child movie clips) using the drawing API, or the movie being zoomed in or out of using the Context menu of Flash Player.

Limits on bitmap caching

There are limits imposed on bitmap caching by file size. These come into effect only in extreme circumstances, but you still need to consider them. For a start, there is a cut-off size of 2,880 pixels in either the x or y direction (so the largest bitmap you can possibly achieve is 2,880 × 2,880); you will not be able to use bitmap caching on movie clips larger than this, because the bitmap size gets too large, and there is a danger of them crashing your computer.

Thinking about it in more general terms, bitmap caching uses more memory when it is enabled, because your computer has to store the vector data and the bitmap data. Bitmaps take up much more memory than vectors in general because vectors store the information needed to reproduce an image as a bunch of algorithms that can re-create it, whereas bitmaps store individual data on each pixel. Let's look at the example of a simple circle, with a radius of 50 pixels (see Figure 7-2). Its area is going to be πr^2, or 3.14 × 2,500 = 7,850 pixels.

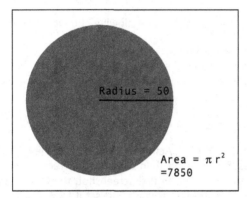

Figure 7-2.
A simple circle

For this circle, a vector representation simply has to store the algorithm that re-creates the circle and the color that the circle's area is set to. A bitmap representation, on the other hand, has to store the position and color of each of the 7,850 pixels!

I don't need to go into any more detail than this for you to see that the bitmap is a lot larger, and the file size can increase exponentially as image sizes increase. You need to bear this in mind for larger movies, as in extreme cases this could affect the performance of your computer—more memory taken up storing these bitmaps for Flash Player means less memory available for other applications.

Filters

You should note that if a filter effect is applied to a movie clip using ActionScript or the Property Inspector, bitmap caching is automatically turned on (the `cacheAsBitmap` property will always return `true`), even if you turn bitmap caching off using ActionScript or the Property Inspector. To prove this, go through the following example:

1. In a new Flash document, add a layer and increase the length of the movie (both layers) to 100 frames.

2. Name the bottom layer object and the top layer actions.

3. Add a simple object to the object layer, such as a filled circle, and turn it into a movie clip using *F8*. Give the instance on the stage a name of mc_myMovieClip.

4. Add a filter to this object using the Filters tab of the Property Inspector. Make it something easily noticeable, like a Drop Shadow or a Glow.

5. Add a keyframe to the actions layer in frame 50 using *F6*.

6. In frame 1 of the actions layer, insert the following ActionScript into the Actions panel (open the panel using Window ➤ Actions):

```
mc_myMovieClip.cacheAsBitmap=false;
var isCached=mc_myMovieClip.cacheAsBitmap;
trace(isCached);
```

7. In frame 50 of the actions layer, insert the following code into the Actions panel:

```
mc_myMovieClip.filters=undefined;
mc_myMovieClip.cacheAsBitmap=false;
var isCached=mc_myMovieClip.cacheAsBitmap;
trace(isCached);
```

Try running this example, and you should see something like Figure 7-3.

So what's happening here? On frame 1, using ActionScript, you've set the `cacheAsBitmap` property of your movie clip as `false`, and then outputted a trace of the value of the `cacheAsBitmap` property afterward. In the first screenshot, the Output panel shows a trace value of `true`—which is a bit strange, as you'd just set it to `false`!

In frame 50, you've done the same thing as in frame 1, except you've used `mc_myMovieClip.filters=undefined;` first of all to programmatically remove your filter. This time the `cacheAsBitmap` property is successfully set to `false`, as the Output panel in the second window proves. So it was the filter that made the difference.

> This example can be found in the code download as `filterTest.fla`.

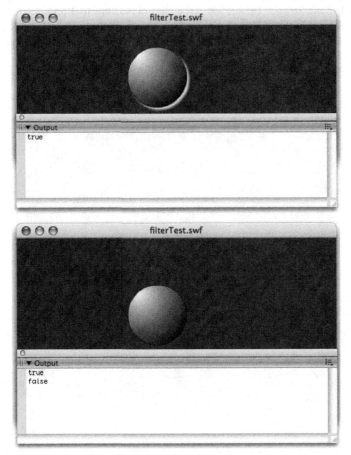

Figure 7-3. Before and after the filter is removed from the example movie clip

Loading external content

Bitmap caching is turned off automatically when an external Flash movie or image is loaded dynamically into a cached movie clip using ActionScript, because when this happens the movie clip is reset—all variables are deleted, all child movie clips are removed, and all movie clip properties are set back to their default values.

Let's prove it with an example:

1. In a new Flash document, call the default layer actions and insert the following code into the Actions panel on the first frame of this layer:

```
this.createEmptyMovieClip("mc_myMovieClip",this.getNextHighestDepth());
mc_myMovieClip.cacheAsBitmap=true;
mc_myMovieClip.loadMovie("sheep.jpg");
trace(this.cacheAsBitmap);
```

2. Save the movie as externalTest.fla, and make sure that an appropriately named image is put in the same location as your movie. You can use my image, sheep.jpg, from the code download, or you can use your own image and filename as you wish.

Test your movie, and you should see the result shown in Figure 7-4.

Figure 7-4. Creating a movie clip and loading an external image into it using ActionScript automatically turns off bitmap caching.

So here, even though you're turning bitmap caching on using ActionScript, the trace still reveals it to be turned off.

> *The files for this example are* externalTest.fla *and* sheep.jpg *in the code download for this chapter.*

Collision detection

As a last point to consider about bitmap caching, you need to bear in mind that results from hit-testing code using MovieClip.hitTest will not be affected by it, as hit-testing is calculated using the vector data of a movie clip, not the bitmap(s) that you will actually see in the movie when bitmap caching is turned on. I haven't included an example for this, because it will likely not affect your work; it's just something that you should be aware of.

Cropping and scrolling with scrollRect

Because scrolling a large amount of complex vector data is, and always has been, a very intensive task for Flash Player, in Flash 8 Macromedia has added a feature to address this: movie clips now have a property called scrollRect. scrollRect can be used to create a viewing window for movie clips that crops them to a specified size and scrolls their contents by a specified offset, which can then be changed to scroll the contents of your movie clips into view over a number of frames. This can help to save dramatically on processing overheads.

You can only use this feature through ActionScript. To use it, you have to create an object to define the viewing window as follows:

```
scrollArea:Object = {x:50,y:50,width:100,height:100};
```

As you can see, four different values are being set here, which are as follows:

- x: Defines the scrolling offset on the x-axis
- y: Defines the scrolling offset on the y-axis
- width: Defines the width of the viewing rectangle
- height: Defines the height of the viewing rectangle

> Be aware that the offset values work in the opposite way from how you might think. A scrolling offset of 10 on the x-axis will shift the contents of a movie clip −10 pixels along the x-axis. A scrolling offset of −20 will shift the contents of a movie clip +20 pixels along the y-axis.

After defining the viewing window as just shown, pass the object to the movie clip that is to be scrolled, like so:

```
scrollArea:Object = {x:50,y:50,width:100,height:100};
mc_myMovieClip.scrollRect=scrollArea; //scroll and crop the movie clip
```

So in this example, mc_myMovieClip is cropped to a size of 100 pixels square, and its contents are shifted by a position vector of (−50, −50). Its _width and _height properties also change to match the cropped size.

Also know that the movie clip will be cropped and scrolled relative to its own internal coordinates, and the viewing window can't be moved. If the contents of the movie clip aren't visible in the cropped window, you need to change the offset values to bring content into view. Let's see this in an example.

1. In a new Flash document, add a layer, and then name the bottom layer object and the top layer actions.

2. Create a new movie clip called mc_myCircle and draw a circle inside it with a diameter of 100 pixels. Position the circle at (0,0) inside the movie clip.

3. Drag an instance of your movie clip on the object layer, and give it the name mc_myMovieClip.

4. Add the following code to the Actions panel in the first frame of the actions layer:

```
var scrollArea:Object = {x:0,y:0,width:100,height:100};
mc_myMovieClip.scrollRect=scrollArea;
```

Test your movie, and you should see something similar to Figure 7-5.

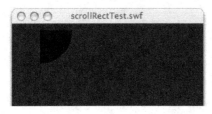

Figure 7-5.
Oops! Only a quarter of the movie clip's content is visible!

So what happened? Well, you haven't offset the content, and the movie clip is cropped from the (0,0) position. The (0,0) position is the top-left corner of the cropped area, not its center.

To see all the content, you need to offset it to bring it into view. Change your code like so:

```
var scrollArea:Object = {x:-50,y:-50,width:100,height:100};
mc_myMovieClip.scrollRect=scrollArea;
```

Test your movie again, and you should see something that looks like Figure 7-6.

> The complete example can be found in the code download as scrollRectTest.fla.

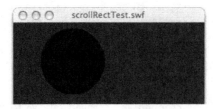

Figure 7-6.
That's better!

You might consider making your scrollRect *window slightly larger than the content you want to display at any one time. As you will notice in Figure 7-6, the circle is clipped very slightly at the edges of the window.*

Note that retrieving the value of a movie clip's scrollRect property actually returns a copy of it, not the original scrollRect. It doesn't return the original, which is a shame because it means you can't set properties of scrollRect like this:

```
mc_myMovieClip.scrollRect.x+=50;
```

You instead have to store a copy, change its properties, and then apply the new values back to the original scrollRect:

```
var scrollRectCopy=mc_myMovieClip.scrollRect;
scrollRectCopy.x+=50;
mc_myMovieClip.scrollRect=scrollRectCopy;
```

It also means that you can't simply delete a movie clip's scrollRect property to delete it. Instead, you have to set it to undefined:

```
mc_myMovieClip.scrollRect=undefined;
```

The real power of scrollRect comes into play when you use it to scroll around a lot of content. Try it!

You will want to turn on bitmap caching when your scrollRect *window contains lots of content that is being scrolled around, but doesn't actually change. As you may have guessed, it's a lot faster to scroll around a bitmap representation of some content than it is to keep redrawing the vector data all the time.*

The Rectangle class

The Rectangle class, another new addition to Flash 8, makes it a lot easier to define and manipulate rectangles. Its syntax is quite similar to that of scrollRect—unsurprisingly, perhaps. It probably also won't surprise you that Rectangle and scrollRect are closely related:

```
flash.geom.Rectangle(x,y,width,height);
```

As you can see, the `Rectangle` class also has four different properties:

- `x`: Defines the x-coordinate of the top-left corner of the rectangle
- `y`: Defines the y-coordinate of the top-left corner of the rectangle
- `width`: Defines the width of the rectangle
- `height`: Defines the height of the rectangle

It's a lot better to use the `Rectangle` class to specify the `scrollRect` of a movie clip instead of what you saw earlier, because the `Rectangle` class has many more properties available to it, giving you a lot more control over it, for example:

```
squareMask = new flash.geom.Rectangle(0,0,100,100);
mc_myMovieClip.scrollRect=squareMask;
```

In the first line, you create a new rectangle, and in the second line, you set it as your `scrollRect` window (with the rectangle's `x` and `y` coordinates being used as offset values for the `scrollRect`). You can now manipulate the window using the `Rectangle` class properties, as mentioned earlier:

```
squareMask = new flash.geom.Rectangle(0,0,100,100);
squareMask.height+=100
bottomLeft=squareMask.bottomLeft;
trace(bottomLeft);
mc_myMovieClip.scrollRect=squareMask;
```

So here, for example, you add a line to increase the height of the rectangle by 100 pixels, and you add two lines that find out the position of the bottom-left corner of the rectangle. There are many more properties to play with—have a look at the flash.geom.Rectangle class page found in the ActionScript 2.0 Language Reference of the Flash 8 help files.

Using scrollRect to overcome size limits

Recall from earlier in the chapter the size limits on bitmap caching: the bitmap can't be allowed to get larger than 2,880 pixels in either direction. Also recall that bitmap caching is turned on automatically when a filter is applied to a move clip. The filter is then applied to the bitmap, not the original vector data. But let's say you wanted to use a 10,000-pixel-wide movie clip with some filters applied to it as a scrolling background for a Flash game. This wouldn't be possible due to the imposed size limits . . . or would it?

You could actually solve this problem using `scrollRect`. Your game window would be unlikely to be more than, say, 800 pixels in width, so you can use a `scrollRect` window to crop the size of the scrolling background and then apply the filters to it. In this way, bitmap caching would be applied only to the cropped selection, not the entire background!

The Show Redraw Regions option

The last and by far the simplest performance-enhancing feature addition we'll look at is the Show Redraw Regions option. This option allows you to see which areas of your movie are redrawn every frame and thereby work out what steps you should take to reduce the amount of redrawing happening, to increase your movie's performance.

To demonstrate this feature, load `satellite.fla` from the code download files. This file contains a simple tweened animation of a satellite orbiting around a sinister alien planet (see Figure 7-7). (Trust me, it's not a giant smartie, so don't get hungry.)

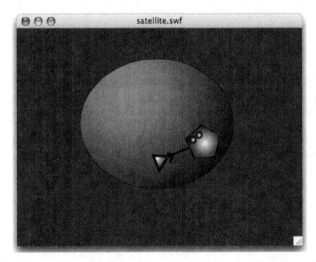

Figure 7-7.
The simple animation example

While you're testing the animation, select View ➤ Show Redraw Regions (or press *CTRL*/⌘+*E*). You should see the output change to what's shown in Figure 7-8.

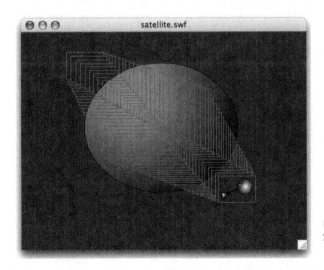

Figure 7-8.
Show Redraw Regions in action

213

The red boxes show exactly what's being redrawn with each passing frame. This is a very useful tool to help you pinpoint exactly what sections of animation are putting the most strain on the renderer while your movie is running. You can then decide how to change your movie to decrease these redraw regions, with the aim of improving performance. You will notice, for example, that regions are redrawn even where the satellite is going behind the moon. This being the case, you might as well delete the satellite altogether from the frames where it isn't visible.

Of course, you're not going to notice significant performance enhancements in a movie of this level of complexity, but it does give you an idea as to what can be achieved using the Show Redraw Regions option.

Summary

Well, this chapter was short and sweet, but that's about all there is to it. A couple of very simple but effective speed-enhancing features have been added to Flash 8 to increase the performance of your movies. Take advantage of them as much as you can!

The next chapter presents an in-depth analysis of the new Flash 8 drawing API, and you'll learn some very clever graphical tricks that can be achieved with it.

8 THE WONDERFUL WORLD
OF BITMAPDATA

by Paul Barnes-Hoggett

Once upon a time, Flash was a great tool for displaying vector artwork and animating it with simple timeline effects. Then along came ActionScript, and we were able to add some funky interactivity to our projects. We could import bitmaps into our Flash movies and do some simple color transformations, but there wasn't really any way to play around with all the information used to make up an image—that is, until `BitmapData` came along. `BitmapData` is a complete API full of great functions allowing you to do all kinds of crazy things with images. In this chapter, I'll show you the following:

- How to create bitmaps in just a few lines of code
- All the features of the `BitmapData` API
- Some cool examples of what you can do with all this `BitmapData` techno-trickery

BitmapData: Creating images on the fly

Now it's time for you to take a look at how to create bitmaps and use them in Flash, including importing your images into Flash, using them to create BitmapData instances, and removing BitmapData instances after you've finished with them.

Creating a BitmapData instance

Creating a new `BitmapData` object is a pretty simple affair, and uses the following constructor:

```
var myBMD:BitmapData = new BitmapData(width:Number, height:Number, ➡
[transparent:Boolean], [fillColor:Number])
```

`width` and `height` are pretty self-explanatory. `transparent` defines whether your bitmap will support per-pixel transparency. Setting this is pretty important for two reasons:

- The `transparent` property is read-only, so this is your only chance at setting it.
- If you have a `BitmapData` instance with transparency, you must be careful to pass **ARGB** (**A**lpha **R**ed **G**reen **B**lue) values instead of just **RGB** ones.

The last property used here is `fillColor`, which allows you to define a default color for your instance. So, let's get started—after all, you're here to do some cool bitmap stuff, right?

1. Create a new Flash movie and save it as `BitmapData1.fla` with the following properties:

2. Select the first frame of your default layer, open the Actions panel, and add the following code to create your very first `BitmapData` object:

```
import flash.display.BitmapData;
var myBMD:BitmapData = new BitmapData(240,270,false,0xF0A12B);
trace("my BitmapData: " + myBMD + " width: " + myBMD.width +➡
  ", height: " + myBMD.height + ", transparent: "+myBMD.transparent);
```

3. Test the movie and you should see the following:

Dude, where's my bitmap?

You just made a `BitmapData` *instance, and it's even tracing out the correct properties—but in your published movie, you see a blank canvas of nothingness! Well, here's the deal: a* `BitmapData` *instance doesn't appear on-screen until you actually attach it to a movie clip. This may seem like a bit of a pain at first, but when you look deeper into what* `BitmapData` *actually is and does later in the chapter, you'll see that it's actually quite a smart move.*

So now that you know you have to attach a bitmap to a movie clip, let's take a look at how you do that using the `MovieClip.attachBitmap` method. This method does exactly what you would expect, and has the following syntax:

movieClip.attachBitmap(bmp:BitmapData, depth:Number,➡
[pixelSnapping:String], [smoothing:Boolean]) : Void

The first two arguments are required; bmp is your BitmapData object and depth is the depth you want your BitmapData instance to be at, just like when you use attachMovie.

pixelSnapping deals with the fact that sometimes a movie clip isn't placed on a whole pixel; it allows you to force the bitmap to snap to the nearest whole pixel, avoiding fuzzy rendering issues. There are three choices for the value of pixelSnapping, as follows:

- auto: This option, which is the default, will snap to the nearest pixel, so long as the movie clip hasn't been scaled or rotated.
- always: This option always snaps to the nearest pixel, regardless of what you've done to the movie clip.
- never: This option switches off snapping.

The final argument, smoothing, will smooth the bitmap data when the movie clip is scaled. This is off by default.

4. Add the following bold lines below the code you've already written, and test the movie.

```
import flash.display.BitmapData;
var myBMD:BitmapData = new BitmapData(240,270,false,0xF0A12B);
trace("my BitmapData: " + myBMD + " width: " + myBMD.width +➡
 ", height: " + myBMD.height + ",transparent: "+myBMD.transparent);
var bmHolder:MovieClip = this.createEmptyMovieClip("bmHolder",1);
bmHolder.attachBitmap(myBMD,1);
```

Now you should see a lovely signal yellow (it's the color of my car) square in the top-left corner of the published movie.

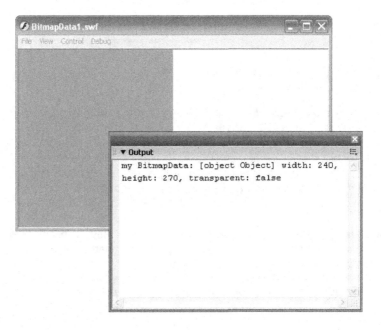

> ### One BitmapData, one movie clip
>
> *It's a good idea to create a separate holder for each* BitmapData *instance. This is because there's not a* removeBitmap *method, and so if you want it offscreen, the best way to deal with it is by putting it in its own movie clip and using* removeMovieClip *when you're done.*

Attaching an image from the library

OK, so this is all well and good—you've made an attractive square of yellow on the screen. Pretty dull, huh? Fortunately, you can also populate a BitmapData instance with information from an image in the library. Let's continue with the example and attach image information from the library.

1. Create a PNG image in your favorite image-editing program or just use the file called sampleImage.png from the download files for this chapter. Just make sure it's 240 pixels by 270 pixels.

2. Import the image to your library using File ➤ Import ➤ Import to Library. If you're familiar with importing PNGs into previous versions of Flash, you'll notice that there are some new options on import that allow you to retain the text and object structure of your PNG files. These options are fairly self-explanatory, so I'll gloss over them here for brevity. You just want a simple, flat image, so check the Import as a single flattened bitmap option at the bottom.

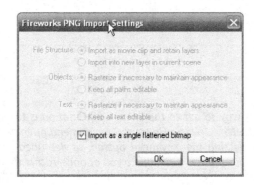

3. Next, double-click the image's symbol in the library, or right/*CTRL*-click and select Properties. This panel should look pretty familiar to you, as not much has changed since MX 2004. However, at the bottom-right-hand corner of the panel is a button labeled Advanced—click it, and the panel will grow to show some more options, which are basically identical to the linkage properties of a movie clip. In the linkage box, check the box labeled Export for ActionScript and, in the Identifier field, enter the linkage name sampleImage.

> **Workflow tip**
>
> *The quickest way to get to the linkage information is to right/CTRL-click the symbol and select* Linkage. *However, I recommend opening the symbol properties and selecting the* Advanced *button, as described previously. This will make more information available to you at once, rather than requiring you to open two panels to get to the information you need. Also, Flash "remembers" your preference for* Advanced *or* Basic *view, so after pressing that button once, you'll always see the advanced properties.*

4. Now that you have your image in the library, it's time to display it on-screen. In order to load library image data into a `BitmapData` instance, you use a static method of `BitmapData` called `loadBitmap`. The function has the following syntax:

```
var attachedBitmap:BitmapData = ➡
BitmapData.loadBitmap(linkageId:String):BitmapData;
```

This basically reads the pixel-level information from an image in the library and uses it to create a `BitmapData` instance with the correct width and height to display the image. It may seem a little confusing that this method is called `loadBitmap` (based on its name, you would probably expect it to be able to load an image from a URL using this method—which you'll look at how to do in the next section). So let's put your newfound knowledge to use—add the following code to your movie, after the last block:

```
//attach Image from the library
var myImageBitmap:BitmapData = BitmapData.loadBitmap("sampleImage");
var bmHolder2:MovieClip = this.createEmptyMovieClip("bmHolder",2);
bmHolder2._x = 240;
bmHolder2.attachBitmap(myImageBitmap,1);
//
```

5. Test the movie and you should see a nice picture next to your now rather drab-looking blob of signal yellow.

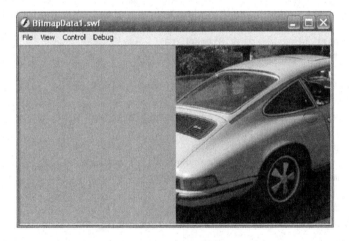

I bet right now this doesn't feel like a particularly groovy addition to the things you can do with Flash—and you're right, it's not too interesting yet—but soon you'll begin to appreciate the benefits. Now let's look at one of the great features of the new `BitmapData` API: `draw`.

Taking a snapshot of a movie clip to use as BitmapData

One of the really neat things you can do with `BitmapData` is capture the visual state of any movie clip at runtime and use it to populate a `BitmapData` instance. Think of this as kind of like the screen grab feature you find in Mac (*CMD+SHIFT+3* or *4*) or Windows (*PRINT SCRN*) operating systems, but at movie clip level. Here's a very quick example to show you how this works:

1. Create a new Flash movie, save it as BitmapData2.fla, and give it the following properties:

2. Create a simple animating movie clip. This can be anything you like: a simple time-line animation, or even something more complicated that you've found elsewhere in the book. If you're lazy like me, you can just use the one included in the code download, inside BitmapData2.fla. Place it on the stage at x: 310, y: 80, and give the movie clip an instance name of anime.

3. Create a new layer on the main timeline and label it actions. Select the first frame, open the Actions panel (Window ➤ Actions), and enter the following code:

```
import flash.display.BitmapData
setInterval(this,"doSnapShot",150);
//
// This will make a snapshot of the 'anime' movieClip
function doSnapShot(){
  var bmd:BitmapData = new BitmapData(anime._width,anime._height,➥
  true, 0x000000);
  bmd.draw(anime);
  var mc = this.createEmptyMovieClip("bmHolder",20);
  mc._x = anime._x - anime._width;
  mc._y = anime._y;
  mc.attachBitmap(bmd,1);
}
```

4. Test the movie, and you should see a snapshot of your animation getting drawn on-screen every 150 milliseconds.

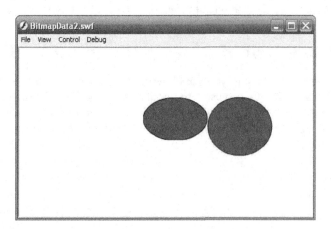

Let's take a look at this code and see what it's doing. The first line, `setInterval(this,` `"doSnapShot",150);`, sets up the `doSnapshot` function to be triggered every 150 milliseconds. In this function, the two key lines are as follows:

```
var bmd:BitmapData = new BitmapData(anime._width,anime._height, true,➡
    0x000000);
bmd.draw(anime);
```

The first line here creates a `BitmapData` instance in much the same way as when you made that lovely yellow rectangle on the screen earlier. This time, however, you're setting the size of `BitmapData` to be the same as the current size of your anime movie clip. This is so that when you take your snapshot, it's big enough to capture all the information you need. Populating the `BitmapData` instance couldn't be simpler—you simply call `BitmapData.draw(anime)`, which basically grabs all the pixel information for `anime` and dumps it into your `BitmapData` instance. The last lines attach that bitmap to a new movie clip, which you should be pretty used to by now. There are more optional arguments for the `draw` method, and you'll look at these later in the chapter.

> *You may have noticed that the edges of the circle at their outermost points in the x and y directions have been cropped, so that instead of a smooth circle, you see flattened edges. The main reason for this is the way Flash draws and measures strokes. Basically, the stroke is drawn with its midpoint where the fill ends. So, if you draw a 50-pixel-diameter circle with a 2-pixel stroke, what you see is a 48-pixel-diameter fill with 2 pixels on either side of it—a 52-pixel-wide circle, as shown in Figure 8-1.*

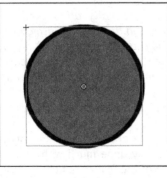

Figure 8-1.
This circle is 50 pixels wide, according to the Properties panel. With a two-pixel stroke, you can see that it overflows the bounding box by 1 pixel on each edge.

5. What does this mean for your `bitmap.draw()` method for copying movie clips? Well, there are actually two issues at play here. First off, the actual width of the movie clip is bigger than the `_width` property by two pixels. So let's remedy this by changing the creation of the `BitmapData` instance to the following:

```
var bmd:BitmapData = new BitmapData(anime._width+2,anime._height+2,➡
    true, 0x000000);
```

6. Publish the movie again, and you should see that the right and bottom edge of the circle now look OK, but the top and left edges are still cut off. This is because the draw method only captures pixels in the positive x and y directions. The only real way to get around this is to ensure that none of your movie clip overshoots into negative x and y directions. Open your animation and, at each keyframe, move the symbol to x: 1, y: 1, which will mean that the stroke can be properly captured.

BitmapData: clean up after yourself

BitmapData objects reside in memory until you get rid of them, and because not all of your instances may be visible on screen, it can be easy to forget about them. BitmapData instances can use up a lot of RAM. Each pixel takes up 4 bytes of memory, so a 300 × 300 instance will use up 4 × 300 × 300 = 360000 bytes (or about 350K); so if you're not careful, BitmapData instances can really choke the player. Fortunately, the thoughtful people at Macromedia have provided a simple way to tidy up after yourself: BitmapData. dispose(). Basically, whenever you're done with a BitmapData instance, make sure you clean up by using the following:

```
myBitMapData.dispose();
```

And don't forget to use the following when you remove your holder movie clip, too:

```
myBitMapData.dispose();
bitmapHolder.removeMovieClip();
```

> **But why can't I just use delete?**
>
> You might think that you could just use delete to get rid of BitmapData. The trouble with that is that you can't be absolutely sure that your BitmapData instance has been deleted. Memory management and the built-in Flash garbage collector (the thing that makes sure deleted objects free up memory) are way beyond the scope of this chapter, but just be aware that sometimes when you delete an object, other references to that object may keep the object in memory; dispose gets around this.

OK, I've now given you a whirlwind tour of how to get your BitmapData instance populated and displayed on-screen, but you haven't actually done much with them yet. The next section of this chapter will run you through each of the features of the BitmapData API before you take things a little further with some examples.

BitmapData API

Now that you know how to create a `BitmapData` instance, let's have a quick run-through of the `BitmapData` API so you know what tools you have in your pixel-pushing arsenal.

Properties

The interesting thing about a `BitmapData` instance is that once you've created it, you can't directly change any of its properties. This may seem like a bit of a pain at first, but see it as a small price to pay for such a cool tool. Besides, there are ways around these limitations, which are described in the following table.

property	description	workaround
height	Sets the height of the bitmap image in pixels.	Change the height of the enclosing movie clip.
width	Sets the width of the bitmap image in pixels.	Change the width of the enclosing movie clip.
rectangle	Defines the rectangle that sets the size and location of the bitmap (for more details on the new `Rectangle` class, see Chapter 7).	Use the enclosing movie clip to manipulate the size of the bitmap image on-screen.
transparent	Defines whether the image will support per-pixel transparency	This one is a bit trickier—you need to create a new `BitmapData` instance with the desired value and then copy data from your old `BitmapData` instance into it. (It's unlikely you would want to change this property once the `BitmapData` has been created, but I included this workaround for completeness.)

Methods

In this section, I'll give you a whistle-stop tour of the `BitmapData` API. First, you'll create a simple template Flash movie to use for each of these methods. By the end of this section, you should have yourself a nice visual library that you can refer to when you're wondering how these methods work. You'll start by using the `loadBitmap` function, which will be used for all your template movies.

loadBitmap

`BitmapData.loadBitmap(id:String):Void`

As mentioned before, `loadBitmap` is used to create a `BitmapData` object populated with the pixel-level information of a library item with the specified linkage. Let's use this now to create a template movie.

1. Create a new Flash document, save it as `bitmapMethodTemplate.fla`, and give it the following properties:

2. Import an image of size 300 × 200 into the library. You can use `sampleImage2.png` from the chapter downloads if you like, or use your own. Double-click the image's symbol in the library and, if the advanced (linkage info) part of the panel isn't visible, click the Advanced button in the bottom-left corner to expand it. Check the box marked Export for ActionScript and give the symbol a Linkage Identifier of sourceImage.

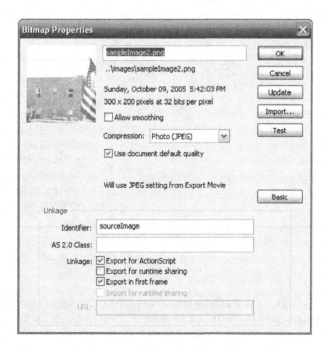

3. Rename the default layer actions and enter the following code into frame 1:

```
import flash.display.BitmapData;
// create & display source Image;
var sourceImage:BitmapData;
var sourceHolder:MovieClip;

sourceImage = BitmapData.loadBitmap("sourceImage");
sourceHolder = this.createEmptyMovieClip("sourceHolder",1);
sourceHolder.attachBitmap(sourceImage,1);
```

4. Test the movie, and you should see something similar to the following (it will depend on what image you chose):

> *That's all you need to know about* loadBitmap. *If you would like to use the movie as a template for the rest of the method code samples, complete steps 5 through 10, which follow.*

5. Encapsulate the code you just wrote into an `initialize` function by adding the following bold lines to your code. While not strictly necessary, it's good practice; and as you start to have more code on the page, it's easier to understand when code is wrapped up in functions like this.

```
import flash.display.BitmapData;
// create & display source Image
var sourceImage:BitmapData;
var sourceHolder:MovieClip;
//
function initialize(Void):Void{
  sourceImage = BitmapData.loadBitmap("sourceImage");
  sourceHolder = this.createEmptyMovieClip("sourceHolder",1);
  sourceHolder.attachBitmap(sourceImage,1);
}

// get it running:
initialize();
```

6. Create a new layer on your main timeline and call it text. Place the following text fields on that layer:

a. A dynamic text field with an instance name of `methodText` and the following properties:

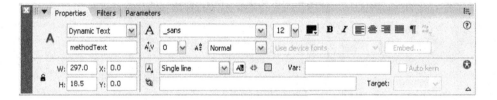

b. A dynamic text field with an instance name of `methodSyntaxText` and the following properties:

c. A static text field with the text SOURCE IMAGE: and the following properties:

d. A static text field with the text OUTPUT IMAGE: and the following properties:

7. Almost there! Add the following bold code to your actions layer:

```
import flash.display.BitmapData;
// create & display source Image
var sourceImage:BitmapData;
var sourceHolder:MovieClip;
//
var theMethod:String = "loadBitmap";
var theMethodSyntax:String = "public static loadBitmap(id:String) :➥
 BitmapData";
//
function initialize(Void):Void{
  sourceImage = BitmapData.loadBitmap("sourceImage");
  sourceHolder = this.createEmptyMovieClip("sourceHolder",1);
  sourceHolder.attachBitmap(sourceImage,1);
  sourceHolder._y = 85
  //
  methodText.text = theMethod;
  methodSyntaxText.text = theMethodSyntax;
}
```

Now when you publish, you should see something like this:

8. Next, add a function called `alter()`, which will be in charge of displaying the image that's output. Add the following code after the `initialize()` function:

```
var outputImage:BitmapData;
var outputHolder:MovieClip;
//
function alter(Void):Void{
  outputImage = BitmapData.loadBitmap("sourceImage");
  outputHolder = this.createEmptyMovieClip("outputHolder",2)
  outputHolder.attachBitmap(outputImage,1);
  outputHolder._y = 310;
}
```

9. Finally, type `alter();` on the line after you call `initialize()`. Your completed code should now look like the following:

```
import flash.display.BitmapData;
// create & display source Image
var sourceImage:BitmapData;
var sourceHolder:MovieClip;
//
var theMethod:String = "loadBitmap";
var theMethodSyntax:String = "public static loadBitmap(id:String) :➥
BitmapData";
```

```
//
function initialize(Void):Void{
sourceImage = BitmapData.loadBitmap("sourceImage");
sourceHolder = this.createEmptyMovieClip("sourceHolder",1);
sourceHolder.attachBitmap(sourceImage,1);
sourceHolder._y = 85;
//
methodText.text = theMethod;
methodSyntaxText.text = theMethodSyntax;
}
//
var outputImage:BitmapData;
var outputHolder:MovieClip;
//
function alter(Void):Void{
        outputImage = BitmapData.loadBitmap("sourceImage");
        outputHolder = this.createEmptyMovieClip("outputHolder",2)
        outputHolder.attachBitmap(outputImage,1);
        outputHolder._y = 310;
}
// get it running:
initialize();
alter();
```

10. Test the movie, and you'll see something like the following:

11. Save the file, and then save a copy as `bitmapMethodLoadBitmap.fla`. You'll find this useful when you want to grab sample snippets of code and see them in action.

> *I know those last few steps may have seemed like a bit of overkill, but I think it's better to build something that you can refer back to as a quick reminder of what* `BitmapData` *is supposed to do than to put together some throwaway elements. You've now built yourself the initial framework for a* `BitmapData` *function browser. Don't you feel good about yourself?*

draw

You visited `draw` in the "Taking a snapshot of a movie clip to use as BitmapData" section. But `draw` goes much deeper than that. If you look at the full syntax for `draw`, you'll see the following:

```
public draw(source:Object, [matrix:Matrix], ➡
[colorTransform:ColorTransform], [blendMode:Object],➡
[clipRect:Rectangle], [smooth:Boolean]) : Void;
```

As you can see, `draw` allows you to take a snapshot of a movie clip and then apply a number of transformations to it. You can transform the shape of the resulting image by specifying a transform matrix, alter the color of the snapshot by specifying a color transform, and even specify a blend mode to apply when creating your snapshot. The last two arguments specify a clipping rectangle for the image, and whether or not the image is smoothed when scaled (the default is `false`).

Lots of scary-looking stuff, huh? Well, don't worry too much—once you start playing with the `draw` method, you'll get used to it soon enough. I'm going to get you started by demonstrating how to specify a matrix in your `draw` method.

Using a matrix. The matrix parameter specifies a matrix used to scale, rotate, or translate the coordinates of the bitmap. Matrix objects are out of the scope of this chapter, but see Chapter 3 for further examples of using them. To see a matrix transformation in action, run through the following example.

1. Open `bitmapMethodTemplate.fla` and save it as `bitmapMethodDrawMatrix.fla`.

2. At the top of the code, you set the variables for `theMethod` and `theMethod➡Syntax`, like so:

```
var theMethod:String = "draw (using transform matrix)";
var theMethodSyntax:String = "public draw(source:Object, ➡
[matrix:Matrix], [colorTransform:ColorTransform], ➡
[blendMode:Object], [clipRect:Rectangle], [smooth:Boolean]) : Void";
```

3. I'm going to provide a simple example to show how to use a matrix to alter the way a copied `BitmapData` instance looks on-screen. Replace the `alter()` method with the following code:

```
function alter(Void):Void{
  var m:Matrix = new Matrix();
  m.rotate(Math.PI*45/180);
  m.translate(150,0);
  outputImage = new BitmapData(sourceHolder._width, ➡
  sourceHolder._height, true, 0x000000);
  outputImage.draw(sourceHolder,m);
  //
  outputHolder = this.createEmptyMovieClip("outputHolder",2);
  outputHolder.attachBitmap(outputImage,1);
  outputHolder._y = 310;
}
```

4. Test your movie and you should see something like this:

As you can see, the matrix has taken the original pixel data, rotated it 45 degrees, and moved it 150 pixels to the right. You should notice that the bottom of the image is cut off. This is because you've specified the width and height of BitmapData to be the width and height of the unscaled, unrotated, untranslated original. Obviously you need to sort this. I'm not going to go into too much detail here, but basically, what you do is create a point (`flash.geom.point`) equivalent to the `width` and `height` of the original. You then transform that point using the matrix to work out how big you actually need to make your output image.

5. As you can see, the `BitmapData` instance was not created with the correct dimensions. Insert the following code inside the `alter()` function to rectify this, as follows:

```
function alter(Void):Void{
    var m:Matrix = new Matrix();
    m.rotate(Math.PI*45/180);
    m.translate(150,0);
    //
    var p = new Point(sourceHolder._width, sourceHolder._height);
    var p2 :Point= m.transformPoint(p);
    //outputImage = new BitmapData(p2.x, p2.y, true, 0x000000);
    outputImage = new BitmapData(sourceHolder._width, ➥
    sourceHolder._height, true, 0x000000);
    outputImage.draw(sourceHolder,m);
    //
    outputHolder = this.createEmptyMovieClip("outputHolder",2);
    outputHolder.attachBitmap(outputImage,1);
    outputHolder._y = 310;
    outputHolder._x = 110;
}
```

6. This should now fix the issue, and the image should no longer be cropped.

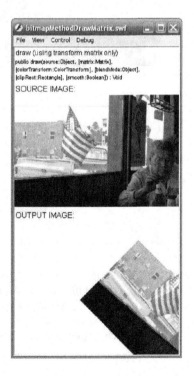

getPixel

The `getPixel` function returns an integer that represents an RGB pixel value from a `BitmapData` object at a specific point. To see this in action, do the following:

1. Open the template file and save a copy as `bitmapMethodGetPixel.fla`.

2. Add a dynamic text field on the stage and give it the following properties:

3. Add the following code below the `initialize` function:

```
this.onMouseMove = function(){
  var x = sourceHolder._xmouse
  var y = sourceHolder._ymouse
  //
  var rgb:Number = sourceImage.getPixel(x,y)
  methodOutputText.text = rgb.toString();
}
```

4. Test the movie and roll your mouse over the source image. You should see something like this:

As you roll over the image, you'll see the output number change. Riveting, huh? So, the number you see is the base-10 representation of the RGB value of the pixel. Now, I'm guessing you would much rather see this number represented as a hex or RGB value, so next you'll add some nice helper functions to convert your indecipherable base-10 number to RGB and hex.

5. Add the following bold code to your file to convert the number to a more meaningful output:

```
this.onMouseMove = function(){
  var x = sourceHolder._xmouse;
  var y = sourceHolder._ymouse;
  //
  var rgbVal:Number = sourceImage.getPixel(x,y);

  var outStr:String = "base 10:\t"+rgbVal.toString();
  //
  var hex:String = rgbVal.toString(16).toUpperCase();
  outStr += "\nhex:\t\t"+hex;
  //
  var rgbObj:Object = hexToRGB(hex);
  outStr += "\nRGB:\t\tr:\t"+rgbObj.r+"\tg:\t"+rgbObj.g+"\tb:\t"➥
  +rgbObj.b;
  methodOutputText.text = outStr;

}
function hexToRGB(hex:String):Object {
  var rgb24 = (isNaN(hex)) ? parseInt(hex, 16) : hex;
  var r = rgb24 >> 16;
  var g = (rgb24 ^ (r << 16)) >> 8;
  var b = (rgb24 ^ (r << 16)) ^ (g << 8);
  return {r:r, g:g, b:b};
}
```

6. Finally, test your movie and you should now see something more like the following image—much more useful!

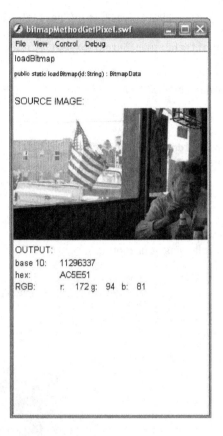

getPixel32

This is basically the same as `getPixel`, but will return an ARGB number. The syntax is also the same.

```
public getPixel32(x:Number, y:Number) : Number
```

setPixel

OK, now that you've seen `getPixel`, let's take a look at its counterpart: `setPixel`. This function will set the color of a single pixel in your `BitmapData` instance. Let's take a look at this in action.

1. Open your template file and save a copy as `bitmapMethodSetPixel.fla`. Set the text variables as follows:

```
var theMethod:String = "setPixel";
var theMethodSyntax:String = "public setPixel(x:Number, y:Number, ➡
color:Number) : Void"
```

2. Insert the following code in the `initialize` function just before the closing curly brace:

```
outputImage = BitmapData.loadBitmap("sourceImage");
outputHolder = this.createEmptyMovieClip("outputHolder",2)
outputHolder.attachBitmap(outputImage,1);
outputHolder._y = 310
```

3. Add the following code after the `initialize` function:

```
this.onMouseMove = function(){
var x = outputHolder._xmouse
var y = outputHolder._ymouse
var col:Number = 0xF0A12B;
//
outputImage.setPixel(x,y,col)
}
```

4. Test your movie and move your mouse over the lower image. You should see a nice trail of yellow following your mouse.

While this may seem pretty basic on its own, this can actually be a pretty powerful tool. You could use it as part of a freehand drawing tool, or even a tool to "paint" image pixels from one bitmap to another.

setPixel32

This function works in essentially the same way as setPixel, except you have to pass it an ARGB number. The syntax is also the same as for setPixel.

```
public setPixel32(x:Number, y:Number, color:Number) : Void
```

colorTransform

This function performs a color transform on a section of your BitmapData instance. You simply specify a rectangle and colorTransform to use, and presto, you have yourself a transformed image! This is similar to being able to change the color properties of a symbol onstage using the Color ➤ Advanced menu in the Properties panel. The great thing about using colorTransform with your BitmapData instance is that you can specify a region of the image rather than being stuck with changing the whole thing. You can also lay one color transform over the top of another. Let's take a look at this in action.

1. Open your template file and save it as BitmapMethodColorTransform.fla. Set the text variables as follows:

```
var theMethod:String = "colorTransform";
var theMethodSyntax:String = "public colorTransform(rect:Rectangle,➡
colorTransform:ColorTransform) : Void"
```

2. Change the alter() function in the code so it looks like the following:

```
function alter(){
  //
  outputImage = BitmapData.loadBitmap("sourceImage");
  outputHolder = this.createEmptyMovieClip("outputHolder",2);
  outputHolder.attachBitmap(outputImage,1);
  outputHolder._y = 310;
  //
  var rect:Rectangle = new Rectangle(30,30,120,120);
  var colTrans:ColorTransform = new ColorTransform(.66,.94,.10,1,➡
  71,-51,-41,0);
  //
  outputImage.colorTransform(rect,colTrans);
}
```

3. Test your movie, and you should see a nice yellow rectangle somewhere over the American flag.

Your color transform is created with the following syntax:

```
var myTransform:ColorTransform = ➡
  new ColorTransform([redMultiplier:Number],
[greenMultiplier:Number],➡
  [blueMultiplier:Number], [alphaMultiplier:Number],
[redOffset:Number],➡
  [greenOffset:Number], [blueOffset:Number], [alphaOffset:Number])
```

Now, I know that looks like a lot, but bear with me, it's not that bad, I promise! Just take a look at your Advanced Effect Color panel and it will become clearer. You can see this panel by selecting a symbol on the stage, choosing Color ➤ Advanced, and clicking on the Settings button (see Figure 8-2).

So, the first four arguments in the color transform are simply the values in the first column of the panel expressed as multiples rather than percentages (if you want 66% red, you pass 0.66 as the value); and the last four are the values from the second column.

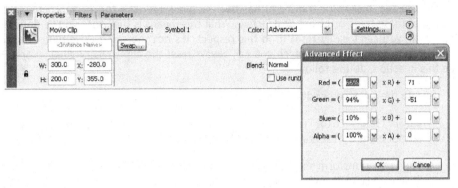

Figure 8-2. The Advanced Effect Color panel gives you a good clue as to what's going on with the `colorTransform` syntax.

Next, you'll take a look at what happens when you do two color transforms on the same `BitmapData` instance.

4. Add the following lines at the end of your `alter()` function:

```
var rect:Rectangle = new Rectangle(100,100,160,40);
var colTrans:ColorTransform = ➡
  new ColorTransform(0.2,.94,0.7,1, 71,-51,-41,0);
outputImage.colorTransform(rect,colTrans);
```

5. Now test your movie, and you should see another color transform has been applied over your yellow box.

As you can see, one color transform has been applied over the top of another. Bear in mind that these transforms are destructive. What this means is that once you've done the transform, you can't easily reset it; in this respect, it's not the same as setting the color property of a movie clip (for which you can always reset the clip to its original colors). To see this in action, do the following:

6. Add the following code at the end of your `alter()` function:

```
var colTrans:ColorTransform = new ColorTransform(1,1,1,1, 0,0,0,0);
outputImage.colorTransform(rect,colTrans);
```

7. This color transform should be like resetting the values in the Settings panel for an advanced color transform on a movie clip. But test your movie, and you'll see that it hasn't reset anything—in fact, it hasn't done anything!

fillRect

`fillRect` simply fills a specified rectangle with a specified color. It's a pretty simple one to get your head around, so you'll use it to do something a bit more interesting than simply demonstrate the effect in action. Open your template file, grab ahold of your mouse, and follow me, soldier.

1. Save a copy of your template file as bitmapMethodFillRect.fla. Alter the text variables as follows:

```
var theMethod:String = "fillRect";
var theMethodSyntax:String = "public fillRect(rect:Rectangle,➥
 color:Number) : Void";
```

2. Amend the first line of the `alter()` function (the one that creates `outputImage`), so it looks like this:

```
outputImage = new BitmapData(sourceImage.width,sourceImage.height,➥
 false, 0xEAEAEA)
```

3. Add the following code after the `alter()` function to create an `onMouseMove` function:

```
function onMouseMove(){
  var x:Number = sourceHolder._xmouse
  var y:Number = sourceHolder._ymouse
  if(x>0 && x<sourceHolder._width && y>0 && y<sourceHolder._height){
    var colValue:Number = sourceImage.getPixel(x,y)
    var rect = new Rectangle(x-3,y-3,6,6)
    outputImage.fillRect(rect,colValue)
  }
}
```

4. Test the movie, and initially you'll see a blank gray rectangle in place of the source image. Now roll your mouse over the source image, and you should start to see something like the following:

This example makes use of `getPixel` (which you took a look at earlier), and uses it to "paint" rectangles of color onto your output image for a nice abstract painting effect. Try increasing the size of the rectangle to get a more abstract effect, or reducing it to start painting a more realistic picture.

hitTest

Just like `MovieClip`'s `hitTest` function, `BitmapData` instances also have their own `hitTest` function. This function is able to perform pixel-level hit detection between a `BitmapData` instance and a point, rectangle, or other `BitmapData` instance. You can even specify an alpha level threshold to tell Flash what to actually consider when performing the hit calculation. The syntax is as follows:

```
public hitTest(firstPoint:Point, firstAlphaThreshold:Number,➡
  secondObject:Object, [secondBitmapPoint:Point], ➡
  [secondAlphaThreshold:Number]) : Boolean
```

This performs pixel-level hit detection between one bitmap image and a point, rectangle, or other bitmap image. No stretching, rotation, or other transformation of either object is considered when doing the hit test.

If an image is an opaque image, it's considered a fully opaque rectangle for this method. Both images must be transparent images to perform pixel-level hit testing that considers transparency. When you're testing two transparent images, the alpha threshold parameters control what alpha channel values, from 0 to 255, are considered opaque.

243

clone

clone simply makes an exact copy of a BitmapData object and returns it. This is another simple way of creating a BitmapData object prepopulated with information. Think of it as a kind of cut-down version of draw, specifically for copying BitmapData instances. Let's take a quick look at this in action.

1. Open your template file, save a copy as bitmapMethodClone.fla, and set your text variables to the following:

```
var theMethod:String = "clone";
var theMethodSyntax:String = "public clone() : BitmapData";
```

2. Change your alert() function so it looks like this:

```
function alter(Void):Void{
  outputImage = sourceImage.clone();
  //
  outputHolder = this.createEmptyMovieClip("outputHolder",2);
  outputHolder.attachBitmap(outputImage,1);
  outputHolder._y = 310;
}
```

3. Test your movie and you should see the following:

As you probably guessed, the output image is an exact copy of the original. Let's move on—you have a lot of ground to cover before sunset!

copyPixels

This method provides a way to copy an area of pixel data from one `BitmapData` instance to another. Let's take a look at this in action to appreciate the power of what it can do.

1. Open your template file and save a copy as `bitmapMethodCopyPixels.fla`. Change the text variables to look like the following:

```
var theMethod:String = "copyPixels";
var theMethodSyntax:String =➡
  "public copyPixels(sourceBitmap:BitmapData, sourceRect:Rectangle,➡
  destPoint:Point, [alphaBitmap:BitmapData], [alphaPoint:Point],➡
  [mergeAlpha:Boolean]) : Void";
```

2. Change the code in your `alter()` function to this:

```
function alter(){
  outputImage = new BitmapData(sourceImage.width,sourceImage.height,➡
  false, 0xEAEAEA);
  outputHolder = this.createEmptyMovieClip("outputHolder",2);
  outputHolder.attachBitmap(outputImage,1);
  outputHolder._y = 310;
}
```

3. As you can see, you're going down the same path as the `fillRect` example. You're now going to add a `mouseMove` function for interactivity. Insert the following code after the `alter()` function:

```
function onMouseMove(){
  var pt = new Point(sourceHolder._xmouse,sourceHolder._ymouse);
  if(pt.x>0 && pt.x<sourceHolder._width➡
  && pt.y>0 && pt.y<sourceHolder._height){
    var rect = new Rectangle(pt.x-15,pt.y-15,30,30);
    outputImage.copyPixels(sourceImage,rect,pt);
  }
}
```

4. Test your movie, and you'll see that as you move your mouse over the top image, the gray canvas area is painted with a copy of the source image.

This does pretty much as you would expect—and if it only did this, it would still be a pretty useful method—but there's more. There are some optional arguments:

```
public copyPixels [plain code font] (sourceBitmap:BitmapData, ➥
sourceRect:Rectangle,
destPoint:Point, [ italic]
[alphaBitmap:BitmapData],
[alphaPoint:Point],
[mergeAlpha:Boolean]) [bold code]
 : Void [plain code]
```

This is where the method gets really cool. Basically, what you can do is use another bitmap as a kind of alpha mask for copying your pixels. Let's take a look at what you can do with this.

5. Import a 30 × 30 image that has some transparency on it into the library (or just use the brush.png file included in the downloads).

6. Double-click the symbol in the library and give it a linkage name of brush.

7. Above your initialize() function, create a new BitmapData instance named brush:

```
var brush:BitmapData= BitmapData.loadBitmap("brush");
```

8. You don't need to worry about attaching this `BitmapData` to a movie clip, as you aren't actually going to be looking at it, so you can move on and add the following to your `copyPixels()` function:

```
outputImage.copyPixels(sourceImage,rect,pt, brush, new Point(0,0));
```

9. When you now test the movie, your copied area has smooth edges. Imagine all the fun you could have with photo-paintbrushes.

copyChannel

The `copyChannel` function allows you to take the channel information from one bitmap (or a portion of it) and copy it into the channel of another `BitmapData` instance. The source and destination channels are specified by passing in a number for the source and destination channel, according to the following codes:

Channel	Number
Red	1
Green	2
Blue	4
Alpha	8

The easiest way to see how this method works is to see it in action.

1. Open the template file and save a copy of it as `bitmapMethodCopyChannel.fla` with the following text variables:

```
var theMethod:String = "copyChannel";
var theMethodSyntax:String = "public copyChannel(➥
    sourceBitmap:BitmapData, sourceRect:Rectangle, destPoint:Point,➥
    sourceChannel:Number, destChannel:Number) : Void";
```

2. The `alter()` function will simply take the red, green, and blue channels from the source image and copy each of them into a third of your output image. Change the `alter()` code to look like this:

```
function alter(){
    outputImage = new BitmapData(sourceImage.width,sourceImage.height,➥
    false, 0x000000);
    //
    outputHolder = this.createEmptyMovieClip("outputHolder",2);
    outputHolder.attachBitmap(outputImage,1);
    outputHolder._y = 310;
    //
    var sw:Number = sourceImage.width/3;
    var sh:Number = sourceImage.height;
    outputImage.copyChannel(sourceImage, new Rectangle(0,0,sw,sh),➥
    new Point(0,0),1,1);
    outputImage.copyChannel(sourceImage, new Rectangle(sw,0,sw,sh),➥
    new Point(sw,0),2,2);
    outputImage.copyChannel(sourceImage, new Rectangle(sw*2,0,sw,sh),➥
    new Point(sw*2,0),4,4);
    //
}
```

So why do I specify 1, 2, 4, or 8 for the channel?

You may be wondering why you need to specify a number for the channel, and why Macromedia decided to make those numbers 1, 2, 4, or 8. Well, it makes more sense when you think of these numbers as the binary version of 1, 10, 100, and 1000. Without going into all the details of how Flash interprets these (if you're interested, have a look into bitwise operations), it's basically a very quick way of differentiating between the channels, and far quicker than interpreting strings like "red," "green," or "blue." Remember, when dealing with BitmapData, *Flash has to deal with thousands of pixels of information, and the quicker it can do this, the better.*

3. Test your movie, and you'll see that the channels have been copied to the output image, as shown:

floodFill

This method is rather like the paint bucket tool you find in many illustration programs. What it does is fill a specified pixel, and all adjacent pixels of the same color, with a specified color. Let's see what you can do with this one.

1. Open your template file and save a copy as bitmapMethodFloodFill.fla. Set the text variables as follows:

```
var theMethod:String = "floodFill";
var theMethodSyntax:String = "public floodFill(x:Number, y:Number,➥
    color:Number) : Void";
```

2. Your alter() function will simply display a copy of the source image below it. Until now, you've been using loadBitmap to populate outputImage. This time, you'll use clone() just to mix it up a bit. Change your alter() function to the following:

```
function alter(){
  outputImage = sourceImage.clone();
  //
  outputHolder = this.createEmptyMovieClip("outputHolder",2);
  outputHolder.attachBitmap(outputImage,1);
  outputHolder._y = 310;
  //
}
```

3. Now add an `onMouseMove` function below the `alter()` function to see `floodFill` in action.

```
function onMouseMove(){
  var pt = new Point(sourceHolder._xmouse,sourceHolder._ymouse);
  if(pt.x>0 && pt.x<sourceHolder._width && pt.y>0 && ➡
pt.y<sourceHolder._height){
    outputImage.floodFill(pt.x,pt.y,0xF0A12B);
  }
}
```

4. Test your movie and move your mouse over the top image. If you don't see much at first, try moving over the burned-out areas of sky in the top-right part of the image. You should see something like this:

As you roll the mouse over the more detailed areas of the image, quite often only one pixel is getting colored in on the output image. However, when you roll over the sky, you should see big blocks of color getting filled in. As you can see, floodFill isn't terribly useful as-is for photographic images, but when you're dealing with simpler artwork (e.g., if you've taken a snapshot of a movie clip), it could really come into its own.

getColorBoundsRect

This method will return a rectangle that fully encloses all pixels of a specified color in a BitmapData instance. In order to get this to work, you specify a mask and the color value that you're looking for. Let's look at this in action to see how it works.

1. OK kids, you should know the drill by now—open the template file and save a copy as bitmapMethodGetColorBoundsRect.fla with the following text variables:

```
var theMethod:String = "getColorBoundsRect ";
var theMethodSyntax:String = "public getColorBoundsRect(mask:Number,➡
 color:Number, [findColor:Boolean]) : Rectangle";
```

2. For this movie, you're not going to show an output image, but rather draw a rectangle over the source image to show the bounding rectangle. Change your alter() function to look like this:

```
function alter(){
  outputHolder = this.createEmptyMovieClip("outputHolder",2)
  outputHolder._y = 85
}
```

3. Next, you'll make an onMouseMove() function to track what pixel you're currently over, find the bounding rectangle, and draw it on top of the original. Add the following code to your movie:

```
function onMouseMove(){
  var pt = new Point(sourceHolder._xmouse,sourceHolder._ymouse);
  if(pt.x>0 && pt.x<sourceHolder._width && pt.y>0 &&➡
  pt.y<sourceHolder._height){
    var col = sourceImage.getPixel32(pt.x, pt.y);
    var rect:Rectangle = sourceImage.getColorBoundsRect(col,➡
    col, true);
    with (outputHolder){
      clear();
      lineStyle(0,0xFF0000);
      moveTo(rect.left,rect.top);
      lineTo(rect.right,rect.top);
      lineTo(rect.right,rect.bottom);
      lineTo(rect.left,rect.bottom);
      lineTo(rect.left,rect.top);
    }
  }
}
```

4. Test your movie and move your mouse over the image. You'll see a red rectangle defining the area that encloses the rolled-over color—something like the following:

scroll

This method simply shifts pixel data in the `BitmapData` instance according to an x and y offset. Areas that are outside the bounds of the scroll are left unchanged. Take a look at the Flash documentation for more detail on this method.

applyFilter

If you've been a good student and worked through this book in order, you'll know that Flash 8 has a wonderful new feature that allows you to apply filters to movie clips. You can also apply these filters to `BitmapData` instances. The syntax for this is as follows:

```
public applyFilter(sourceBitmap:BitmapData, sourceRect:Rectangle,
destPoint:Point, filter:BitmapFilter) : Number
```

You simply specify the filter you want to apply, and presto—lovely filtered images. Follow the steps that follow to see this in action.

1. Open your template movie and save it as `bitmapMethodApplyFilter.fla` with the following text variables:

```
var theMethod:String = "applyFilter";
var theMethodSyntax:String =
"public applyFilter(sourceBitmap:BitmapData, sourceRect:Rectangle,
destPoint:Point, filter:BitmapFilter) : Number";
```

2. Change your `alter()` function to look like this:

```
function alter(){
  outputImage = new BitmapData(sourceImage.width,sourceImage.height);
  //
  outputHolder = this.createEmptyMovieClip("outputHolder",2);
  outputHolder.attachBitmap(outputImage,1);
  outputHolder._y = 310;
  //
  outputImage.applyFilter(sourceImage, sourceImage.rectangle,➥
  new Point(0,0), new BlurFilter());
  //
}
```

3. Test your movie, and you'll see the original image has been copied to your output image with a nice bit of blur on it.

As you can see, the filter has been applied to `BitmapData`. This is all well and good, but sometimes a filtered output image will be larger than the original, and you'll want to see the full effect of the filter. How can you do this without complicated math to work out how big the resulting image will be? Enter `generateFilterRect`.

generateFilterRect

So, you want to apply a filter that's going to result in a larger image footprint, huh? Fear not, `generateFilterRect` is here to help you. If you supply it with the rectangle you would like to apply the filter to, it will return a rectangle that describes the output size.

Like most of these `BitmapData` methods, it's easier to visualize, so let's take a look at this in action.

1. Once again, open your template movie, save it as bitmapMethodGenerateFilter➥ Rect.fla, and set the text variables as follows:

```
var theMethod:String = "generateFilterRect";
var theMethodSyntax:String = "public generateFilterRect➥
(sourceRect:Rectangle, filter:BitmapFilter) : Rectangle";
```

2. Change your `alter()` function to the following:

```
function alter(){
  var filter:BlurFilter = new BlurFilter();
  var rect:Rectangle = sourceImage.generateFilterRect➥
  (sourceImage.rectangle, filter);
  outputImage = new BitmapData(rect.width,rect.height);
  //
  outputHolder = this.createEmptyMovieClip("outputHolder",2);
  outputHolder.attachBitmap(outputImage,1);
  outputHolder._y = 310;
  //
  outputImage.applyFilter(sourceImage, sourceImage.rectangle,➥
  new Point(filter.blurX,filter.blurY), filter);
  //
}
```

3. This time when you test your movie, you'll see your output image has nice blurry edges, rather than a blur that stops abruptly at a sharp edge.

noise

The `noise` method fills a `BitmapData` instance with computer-generated noise. You can specify whether to fill the instance with monochrome or colored noise, and even whether to put noise only on certain channels. Take a look at the tutorial on "oldifying" an image (in the "Changing the look of an image to suit a site style" section near the end of this chapter) to see it in action.

pixelDissolve

This method allows you to dissolve an image by filling in random pixels with solid color. For brevity, consult the Flash documentation for more details on this.

Merge

The `merge` function is used to merge two images by specifying how much of each channel is used from the source image, and how much is used from the original image. The syntax is as follows:

```
public merge(sourceBitmap:BitmapData, sourceRect:Rectangle,➥
destPoint:Point, redMult:Number, greenMult:Number, blueMult:Number,➥
alphaMult:Number) : Void;
```

The multipliers should have values between 0 and 256. The larger the number, the more weighting is given to the source image. Let's take a look at this in action.

1. Open your template file and save a copy as bitmapMethodMerge.fla with the following text variables:

```
var theMethod:String = "merge";
var theMethodSyntax:String = "public merge(sourceBitmap:BitmapData,➥
sourceRect:Rectangle, destPoint:Point, redMult:Number,➥
greenMult:Number, blueMult:Number, alphaMult:Number) : Void";
```

2. Amend your `alter()` function to look like this:

```
function alter(){
  outputImage = new BitmapData(sourceImage.width,sourceImage.height,➥
  false, 0xAACC00)
  //
  outputHolder = this.createEmptyMovieClip("outputHolder",2)
  outputHolder.attachBitmap(outputImage,1);
  outputHolder._y = 310
  //
  outputImage.merge(sourceImage, sourceImage.rectangle,➥
  new Point(0,0),128,200,0)
  //
}
```

3. When you test your movie, you should see that the resulting image has copied half of the red channel, most of the green channel, and none of the blue channel into the destination image.

perlinNoise

Perlin noise is a type of computer-generated noise that's generated by combining and interpolating between several individual noise-generating functions (known as octaves). When these are combined, you're left with an organic-looking area of noise that works really well when you want to add texture without your image looking too computer generated. This method is covered in detail later in this chapter, in the "Making an image feel like a movie" section, in which you'll use it to create clouds—but it can also be used to create realistic looking flames, mountain ranges, and even wood grain! It's also used in Chapter 3, when Craig Swann and Glen Rhodes demonstrate the Displacement Map filter.

paletteMap

This advanced function is used to remap color channel values in a `BitmapData` instance. It can be used to shift colors in an image, and also for advanced color manipulation, such as changing levels and curves (in much the same way as you can with image manipulation tools in programs like Photoshop). A good description of this method would warrant an entire chapter in itself, and is way beyond the scope of this book. For more detail, take a look at the Flash 8 documentation.

threshold

This method allows you to test the pixel values of an image against a specified formula, and then set pixels that satisfy the criteria to a new color value. For more details, consult the Flash 8 documentation.

Using BitmapData to do some cool stuff

Now that you've had a brief introduction to the tools that are available with `BitmapData`, I'm sure you would like to get a quick head start into doing some cool stuff, right? When I first started playing around with the `BitmapData` class, I was soon hooked, and before long found myself using it in several key areas of my work: making lightweight movie effects, doing image transitions, and manipulating images to fit in with a site style. This next section will run you through three complete work examples to give you a few ideas of where to start performing your own pixel trickery. They are as follows:

- Making an image feel like a movie
- Transitioning stylishly from one image to another
- Changing the look of an image to suit a site style

Making an image feel like a movie

So here's the deal: you want to have some nice movie effects in your project, but you don't have all the bandwidth in the world to play with. Time to bring `BitmapData` to the table to make a static image move. For this example, you're going to use Perlin noise to make some realistic clouds move across the sky of an image. In order for this to work, you really need an image without any clouds in the sky to begin with, so you don't get left with any annoying non-moving clouds along the way. If you've downloaded the source files from the website, you can use the `cloudsBase.jpg` image.

   1. Create a new Flash movie, save it as `clouds.fla`, and give it the following properties:

2. Next, import your image into the library. Give it a linkage name of BackgroundImage by double-clicking on the image's symbol in the library, checking Export for ActionScript, and entering the linkage name in the appropriate field.

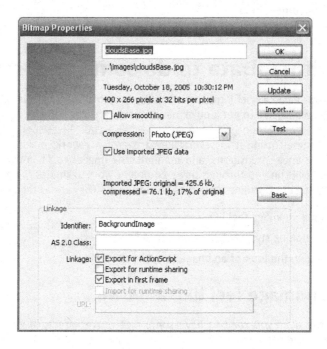

3. Next, rename layer 1 of your main timeline to Actions, select the first frame, and add the following `import` statements:

```
import flash.display.BitmapData;
import flash.filters.ColorMatrixFilter;
import flash.geom.Point;
```

4. Add the following code following the `import` statements to attach the bitmap from the library:

```
var bg:MovieClip = this.createEmptyMovieClip("background",➥
this.getNextHighestDepth());
var bgBmp:BitmapData = BitmapData.loadBitmap("BackgroundImage");
bg.attachBitmap(bgBmp, 1);
```

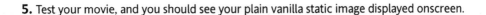

5. Test your movie, and you should see your plain vanilla static image displayed onscreen.

6. So far, so good. However, there's still no hint of a cloud in the sky—let's get to fixing that next. The next few stages are going to concentrate on making the clouds, and it's going to be a lot easier to see your clouds taking shape without the background distracting you; so for now, comment out the line of code that attaches the bitmap.

```
var bg:MovieClip = this.createEmptyMovieClip("background",➥
this.getNextHighestDepth());
var bgBmp:BitmapData = BitmapData.loadBitmap("BackgroundImage");
//bg.attachBitmap(bgBmp, 1);
```

7. The next thing you're going to do is create a new `BitmapData` instance the same size as your base image, and fill it with Perlin noise. Add the following code just below your last block of code:

```
var cloudsBmp:BitmapData = new BitmapData(bgBmp.width, bgBmp.height,➥
true, 0x000000);
var clouds:MovieClip = this.createEmptyMovieClip("clouds_mc",➥
this.getNextHighestDepth());
clouds.attachBitmap(cloudsBmp, 1);
```

8. In order to fill your new `BitmapData` instance with cloud-like texture, you'll simply apply Perlin noise to it. Let's encapsulate this as a function call (it will make life easier later on in the tutorial). Add the following code after your last bit:

```
var seed:Number = Math.random()*100000;
function makeClouds(){
   cloudsBmp.perlinNoise(275, 75, 4,seed, false, true, 1|2|4, true);
}
makeClouds();
```

9. Test your movie, and you'll see a rather monochrome-looking cloud-like texture.

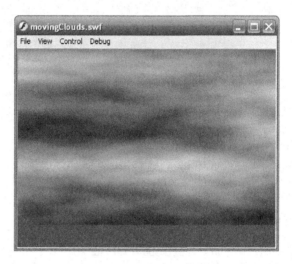

I suppose you're wondering what all those parameters mean? Let's take a quick look at the `perlinNoise` syntax:

```
public perlinNoise(baseX:Number, baseY:Number, numOctaves:Number,➡
randomSeed:Number, stitch:Boolean, fractalNoise:Boolean,➡
[channelOptions:Number], [grayScale:Boolean], [offsets:Object]) : Void;
```

What follows is a quick guide to how the parameters affect your example—consult the Flash documentation for a full explanation of what each of these are and do.

Argument	Effect
baseX	Stretches the clouds in the x direction. The larger the number, the more stretched the clouds will be.
baseY	Stretches the clouds in the y direction. The larger the number, the more stretched the clouds will be.
numOctaves	Defines how much detail there is in the clouds, with more octaves creating greater detail. Note that higher numbers make the calculation slower.
randomSeed	Creates a different effect depending on the number—just like a random seed in a fractal-generation program.
stitch	Gives similar edges to the noise generated if set to true, making it easier to tile noise filters. (You don't need to worry about this for this effect, so leave it as false.)
fractalNoise	Creates a more even result for your effect if set to true. (That is, it creates a more overcast day!)
channelOptions	Specifies the channels you want to apply the effect to. As you're going to be using a grayscale-generated noise pattern, this has no real effect. (Just don't include the alpha channel, 8, or your effect won't look very realistic.)
grayscale	Specifies whether the Perlin noise should be grayscale. Leave this set to true, unless you're looking for a more psychedelic effect!
offsets	Defines an array of points that specifies how much to offset each octave (layer) of Perlin noise. (You'll see this in action later in the tutorial.)

10. Let's move on to animating the clouds. With perlinNoise, you can specify an offset for each octave of noise—by changing these offsets over time, you'll end up with some nice moving clouds. First, you need to set up some initial variables. Add the following just below the last bit of code:

```
var offsets:Array = [new Point(), new Point(), new Point(),➡
new Point()];
var speeds:Array = [0.8, 0.4, 0.1, 0.22];
```

11. Now you want to change these offsets over time. Add the following bold code to your `makeClouds()` function:

```
function makeClouds(){
  var numOctaves:Number = offsets.length;
  for(var i:Number=0; i<numOctaves; i++){
    offsets[i].x += speeds[i];

  }
  cloudsBmp.perlinNoise(275, 75, numOctaves,seed, false, false,➥
  1|2|4, true, offsets);
}
```

12. Finally, add the following `onEnterframe` function and test your movie. You should see the clouds moving gently from right to left.

```
onEnterFrame = function(){
  makeClouds();
}
```

13. Next, you want to look at blending your clouds into your background image. The first step is to specify a blend mode for the cloud's movie clip. Add the following just after the `clouds.attachBitmap(cloudsBmp, 1);` line of code from step 7:

```
clouds.blendMode = "overlay";
```

14. Now when you publish your movie, you should see the background blue color of the stage peeping through the clouds:

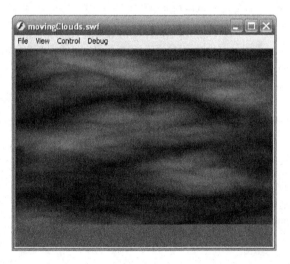

15. Let's bring back your background image. Uncomment the `bg.attachBitmap`➡
(`bgBmp`, 1) line of code and test your movie. You should see something like the
following:

So now you're getting somewhere. You're seeing a vaguely cloud-like effect moving gently
across the image, but it's still nowhere near realistic enough. The clouds are in front of the
mountains and telephone poles. One nice side effect of the blend effect you've used is
that you get cloud-like shadows on the road. I kind of like these, and it was an unexpected
bonus when I was building this example, so you're going to keep them. What you really
need is to hide the clouds from the middle ground, distance, and vertical surfaces like the
flag and the telephone poles. In order to do this, you need to introduce a new bitmap to
mask out these areas. The following steps show how I made the mask using Photoshop,
but you can use any image-editing program you wish. If you would rather just use the image
I've already created for you, you can find it in the code download files as `cloudMask.png`.

1. Open the image in Photoshop and use the Magnetic Lasso tool to create a rough
outline of the area to be masked (don't worry about getting it exactly right, you'll
sort this in the next step).

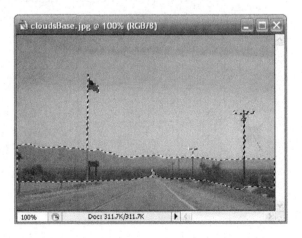

2. Move into Quick Mask mode. This mode allows you to use the Paintbrush (and other drawing tools) to fine-tune your mask area. What you're looking for here are smooth edges between your masked and non-masked areas. I prefer using this method as it allows me finer control over how much feathering is used in each area.

3. When you're satisfied with your masked area, go back into standard mode and invert the selection (*CTRL/CMD+SHIFT+I*).

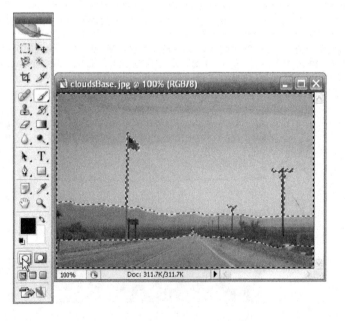

4. Next, create a new layer and fill the selected area with black pixels by pressing *CTRL/CMD+BACKSPACE*. Switch the visibility of the background layer off, and select File ➤ Save for Web. Export the image as a PNG to retain the transparent area.

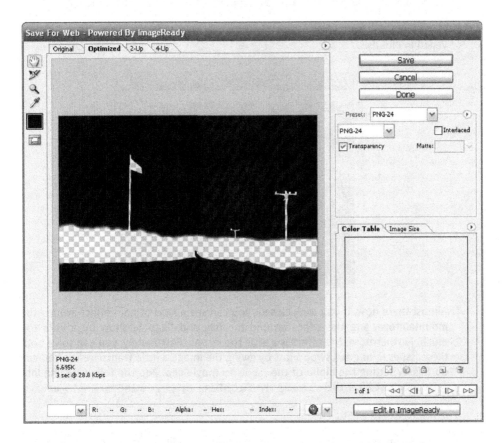

5. Import your image into Flash and give it a linkage name of cloudsMask.

If you're anything like me, you'll probably have skipped the last few steps and used the mask image from the chapter download. However, I thought it was worth running through those steps in case you're using your own image. Let's crack on!

1. Now that you have your image in the library, you can get to using it. You could simply create a movie clip symbol containing the image, and mask your clouds by masking the enclosing movie clip, but that wouldn't really be in the spirit of the chapter, so let's do the masking using BitmapData instead. In essence, the only channel you're interested in here is alpha—so next, you'll use copyChannel to add an alpha channel to the clouds. Add the following code just below the clouds.blendMode = "overlay"; line from step 13 of the first set of steps in the example:

```
var mask:BitmapData = BitmapData.loadBitmap("cloudsMask");
```

2. Then, in your `makeClouds` function, add the following line just below the `perlinNoise` method:

```
cloudsBmp.copyChannel(mask,cloudsBmp.rectangle, new Point(),8,8);
```

3. Now when you test your movie, you can see that the mountains are no longer veiled in clouds:

4. Almost there now. If you look closely, you can see a kind of halo effect around the mountaintops, and the edges around the flag and flagpole show up a little too much. Furthermore, the effect is a little too strong. Fortunately, you can solve both these issues in one fell swoop just by giving the image a little transparency. You can do this by setting the alpha of the `clouds` movie clip. Pop the following line into your code just after the `clouds.attachBitmap(cloudsBmp, 1);` line:

```
clouds._alpha = 50;
```

5. Test your movie and you'll see a much subtler rendition of clouds rolling across Route 66.

> Another, quicker way to do this is to open your mask image in Photoshop and knock the transparency back to 70%. Although this is a neater solution overall, it's less flexible in terms of being able to tweak the alpha value in Flash to get the balance just right.

6. Once I had gotten this far, I was pretty much done, although I now felt that the image was a little too dark. This can be fixed using a brightness filter. Add the following code just after the `bg.attachBitmap(bgBmp, 1);` line (shown in step 4 of the first series of steps in this exercise) to boost the brightness of the background image:

```
var cm:ColorMatrixFilter = new ColorMatrixFilter([1,0,0,0,35,0,1,0,➡
0,35,0,0,1,0,35,0,0,0,1,0]);
bgBmp.applyFilter(bgBmp,bgBmp.rectangle, new Point(0,0),cm);
```

7. When you test your movie now, you can see you've lifted the image a little so that it's a bit more punchy.

8. At this point, you should have yourself a really nice subtle cloud movement on the base image. There's just one thing that doesn't quite look right: the clouds are moving right to left, but the flag shows that the wind is coming from the left. This is an easy problem to fix—change the code so that your speeds get subtracted from your offsets instead of added to them, and you're done.

```
for(var i:Number=0; i<numOctaves; i++){
  offsets[i].x -= speeds[i];
}
```

Transitioning from one image to another

When I worked on the websites for Select Model Management (www.selectmodel.com) and Ellison / Lee (www.ellisonlee.com), I spent a long time looking at how you could transition between two images. Without having pixel-level control of an image, you were left with three main options—alpha one image in over another, fade to solid color and then out again to reveal the image, or use masking to hide/show the new image. These transitions are all well and good, but the methodology is a bit of a handful.

However, with `BitmapData` you can approach the problem in an easier, cleaner manner than ever before—manipulating `BitmapData` is significantly better than doing heavy alpha transitions on movie clips. I'm going to whet your appetite for these new types of transitions with a kind of color parallax effect to swap between two images. For this, you'll need two images of the same size. If you've downloaded the source material for this chapter, you can use `flyover1.jpg` and `flyover2.jpg`, and you'll be good to go. Otherwise, pick two images you would like to use, strap yourself in, and get ready for the ride.

1. Create a new Flash movie with the following properties (if you've used different images, set the movie to be the size of the images), and then save it as `transitions.fla`.

2. Import your images directly into the library and give them linkage names of image1 and image2.

3. To save you from having to write loads of `import` statements as you progress through the tutorial, let's get them out of the way to start with. If you're unsure of why you're importing all these classes, be patient and all will become clear as you go (or just flip through the next few pages and spoil the surprise). Rename layer 1 on your main timeline to Actions, select the first frame, and open your Actions panel. Insert the following code:

```
import flash.display.BitmapData;
import flash.geom.Rectangle;
import flash.geom.Point;
import mx.utils.Delegate;
import mx.transitions.Tween;
import mx.transitions.easing.*;
```

4. Next, you'll declare the variables you'll be using. You'll be using three `BitmapData` instances for this transition. Basically, you're going to load the two images into `BitmapData` instances, and then these will be used for creating your transitioning image (the only one that actually renders on-screen). Add the following code below the `import` statements:

```
var image1:BitmapData;
var image2:BitmapData;
var image3:BitmapData;
```

> As you move through the tutorial, you'll be adding more variables at this point in the code. Although you could put these variable declarations anywhere outside of a function for them to be available to any function on the frame, it makes for good housekeeping to put these all in the same place at the top of the code.

5. If you've worked through some of the method examples, you'll be familiar with my practice of creating an `initialize` function to perform initial setup. Not wanting to upset the applecart, let's do that now. Add the following code below your variable declarations:

```
function initialize(){
   image1 = BitmapData.loadBitmap("image1");
   image2 = BitmapData.loadBitmap("image2");
   image3 = image1.clone();
   sourceHolder = this.createEmptyMovieClip("sourceHolder",1);
   sourceHolder.attachBitmap(image3,1);
}
initialize();
```

6. Test your movie, and you should see something like this:

What you've done here is create your three `BitmapData` instances. `image1` and `image2` will never get rendered onstage, and are merely used as source material to render `image3`, your output image.

7. Next, you need to initiate your transition. You do this by having a simple `onPress` function associated with the movie clip. Add the following line inside your `initialize()` function, at the bottom of it:

```
sourceHolder.onPress = Delegate.create(this,swapImage);
```

269

> *I use* `Delegate.create` *here to avoid any possible scope issues. A full discussion of scope within functions is way beyond the scope of this chapter, but if you've ever had problems when functions execute and you find that it's down to the scope the function is executing in (i.e., what the function thinks* `this` *is), have a look at the* `Delegate.create` *function—it will save you hours of head-scratching.*

8. Now that you've given the `sourceHolder` the name of a function to execute when it's pressed, you had better go ahead and write it. Before you jump ahead and write the function, though, you need to declare a couple of variables that you'll use in the transition. Add the following code just below the other variable declarations at the top of the code:

```
var bluePos:Number;
var endPos:Number;
```

9. You're now ready to write the `swapImage` function. This function simply resets the `bluePos` and `endPos` variables and then assigns a new function, `doTransition`, to the image holder's `enterFrame` handler. Add the following code to your movie at the bottom of the code:

```
function swapImage(){
bluePos = 0;
endPos = image1.width;
this.onEnterFrame = doTransition;
}
```

If you're wondering why I've put the setting of `endPos` in the `swapImage()` function, which gets called every time someone clicks an image (even though the width of the image never changes), bear with me; all will become clear.

10. Now you need to write the `doTransition` function. What this needs to do is recreate the `image3` `BitmapData` each frame until the transition is done. Add the following code to your movie:

```
function doTransition(){
bluePos+=10
image3.copyChannel(image1,image1.rectangle, new Point(bluePos,0),4,4);
if(bluePos==endPos){
  delete this.onEnterFrame
}
}
```

11. Now test your movie and click the image. As you can see, the blue channel is shifted 10 pixels to the right each frame. As it moves across, the area to the left of the image doesn't have its blue channel shifted, so you're left with artifacts on the image.

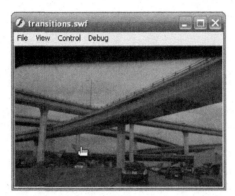

12. Let's fill up the shifted area with the blue channel from your new image. Add the following code just under the first `copyChannel` method call:

```
image3.copyChannel(image2,new Rectangle(endPos-bluePos,0,bluePos,➡
image1.height),new Point(0,0),4,4);
```

13. Now when you test your movie, you should see the blue channel from the second image being pulled across, something like the following:

14. Now that you've seen how to copy one channel, you can go ahead and copy the others. Add the following variable declarations:

```
var greenPos:Number;
var redPos:Number;
```

15. Next, add the following lines of code to the `swapImage()` function, just below the `bluePos = 0;` line:

```
greenPos = 0;
redPos = 0;
```

16. At the beginning of your `doTransition()` function, add the following lines of code:

```
redPos +=4;
greenPos +=2;
//
image3.copyChannel(image1,image1.rectangle, new Point(redPos,0),1,1);
image3.copyChannel(image2,new Rectangle(endPos-redPos,0,redPos,➥
image1.height),new Point(0,0),1,1);
//
image3.copyChannel(image1,image1.rectangle, new Point(greenPos,0),2,2);
image3.copyChannel(image2,new Rectangle(endPos-greenPos,0,greenPos,➥
image1.height),new Point(0,0),2,2);
```

17. As your green channel is the slowest-moving channel, you need to change your end-state test—so change the code that checks for the transition to end to the following:

```
if(greenPos>=endPos){
    delete this.onEnterFrame
}
```

18. Test your movie and have a look to see how you're coming along. You should see the channels moving off to the right as you want them to, but unfortunately, your speedy red and blue channels don't stop copying until the tortoise-like green channel has finished.

This is like the effect you saw after step 11. Now you'll add some checks to make sure they don't overshoot.

19. What you need to do is copy a channel only when its position is less than the end position. Add the following bold lines to your doTransition() function so it looks like this:

```
function doTransition(){
  bluePos+=10;
  redPos +=4;
  greenPos +=2;
  if (bluePos<=endPos){
    image3.copyChannel(image1,image1.rectangle, new Point(bluePos,0)➡
    ,4,4);
    image3.copyChannel(image2,new Rectangle(endPos-bluePos,0,➡
    bluePos,image1.height),new Point(0,0),4,4);
  }
  if(redPos <=endPos){
    image3.copyChannel(image1,image1.rectangle, new Point(redPos,0)➡
    ,1,1);
    image3.copyChannel(image2,new Rectangle(endPos-redPos,0,redPos,➡
    image1.height),new Point(0,0),1,1);
  }
  if(greenPos <= endPos){
    image3.copyChannel(image1,image1.rectangle, new Point(greenPos,0)➡
    ,2,2);
    image3.copyChannel(image2,new Rectangle(endPos-greenPos,0,➡
    greenPos,image1.height),new Point(0,0),2,2);
  }
  if(greenPos>=endPos){
    delete this.onEnterFrame
  }
}
```

20. Now when you test your movie, you should see the colors shift with the intended parallax effect, and you end up with your new image.

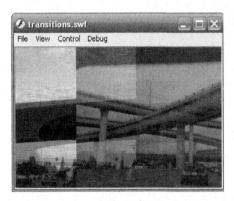
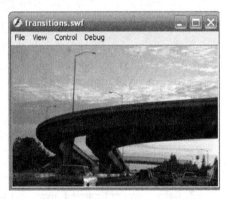

OK, so you now have a more interesting transition than your plain old alpha fade. However, at the moment, it lacks subtlety and doesn't have any gentle slowing down at the end, so the effect is a little jarring. In the next part of the tutorial, you'll take a look at improving this to achieve a subtler effect.

1. Instead of simply incrementing your red, blue, and green positions on each frame, you're going to use the `Tween` class to work out what your offset values should be for each frame. Doing this gives you much greater flexibility for tweaking the numbers. Amend your `swapImage()` function to look like the following:

```
function swapImage(){
    bluePos = 0;
    greenPos = 0;
    redPos = 0;
    endPos = image1.width;
    new Tween(this,"bluePos",Elastic.easeInOut,bluePos,endPos,1.1,true);
    new Tween(this,"redPos",Elastic.easeInOut,bluePos,endPos,1.2,true);
    var t = new Tween(this,"greenPos",Elastic.easeInOut,bluePos,➡
    endPos,1.3,true);
    t.onMotionStopped = Delegate.create(this,killTransition);
    this.onEnterFrame = doTransition;
}
```

> ### *The Tween Classes*
>
> *Hidden away in the depths of Flash MX 2004 were a set of classes in the package* `mx.transitions`. *This included a* `Tween` *class and a whole package of easing equations (in* `mx.transitions.easing`*). These classes allowed you to do the sort of tweens that you can do on the timeline, and then some. A full discussion of these is out of the scope of this chapter, but basically, you can get any property of any object to change over time (or frames), and get it to ease in, ease out, or—as you're doing here—ease both in and out. For more details on this fantastically useful set of classes, see* www.actionscript.org/tutorials/advanced/Tween-Easing_Classes_Documented.

2. These tweens will change the red, blue, and green positions over time (1.1, 1.2, and 1.3 seconds to be precise). When a tween is finished, it calls a user-defined `onMotionStopped` function. You've specified a function called `killTransition` for the slowest transition, green. Add the following function to your code, below the `doTransition()` function:

```
function killTransition(){
    delete this.onEnterFrame
}
```

3. Before you get carried away and test the movie, change the `doTransition()` function to look like the following (I've commented out the lines you don't need so you can see what I'm getting rid of, but you can just delete it if you prefer):

```
function doTransition(){
  //bluePos+=10;
  //redPos +=4;
  //greenPos +=2;
  //if (bluePos<=endPos){
    image3.copyChannel(image1,image1.rectangle, new Point(bluePos,0)➡
    ,4,4);
    image3.copyChannel(image2,new Rectangle(endPos-bluePos,0,➡
    bluePos,image1.height),new Point(0,0),4,4);
  //}
  //if(redPos <=endPos){
    image3.copyChannel(image1,image1.rectangle, new Point(redPos,0)➡
    ,1,1);
    image3.copyChannel(image2,new Rectangle(endPos-redPos,0,redPos,➡
    image1.height),new Point(0,0),1,1);
  //}
  //if(greenPos <= endPos){
    image3.copyChannel(image1,image1.rectangle, new Point(greenPos,0)➡
    ,2,2);
    image3.copyChannel(image2,new Rectangle(endPos-greenPos,0,➡
    greenPos,image1.height),new Point(0,0),2,2);
  //}
  //if(greenPos>=endPos){
    //killTransition();
  //}
}
```

4. Now test your movie, and you'll see a far more pleasing color parallax transition.

Taking the transition further

This should be just a starting point for your creativity. You could try out different transition times and different easing equations, or even use different methods of the BitmapData *images you want to transition.*

Changing the look of an image to suit a site style

Sometimes you may want to apply a similar style to a series of images. In the following example, I'm going to show you how to "oldify" an image by giving it a sepia tint and adding some noise to it to make it seem a bit less crisp. The image I've chosen is a picture of me outside a café in Monterey, California, where John Steinbeck stayed, got drunk, and wrote *Cannery Row*—sufficient reason to "oldify" the image, I think. You, of course, can use any image you like.

1. Create a new Flash movie, save it as `oldifying.fla`, and give it the following properties:

2. Create an image with dimensions 200 × 267 (or use my lovely holiday snapshot, `paulOnHoliday.jpg`, from the code download files) and import it into the library.

3. Double-click the image in the library to bring up the Properties panel, and click the Advanced button at the bottom-right of the panel if the linkage part of the panel isn't visible. (If you've been following the chapter up to now, it should be open by default.) Give the image a Linkage Identifier name of sampleImage:

4. Rename the default layer actions and add the following `import` statements to the Actions panel at frame 1:

```
import flash.display.BitmapData;
import flash.filters.BitmapFilter;
import flash.filters.ColorMatrixFilter;
import flash.geom.Point;
import flash.geom.Matrix;
import flash.geom.ColorTransform;
```

5. After these, insert the following code:

```
//attach Image from the library
var myImageBitmap:BitmapData = BitmapData.loadBitmap("sampleImage");
var bmHolder:MovieClip = this.createEmptyMovieClip("bmHolder",1);
bmHolder.attachBitmap(myImageBitmap,1);
```

6. Test the movie and you should see your image in all its colorful glory at the top left of the movie window.

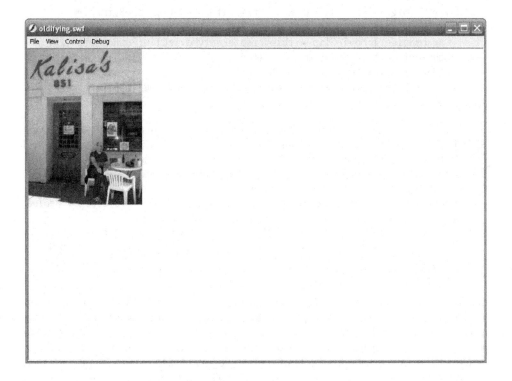

7. While this picture is no doubt glorious, it's a little too colorful for your purposes. What you're now going to do is create a black-and-white copy of your original. To do this, you'll use `applyFilter()` to apply a `ColorMatrix` filter, which will suck all the color out of your image. Add the following code after the code that was used to display the first bitmap:

```
function getDesaturationFilter():BitmapFilter{
// coefficients by Paul Haeberly
//http://www.sgi.com/misc/grafica/matrix/
var r = 0.212671;
var g = 0.715160;
var b = 0.072169;
return new ColorMatrixFilter(
[r, g, b, 0, 0,
r, g, b, 0, 0,
r, g, b, 0, 0,
0, 0, 0, 1, 0]);
}

var myImageBitmap2:BitmapData = new BitmapData(myImageBitmap.➥
width,myImageBitmap.height)
var bmHolder2:MovieClip = this.createEmptyMovieClip("bmHolder2",2);
bmHolder2.attachBitmap(myImageBitmap2,1);
bmHolder2._x = 200;
myImageBitmap2.applyFilter (myImageBitmap, myImageBitmap.rectangle,➥
new Point(0,0),getDesaturationFilter());
```

So what are those magic numbers? Basically, what's going on here is that you're taking some information from each of the source red, green, and blue channels of the image and copying that resultant value into the destination channels, doing some math—you're taking the RGB values of the source pixels and working out a `baseValue` like this:

$$baseValue = 0.212671*redValue + 0.715160*greenValue + 0.072169*blueValue$$

You then set the RGB values of the destination pixels to that same `baseValue`. You don't need to worry too much about how this is worked out (if you do, check out the matrix examples in Chapter 3 for more clues, or check out the resources that follow), just be aware that that's what it does.

But the question remains, how did clever old Paul come up with those magic numbers? Well, truth be told, I didn't. Although all this color matrix fanciness is brand new in Flash, it has been used in other languages for a long time, and so there are a few very valuable resources on the Web for finding out this kind of stuff. Although the text can be quite heavy reading, you can find out lots of useful snippets of information if you look hard enough. A good exhaustive set of information on all things color based can be found at www.faqs.org/faqs/graphics/colorspace-faq (look for section C-9 to see where I got those magic numbers from).

Another very useful page relating to color matrices in particular can be found at www.sgi.com/misc/grafica/matrix.

Finally, if you're a total Flash-head like me, you probably far prefer seeing pretty pictures doing stuff to reading heavy texts. For a real eye-opener, check out Mario Klingemann's utterly superlative color matrix utility class and the demo browser that goes with it at www.quasimondo.com/archives/000565.php. This will show you more about what you can do with the color matrix than could ever be covered in this chapter.

8. Test your movie and you should see a grayscale version of your image next to the original.

Although this image is indeed grayscale, it still doesn't really feel right—it's not the look you want in this situation. Black-and-white photos are never truly color neutral, so in the next step you'll transform the color to give a little color depth to the image.

9. After your last block of code, add the following:

```
//
var myImageBitmap3:BitmapData = new BitmapData(myImageBitmap.width,➥
myImageBitmap.height);
var bmHolder3:MovieClip = this.createEmptyMovieClip("bmHolder3",3)
bmHolder3.attachBitmap(myImageBitmap3,1);
bmHolder3._x = 400
myImageBitmap3.draw(myImageBitmap2, new Matrix(), new➥
ColorTransform(1.1,0.94,0.9,1,35,20,-26,0))
```

279

10. As you can see, you're copying the `BitmapData` information from your second black-and-white image, applying a color transform to the data, and using this to populate a new `BitmapData` instance. Test the movie, and you should see the following:

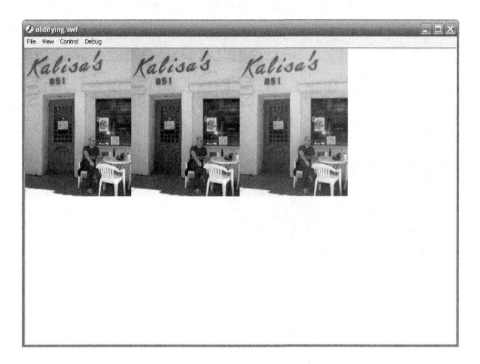

As you can see, the image now has a warmish yellow sepia tone to it. I've deliberately exaggerated the effect here so you can easily see what's going on, but I would recommend being as subtle as possible with something like this. Feel free at this stage to adjust the values in the color transform to get a result that's pleasing to you. Speaking of which, how did I get this new set of magic numbers? Well, I turned my image on the stage into a movie clip. Then I added an Adjust Color filter and knocked the saturation down to 0 (see Chapter 3 for more information on filters). Finally, I set the Color setting in the Property inspector to Advanced and played around with the values until I got a pleasing result (see Figure 8-3).

My resulting color transform would be represented as having the multipliers as the first four arguments (divided by 100—as they're multipliers, not percentages) and the offsets as the last four—that is, `new ColorTransform(1.1,0.94,0.9,1,35,20,-26,0);`.

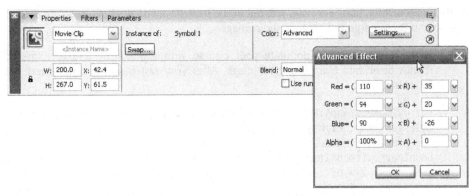

Figure 8-3. The advanced color effect, achieved using the Property inspector

11. So far so good—but the image still looks a little clean, so let's grunge it up a bit by adding some noise (image noise, that is). Insert the following after your last bit of code:

```
var myImageBitmap4:BitmapData = new BitmapData(myImageBitmap.width,➥
myImageBitmap.height);
var bmHolder4:MovieClip = this.createEmptyMovieClip("bmHolder4",4);
bmHolder4.attachBitmap(myImageBitmap4,1);
bmHolder4._x = 600;
myImageBitmap4.noise(1,0,256,1|2|4,true);
```

12. Test your movie, and you'll see a block of monochrome noise at the far right of the stage.

Pretty uninteresting, huh? For now, yes; but in the next step, you're going to create a noisy bitmap and then merge it with your sepia image.

13. Here, you're going to populate your bitmap with some noise and then merge it with pixel data from the third image. After your last block of code, insert the following:

```
var myImageBitmap5:BitmapData = new BitmapData(myImageBitmap.width,➥
myImageBitmap.height);
var bmHolder5:MovieClip = this.createEmptyMovieClip("bmHolder5",5);
bmHolder5.attachBitmap(myImageBitmap5,1);
bmHolder5._x = 0;
bmHolder5._y = 267;
myImageBitmap5.noise(1,0,256,1|2|4,true);
myImageBitmap5.merge(myImageBitmap3, myImageBitmap3.rectangle,➥
new Point(0,0),230,230,230,0);
```

14. This merge function takes `Bitmap3` and merges it with your block of noise, with a strong bias toward the sepia image. Remember, when doing merges, the higher the multipliers, the stronger the bias toward the source image. (If you're a little fuzzy about this, go back and take a look at the `merge` method description earlier in the chapter.) Test the movie and you should see the following:

Your image is now nicely toned, with a bit of grungy noise added to it. This is where most people would leave the transformation, but you can do better than this. The big problem I have with noise generation is that it just never feels quite right. Remember what I said earlier about subtlety when doing these transforms? It's just too regular and obviously computer-generated. What you need to do is randomize the noise a bit. Fortunately, there's something you can use to fuzz up your regular noise—Perlin noise—and that's where you're going next.

15. First up, you're going to create a block of Perlin noise (or cloudy fluff, if you like) so you can see what's being added to the mix. Add the following code to your movie after the last block of code:

```
var myImageBitmap6:BitmapData = new BitmapData(myImageBitmap.width,➡
myImageBitmap.height, false, 0xCCCCCC);
var bmHolder6:MovieClip = this.createEmptyMovieClip("bmHolder6",6);
bmHolder6.attachBitmap(myImageBitmap6,1);
bmHolder6._x = 200;
bmHolder6._y = 267;
myImageBitmap6.perlinNoise(myImageBitmap.width,myImageBitmap.height,➡
3,5,false,false,undefined,true);
```

16. Test your movie, and you'll see an odd-looking smoky blob on your screen. Just so you don't panic and think you've gone wrong somewhere, I'll show you mine:

283

17. Next, you're going to merge your original noise to this smoky blob so you can get a better idea of the noise filter you'll be using. After the last line of code, add the following:

```
myImageBitmap6.merge(myImageBitmap4, myImageBitmap.rectangle,➡
new Point(0,0),140,140,140,0);
```

18. What this does is merge the two noise filters together with a slight bias toward the original, snowstorm-style noise. Test your movie and you should see something like this:

As you can see, the resulting pattern has a more organic unevenness to it—the next step will be to merge this with your image.

19. After the last block of code, add the following:

```
var myImageBitmap7:BitmapData = new BitmapData(myImageBitmap.width,➡
myImageBitmap.height, false, 0xCCCCCC);
var bmHolder7:MovieClip = this.createEmptyMovieClip("bmHolder7",7);
bmHolder7.attachBitmap(myImageBitmap7,1);
bmHolder7._x = 400;
bmHolder7._y = 267;
myImageBitmap7.perlinNoise(myImageBitmap.width,myImageBitmap.➡
height,3,5,false,false,undefined,true);
myImageBitmap7.merge(myImageBitmap4, myImageBitmap3.rectangle,➡
new Point(0,0),140,140,140,0);
myImageBitmap7.merge(myImageBitmap3, myImageBitmap3.rectangle,➡
new Point(0,0),230,230,230,0);
```

20. Test the movie, and you'll see an image with a slightly subtler application of noise.

As you can see, the noise pattern is now applied more subtly. This lightness of touch will really help to lift your work and put it ahead of the pack. In this tutorial, I've deliberately shown each stage as a new `BitmapData` instance so you can review the effects side by side. If you were to use this type of effect in a real-life situation, you could actually do it with just the one `BitmapData` instance.

You're so close to the final result that it's tantalizing, but your last result—although close to what you want—has knocked some of the life out of the image. Compare it to the sepia image without any noise on it, and you'll see that all this adding of noise has made the image rather flat. How do you fix this? You up the contrast, of course!

21. In order to change the contrast of an image, you'll need to create a `ColorMatrix` filter that will do all the hard sums for you. For your viewing pleasure, here's a function for creating just that. Add this to your code after your last code block:

```
//contrast should be passed in as a percentage
function getContrastFilter(contrast:Number){
  var f1:Number = contrast/100
  var f2:Number = 128 *(1-f1);
  return new ColorMatrixFilter(
    [f1, 0, 0, 0, f2,
     0, f1, 0, 0, f2,
     0, 0, f1, 0, f2,
     0, 0, 0, 1, 0]);
}
```

22. Now that you have your contrast filter–generating function, it's time to put it into action. Insert the following code after your function declaration:

```
//
var myImageBitmap8:BitmapData = new BitmapData(myImageBitmap.width,➡
myImageBitmap.height, false, 0xCCCCCC);
var bmHolder8:MovieClip = this.createEmptyMovieClip("bmHolder8",8);
bmHolder8.attachBitmap(myImageBitmap8,1);
bmHolder8._x = 600;
bmHolder8._y = 267;
myImageBitmap8.applyFilter (myImageBitmap7, myImageBitmap.➡
rectangle, new Point(0,0),getContrastFilter(115));
```

23. What this does is take your last `BitmapData` instance and apply a filter to it that increases its contrast to 115% of the original. Test your movie to see the results, and you should see something like this:

Finally, you have a nicely aged image displayed on the screen. In true Steinbeck style, sit back, relax, and go fix yourself a nice prohibition-sized drink.

Summary

By now, you should have a pretty good grasp of what `BitmapData` is and what it can do for you. It's a really great interface for manipulating bitmap information with far more power than you've ever had access to before with Flash. It can be very fast compared to movie clip–level color work. However, although working with `BitmapData` is fast in terms of processor speed, you have to bear in mind that `BitmapData` instances can be real memory hogs, and that's why you should use `dispose` whenever you've finished with an image.

This chapter has really only scratched the surface of what's possible with the `BitmapData` API—from here on out, the rest is up to you! Have fun, and above all, be creative.

9 **GETTING CREATIVE WITH FILTERS, MASKS, AND ANIMATION**

by Todd Yard

You've been through the previous chapters. You've seen the new features and possibilities. You've been nearly overcome with excitement in anticipation of using the new capabilities of Flash 8, but being a diligent reader, you haven't been able to put down this fascinating and insightful book long enough to run wild in the application. (An author can hope, can't he?) Well, the wait is over! You're going to apply many of the tools and techniques introduced in the previous chapters to create some outstanding effects that haven't been possible, or at least as easy, in previous versions of Flash. So get your computer on, your software launched, and your mouse in hand as you scratch the surface of what can now be accomplished with filters, masks, and animation in Flash 8.

> *To pack in as many tutorials and effects as possible, the comments have been removed from the code presented in the chapter text, but you can find all the code fully commented in this chapter's downloadable files.*

Neon with Filters

Here's a sweet and simple effect that can be accomplished without any ActionScript (though you'll apply some in the end for a little bit of icing on the cake). If you've ever needed to create a dynamic effect on a movie clip, either purposely at runtime or in development because of constant new directions from clients (that never happens, right?), then filters will be your favorite new friends. Here, you'll create a neon effect on a dynamic text field that could even change its text at runtime, freeing you from having to prerender bitmaps and limit possibilities. The values arrived at in this tutorial are purely personal choices, so tweak as you go to get the effect you desire.

1. Create a new Flash document named neon.fla and make its background black so you can more easily see the neon effect.

2. Select the Text tool and choose a neon-like font. You can use the aptly named freeware TrueType font Neon Thick that's included with this chapter's files.

3. Set the size of the text in the Properties panel to some large number (50 or more—whatever looks good) and set its color to #66FF00.

4. Click on the stage to create a new text field and type EAT AT JOES. Center the text field on the stage and tweak the text properties to your heart's content.

Figure 9-1. Adding a text field to the stage with a neon font

5. Convert the text field into a movie clip named sign and name the instance on the stage sign_mc.

6. With sign_mc selected on the main timeline, add a new Bevel filter in the Filters panel (which should be grouped by default as a tab with the Properties panel). Set both Blur X and Blur Y to 5, Strength to 100%, Quality to Low, Shadow to black, Highlight to white, Angle to 300, Distance to 5, and Type to Inner. Make sure that Knockout is *not* selected.

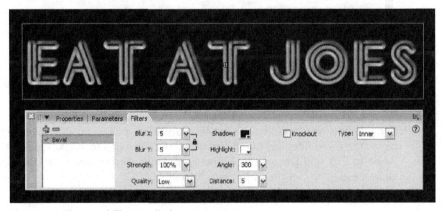

Figure 9-2. The Bevel filter applied

7. Now add a Gradient Glow filter to sign_mc as well. Set Blur X and Blur Y to 0, Strength to 100%, Quality to Low, Angle to 325, Distance to -4, and Type to Outer. Make sure that Knockout is *not* selected. Finally, set the gradient colors to white at 0 (on the very left) and to black at 255 (on the very right).

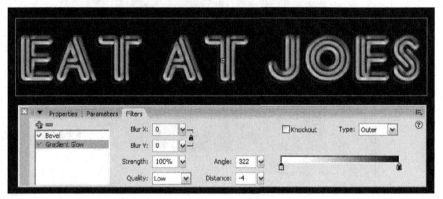

Figure 9-3. The Gradient Glow filter applied

8. Next, add a Glow filter below the Gradient Glow filter from the previous step. Set the Blur X and Blur Y values to 19, the Strength to 60%, and the Quality to Low. Make sure Knockout and Inner glow are *not* selected, and set the swatch color to #66FF00.

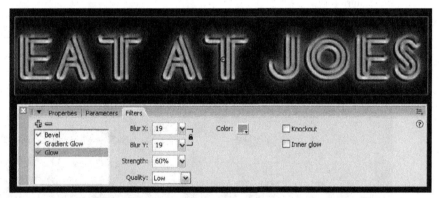

Figure 9-4. The Glow filter applied

9. The last filter you'll add to the movie clip will be a Drop Shadow filter. Add this below the Glow filter. Set Blur X and Blur Y to 0, Strength to 100%, Quality to Low, Angle to 210, and Distance to 3. Knockout, Inner shadow, and Hide object should all be deselected. Set the Color swatch to #CCCCCC.

Figure 9-5. The Drop Shadow filter applied

If you test your movie now, you'll see exactly what you saw in the IDE: a glowing neon effect on your dynamic text—an effect that can immediately be applied to another graphic by simply swapping out the contents of sign_mc or changing the text in the field. To really make it special, though, how about adding a little flicker to the sign? For that, you could tween the Glow filter on the timeline; but to give it a little more randomness (and save you the cost of tweens in file size), you can add some ActionScript.

10. Change the name of the default layer with the sign_mc instance to sign, and add a new layer above it named code.

11. With frame 1 of the code layer selected, add the following to the ActionScript editor:

```
import flash.filters.*;

function onEnterFrame():Void {
  var filters:Array = sign_mc.filters;
  var glow:GlowFilter = filters[2];
  glow.strength = Math.random()*.1 + .6;
  sign_mc.filters = filters;
}
```

If you test your movie now, you'll see a slight flicker applied to the neon effect. The preceding code simply accesses the filters already applied to the sign_mc movie clip in the authoring environment. The third filter was the Glow filter, so you use filters[2] to access it (remember, Arrays start at 0). You then set a random number to the strength variable. Although the IDE uses a range of 0 to 100%, the ActionScript code requires a real percent (between 0 and 1). You then reapply the filters to sign_mc. Voilá—flicker!

If you want to distort the sign in this example to create perspective, you'll have to break the text apart so it's no longer dynamic (using either *CTRL+B* or Modify ➤ Break Apart twice). I did that in the file neon_2.fla, shown in Figure 9-6.

Figure 9-6.
The neon text is broken apart and distorted, but the effect remains unchanged.

Flashlights with alpha masks

Creating a flashlight with a feathered edge and variable transparency has been possible before, but has never been this easy. To achieve this effect in Flash MX 2004, you might have a transparent radial gradient within a large black overlay that hid all underlying graphics. It wasn't perfect, it had its flaws, but it generally worked. Now let's see how to finally do it right!

1. Create a new Flash document named flashlight.fla. Import brick.jpg to the stage from this chapter's download files.

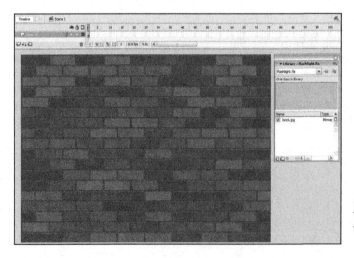

Figure 9-7.
The brick image imported to the stage

2. Rename the default layer brick and create a layer above it named light.

3. Insert a new movie clip symbol named light mask. In Edit Symbols mode for light mask, create two layers named, top to bottom, light and dark.

4. Select the Rectangle tool in the Tools panel and make sure Object Drawing mode is turned on in the Options. Select a black fill at 80% opacity and no stroke. On the dark layer, draw a 550 × 400-pixel rectangle at coordinates (0, 0). This rectangle will darken the brick image on the main timeline.

5. Now select the Oval tool. Set the fill to be a radial gradient going from 20% opacity white to 100% opacity white. Drag the left color slider (20% opacity) to about halfway on the gradient well. Draw a perfect circle in the center of the stage on the light layer. This circle will act as an alpha mask for the dark rectangle. What this means is that the rectangle will be opaque wherever the circle is opaque and transparent wherever the circle is transparent, with variable transparent values to match the circle's variable transparency. Any part of the rectangle that the circle doesn't cover will be 100% opaque as well.

Figure 9-8. A gradient ellipse is drawn to be the light mask over the dark rectangle.

6. With the ellipse still selected, convert it into a movie clip named light and name its instance light_mc. Now set its Blend to Alpha in the Properties panel. Don't worry that it apparently disappears. Flash is now simply using its alpha information, not any of its colors.

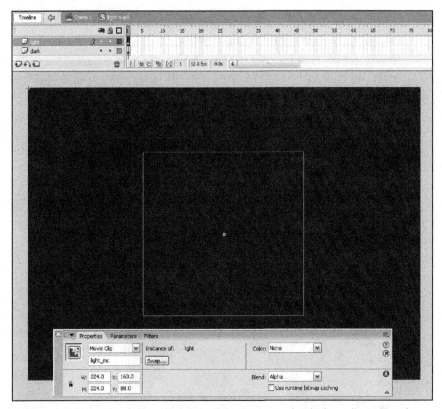

Figure 9-9. With its Blend set to Alpha, the light disappears, but its bounding rectangle remains.

7. Return to the main timeline now and drag an instance of the light mask symbol to the light layer. Center it on the stage and name its instance lightMask_mc. All you'll currently see is the black rectangle covering the brick. Set its Blend to Layer and you should see the light shining through.

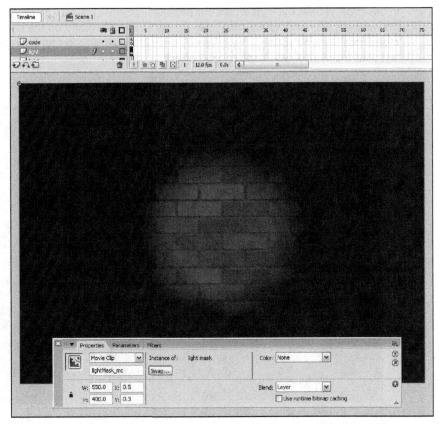

Figure 9-10. The light mask instance has its Blend set to Layer, creating an 8-bit transparency.

8. To get your flashlight to move with the mouse, you'll add a bit of ActionScript. Create a new layer on the main timeline above the light layer, and name it code. Open your ActionScript editor and add the following to the first frame of this layer:

```
onMouseMove();

function onMouseMove():Void {
  lightMask_mc.light_mc._x = _xmouse;
  lightMask_mc.light_mc._y = _ymouse;
  lightMask_mc.light_mc._yscale = 100 - (Math.abs(275-_xmouse)/10);
  var angle:Number = Math.atan2(200-_ymouse, 275-_xmouse);
  lightMask_mc.light_mc._rotation = angle*180/Math.PI;
  updateAfterEvent();
}
```

In this code, you set the light instance inside the light mask instance to be wherever the mouse is. For extra effect, you scale the light vertically based on the horizontal mouse position and rotate it based on its position relative to center stage. If you test your movie now, you'll see the full effect.

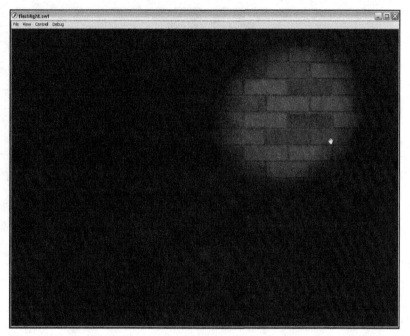

Figure 9-11. The 8-bit transparent mask is moved with the mouse and scaled and rotated based on its stage position.

Now wasn't that easy? Well, you know what? There's another way you can accomplish this that's even easier! Let's take a look.

1. Create a new Flash document named flashlight_2.fla. Import the same brick.jpg to the stage from this chapter's download files.

2. Convert the brick image to a movie clip named brick with the instance name brick_mc.

3. Rename the default layer light brick and create another layer beneath it named dark brick. The light brick layer is the layer you'll be masking with your flashlight, revealing only the circle where the flashlight shines and showing the dark brick layer everywhere else.

4. Drag a new instance of the brick symbol to the stage and drop it on the dark brick layer. Make its Brightness -80% in the Properties panel (you'll have to make the light brick layer invisible to see this). This is the layer that will be revealed behind the masked lighter bricks above.

5. Create a new layer at the top of the stack named light. Use the Oval tool to draw a perfect circle in the center of the stage. Give the circle a radial gradient that goes from 80% opacity white to 0% opacity white. Drag the left color slider to about the

middle of the gradient well. Unlike the alpha mask in the previous exercise, this mask will act like a normal layer mask with opaque areas revealing the masked layers underneath, and transparent areas hiding the masked layers underneath. Shapes in the masked layers that aren't covered with a mask will be completely hidden. For this reason, the center of the gradient is 80% opaque, meaning that anything within this area will be 80% opaque and fade to transparency at the edges of the light.

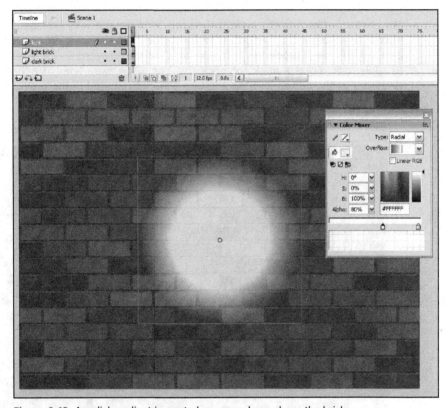

Figure 9-12. A radial gradient is created on a new layer above the bricks.

6. Convert the circle into a movie clip named light and name its instance light_mc.

7. Now you'll create the mask effect through ActionScript. Create a new layer on the top of the stack named code. Open the ActionScript editor and add the following to frame 1 of this layer:

```
init();
function init():Void {
  light_mc.cacheAsBitmap = true;
  brick_mc.cacheAsBitmap = true;
  brick_mc.setMask(light_mc);
  onMouseMove();
}
```

299

```
function onMouseMove():Void {
  light_mc._x = _xmouse;
  light_mc._y = _ymouse;
  light_mc._yscale = 100 - (Math.abs(275-_xmouse)/10);
  var angle:Number = Math.atan2(200-_ymouse, 275-_xmouse);
  light_mc._rotation = angle*180/Math.PI;
  updateAfterEvent();
}
```

The onMouseMove in this code is the same as in the previous exercise. The difference lies in the init function, in which you set both the brick_mc and light_mc cacheAsBitmap properties to true, and use the standard setMask method to apply light_mc as a mask for brick_mc. Just a few extra lines of ActionScript saves you all the nested layering and blend modes required in the previous step. You gotta love that!

Figure 9-13. The same 8-bit mask flashlight effect with less work and no nested clips

Lightning bugs with custom easing

The custom easing facility in Flash 8 offers animators and developers much more explicit control over the way an object tweens. In previous versions, you could set an easing-in or easing-out rate (which used a function curve behind the scenes), but anything past that required a bit of ActionScript and lots of math. Now customizing the rate or effect of an easing tween is as simple as graphically modifying a function curve that uses standard Bezier controls and anchors, similar to the Curves dialog in Photoshop, or animation function curves found in most 2D or 3D animation programs.

You're going to use the custom easing functionality in this next exercise to create a seemingly random flying pattern for a lightning bug whizzing about the screen. Again, this is something that could have been (nearly) accomplished in the past, using motion paths or ActionScript (with lots of tweaking), but could never be done as quickly and easily as it can now. Want to see how?

1. Create a new Flash document named `lightningBug.fla`, make its background black, and change its fps to 24.

2. Create a new movie clip symbol named bug. Inside Edit Symbols mode, create a 5 × 5-pixel ellipse with no stroke and a radial gradient that goes from yellow at full opacity at the center to yellow at 0% opacity at its edges. Align it in the center of the stage.

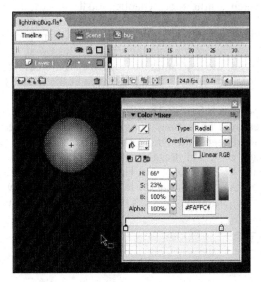

Figure 9-14.
The bug movie clip, made with a radial gradient within a perfect circle

3. Create another new movie clip symbol named bug_animateX. Inside Edit Symbols mode, drag a bug symbol instance to the stage and center it on the registration point.

4. Insert new keyframes to the timeline of bug_animateX at frames 34, 66, and 100, and create a motion tween between each keyframe. The exact position of the keyframes isn't important as long as the total number of frames in this symbol will differ from the symbols you create in further steps (so remember this was 100 frames long).

5. At the second keyframe, move the bug instance to the right by 100 pixels or so. At the third keyframe, move the bug instance to the left to about −100 pixels. Again, the exact position isn't important as long as the bug is set to tween a distance on the x-axis.

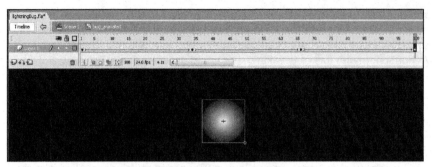

Figure 9-15. The timeline of bug_animateX with new keyframes and motion tweens applied

6. Now, to make this linear tween a little more chaotic, you'll use custom easing. Select frame 1 in the bug_animateX timeline and click the Edit button in the Properties panel. The Custom Ease In/Ease Out window will open and display the function curve. The vertical axis represents the value of the tween property between the two key values set at the keyframes. For instance, in this case it represents the _x value of the movie clip, with 0% being the value at the first keyframe and 100% being the value at the second keyframe. The horizontal axis represents time, which in Flash of course means frames. Therefore, a straight tween between the two values will be represented by a straight line between 0% at frame 1 and 100% at frame 34. To make the tween a little more chaotic, add some new anchor points to the curve by clicking on it and dragging these up or down, and left or right, to create more of a roller coaster than a line. Figure 9-16 shows the function curve I created at frame 1. You can press play at the lower left of the window at any time to see the effect on the bug instance. Click OK when you like what you see.

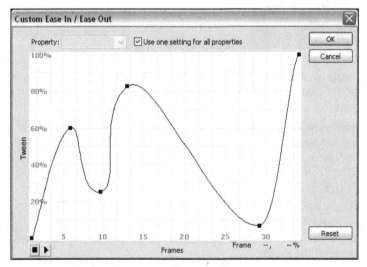

Figure 9-16. The function curve at frame 1 of bug_animateX

7. Create different chaotic function curves at the second and third keyframes. The ones I created are shown in Figures 9-17 and 9-18. Play through your timeline by hitting *ENTER* to see your bug move back and forth on the x-axis.

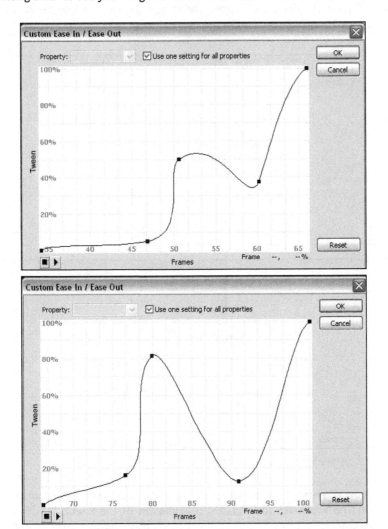

Figures 9-17 and 9-18. Function curves created at the other two keyframes in the bug_animateX symbol

8. Now it's time to do a little nesting of animation. Create a new movie clip symbol named bug_animateY and drop an instance of bug_animateX onto its timeline. Create new keyframes at frames 30, 60, 85, and 110, and add motion tweens between all keyframes. The important thing is that the length of this timeline differs from the length of bug_animateX. The reason for this is that you don't want the animation on the x-axis to match up with the animation on the y-axis as the clip loops. This will create a seemingly random flight pattern for your bug.

9. At the second keyframe of bug_animateY, move the bug_animateX instance to around −80 on the y-axis. At the fourth keyframe (skip the third keyframe), move the bug_animateX instance to around 70 on the y-axis. Edit the custom easing on each of the tweens in the same way as you did for the bug_animateX symbol. Figures 9-19 through 9-22 show the curves I used.

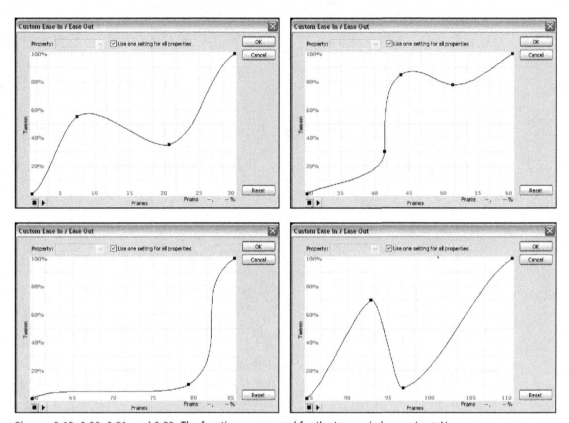

Figures 9-19, 9-20, 9-21, and 9-22. The function curves used for the tweens in bug_animateY

10. OK, now you have a bug animated on the x-axis nested within an animation on the y-axis. This will make for a great 2D animation of the insect. But for something really cool, let's throw in some pseudo-3D. Create another new movie clip named bug_animateScale and drag an instance of bug_animateY onto its timeline. Create keyframes at frames 25, 52, and 75, and add a motion tween between each.

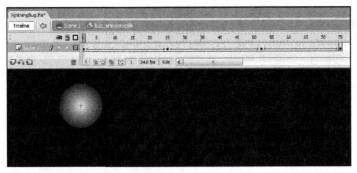

Figure 9-23. A new symbol is created to handle scaling of the bug as it flies toward and away from the viewer.

11. At the second keyframe, scale the bug_animateY instance to 200% on both the x- and y-axes. At the third keyframe, scale it down to 60% on both axes. As before, create a few bumpy function curves for each using the custom easing accessed from the Properties panel. The function curves I used are shown in Figures 9-24 through 9-26.

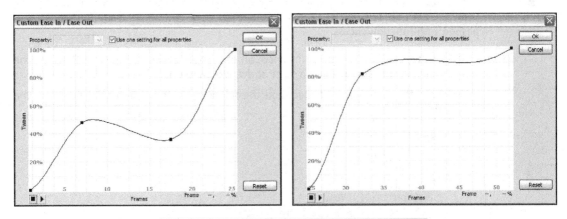

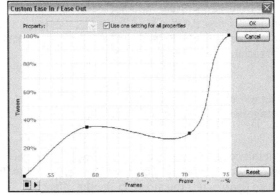

Figures 9-24, 9-25, and 9-26. The function curves used for the tweens in bug_animateScale

12. The tweens are complete! Go back to the main timeline and drop an instance of bug_animateScale onto the main timeline at coordinates (0, 0). What you need now is to keep the bug's registration point at (0, 0) on the main timeline, but have it appear centered on the stage. To do this, select the bug_animateScale instance and convert it into a new movie clip symbol named bugContainer. Double-click this new symbol instance to enter Edit Symbols mode, and move the bug_animateScale instance inside it to coordinates (275, 200). This keeps the bugContainer instance at (0, 0) and yet visually positions the bug in the center of the stage. If you test your movie now, you'll see your bug whizzing about in a seemingly random 3D manner (if you don't, check your file against lightningBug.fla from this chapter's downloadable files).

Of course, what's happening behind the scenes is that inside bugContainer, there's a bug animation on the x-axis, nested within a bug animation on the y-axis, nested within a bug animation on the z-axis (the scale). Each of these animations is over a different number of frames, meaning the animations will never noticeably sync up. In addition, function curves are used on each of the tweens to create more of a chaotic movement than can be accomplished with standard linear tweens.

You could stop this effect at the last step and be perfectly happy, but there's one addition that would make this little lightning bug even cooler. With a little bit of ActionScript, you'll show the path the bug has traveled so you can see how random an animation you accomplished with function curves.

13. Name the bugContainer instance on the main timeline bug_mc. Rename the default layer bug and add a layer above it named code.

14. With the code layer selected, add the following to the ActionScript editor, at the first frame:

```
import flash.geom.*;
import flash.display.*;

init();
function init():Void {
  var w:Number = Stage.width;
  var h:Number = Stage.height;
  matrix = new Matrix();
  stageImage = new BitmapData(w, h, true, 0x00FFFFFF);
  attachBitmap(stageImage, 10);
}

function onEnterFrame():Void {
  stageImage.draw(bug_mc, matrix);
}
```

With this code, you create a new BitmapData object and attach it to the stage so you can see it. On every subsequent frame, you draw the position of the bug onto stageImage. Test the movie to see the effect.

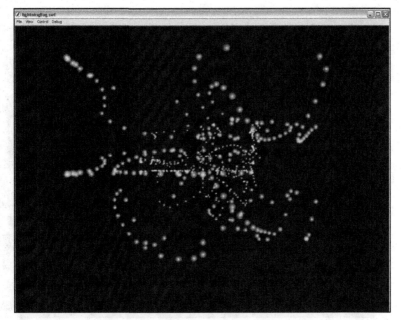

Figure 9-27. `BitmapData` is used to show the lightning bug's traveled path.

Pretty cool, huh? Although the final result can produce an interesting effect, it sort of loses the bug animation. With the next changes (displayed in bold in the following code), a black rectangle at a light transparency is drawn over the stage image each frame, effectively fading the bug's path to the last several frames. This creates a nice motion blur effect and keeps the bug the main focus.

```
import flash.geom.*;
import flash.display.*;

init();
function init():Void {
  var w:Number = Stage.width;
  var h:Number = Stage.height;
  matrix = new Matrix();
  stageImage = new BitmapData(w, h, true, 0x00FFFFFF);
  attachBitmap(stageImage, 10);
  alphaImage = new BitmapData(w, h, true, 0x00FFFFFF);
  alphaImage.fillRect(new Rectangle(0, 0, w, h), 0x11000000);
}

function onEnterFrame():Void {
  stageImage.draw(bug_mc, matrix);
  stageImage.draw(alphaImage, matrix);
}
```

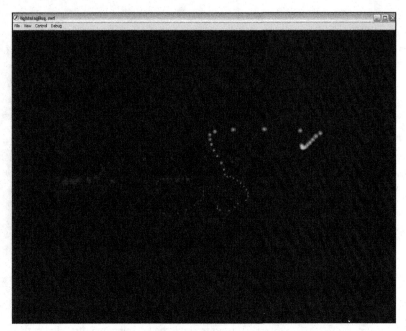

Figure 9-28. Another `BitmapData` instance is used to fade out the bug path by drawing a slightly transparent black rectangle over stageImage.

Another possibility is to tween colors as well as size and position. In the file `lightningBug_2.fla`, you can see color matched to the size of the bug as it animates.

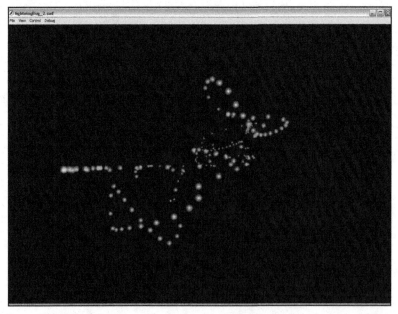

Figure 9-29. `lightningBug_2.fla` shows color tweened as well as size and position.

Flame with displacement maps

This next effect is one of my favorites, namely because it was so difficult to achieve convincingly in previous versions of Flash. Sure, there were particle systems out there, and of course you could always just bring in some successive bitmaps or a video file, but with the pixel manipulation offered in Flash 8, I feel as though fire has been discovered all over again. Let's take a look at how to do this.

1. Create a new Flash document named `flame.fla`. Change the background to black and the fps to 30.

2. Add three new layers above the default and name them code, flame, candle, and table (from top to bottom).

3. On the table layer, use the Rectangle tool to draw a rectangle that covers the lower quarter of the stage. Give it a vertical horizontal gradient that goes from black at the top to a dark brown (#42392C) on the bottom. Convert the rectangle to a movie clip symbol named table and name the instance on the stage table_mc.

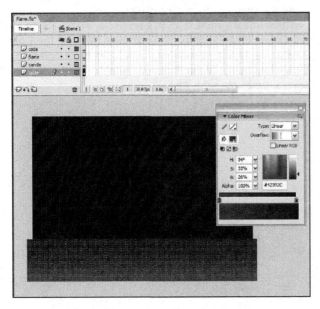

Figure 9-30.
The table graphic before being converted to a movie clip

309

4. On the candle layer, use the Rectangle tool to draw a candle stem, giving it a horizontal linear gradient that simulates a rounded surface (try #38736D to #83C0BA to #53ACA3 to #38736D, spaced evenly on the gradient well). Use the Selection tool to drag slightly down on both the top and bottom sides to create a rounded edge, as shown in Figure 9-31.

Figure 9-31.
The start of the candle graphic, using a rectangle and linear gradient

5. Use the Oval tool to add an ellipse to the top of the stem to represent its top surface. Give it a radial gradient that goes from #53ACA3 at its center to #38736D at its edge. Use the Gradient Transform tool to conform the gradient to the shape of the circle.

6. To create the wick, use the Line tool to draw a curved 1-point line at the top of the candle. Give it a vertical linear gradient that goes from #D3D3D3 to #A7A7A7 (remember that you can now apply gradients to strokes by using the Color Mixer panel and setting the stroke type to Linear or Radial). Set the gradient's overflow method to Repeat, then use the Gradient Transform tool to scale it down vertically so that it repeats several times over the wick.

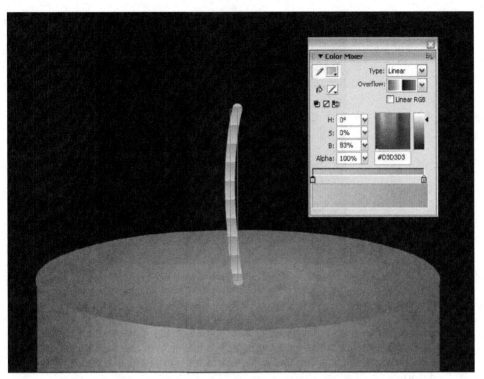

Figure 9-32. The wick is drawn with a linear gradient set to Repeat.

7. Select the candle stem rectangle, ellipse, and wick, and convert them into a single movie clip named candle. Name the instance on stage candle_mc.

8. Create a new movie clip symbol named flame. Inside Edit Symbols mode, rename the default layer rectangle, and on this layer draw a 155 × 155-pixel rectangle with a black fill and 0% opacity at (0, 0). Create a new layer above it named flame. Then import the flame.png file included in this chapter's download files onto this layer and center it over the rectangle. You're doing this so that the area you're distorting to create the animated flame is actually bigger than the flame bitmap itself. This will allow the flame to be distorted outside of its own bounding rectangle.

Figure 9-33. The flame image is centered over a transparent rectangle to increase the bounding rectangle of the movie clip.

9. Return to the main timeline. Drag an instance of the flame symbol to the flame layer and name the instance flame_mc. Position it over the wick, but move it up and to the left slightly. This will compensate for movement that occurs due to the distortion you'll apply.

Figure 9-34. The flame instance is offset from the wick to accommodate for distortion.

10. That's it for the graphic setup. All you have left is the code. Select the code layer in the main timeline and enter the following into the ActionScript editor on the first frame:

```
import flash.filters.*;
import flash.geom.*;
import flash.display.*;

init();
function init():Void {
  initVars();
  initStage();
  onEnterFrame();
}
function initVars():Void {
  phaseRate = 5;
  offsets = [new Point(), new Point()];
  seed = Math.random()
  imageWidth = flame_mc._width;
  imageHeight = flame_mc._height;
  imageRect = new Rectangle(0, 0, imageWidth, imageHeight);
}
function initStage():Void {
}
function onEnterFrame():Void {
}
```

In this code (which is only the first snippet and won't actually *do* anything as of yet), you import the necessary packages at the top, and then call an `init` function that will call all of your other initialization functions. The first, `initVars`, sets up a number of variables that you'll use in the code. `phaseRate` will be used by your Perlin noise that will distort the flame, and signifies how fast the flame will "move." `offsets` is used by the Perlin noise as well, which, together with `phaseRate`, offsets the noise to create the illusion of movement. `seed` is a random number used by the Perlin noise to generate itself. The next two variables store width and height information of flame_mc. Finally, `imageRect` defines a rectangle the width and height of flame_mc. You'll see how this is used next.

11. Enter the following bold code into the ActionScript editor:

```
function initStage():Void {
  displaceImage = new BitmapData(imageWidth, imageHeight, ➥
false, 0xFFFFFFFF);
}
function onEnterFrame():Void {
  for (var i:Number = 0; i < 2; ++i){
    offsets[i].y += phaseRate;
  }
  displaceImage.perlinNoise(50, 30, 2, seed, false, ➥
false, 1, true, offsets);
```

```
   var dMap:DisplacementMapFilter = ➥
new DisplacementMapFilter(displaceImage, ➥
new Point(), 1, 1, 10, 20, "clamp");
   flame_mc.filters = [dMap];
}
```

With these lines, you create a new `BitmapData` object upon the movie's initialization that's the same size as the flame_mc movie clip. With every `enterFrame`, you move the two y offset values by the `phaseRate` set in the `initVars` function. You use these new values to create Perlin noise in the `BitmapData` instance stored in `displaceImage`. `displaceImage`, with its Perlin noise generated, is then used as a displacement map for flame_mc (the values were all arrived at by experimentation and are purely subjective). Test your movie now to see the results so far.

Figure 9-35.
The distorted flame at this point in the exercise

Although the flame shows some good, realistic distortion, it's hopping around a bit too much on the wick. You can do some things to fix this, but it would help if you could see the displacement map you're using to distort the flame.

12. Add the following bold lines to the code, which will allow you to see the displacement map:

```
function initStage():Void {
  displaceImage = new BitmapData(imageWidth, imageHeight, ➥
false, 0xFFFFFFFF);
  createEmptyMovieClip("background_mc", 0);
  backgroundImage = new BitmapData(imageWidth, imageHeight, ➥
false, 0xFF000000);
  background_mc.attachBitmap(backgroundImage, 0);
}
function onEnterFrame():Void {
  for (var i:Number = 0; i < 2; ++i){
    offsets[i].y += phaseRate;
  }
  displaceImage.perlinNoise(50, 30, 2, seed, ➥
false, false, 1, true, offsets);
  var dMap:DisplacementMapFilter = ➥
new DisplacementMapFilter(displaceImage, ➥
new Point(), 1, 1, 10, 20, "clamp");
  flame_mc.filters = [dMap];
  backgroundImage.draw(displaceImage, new Matrix());
}
```

The last three lines in the `initStage` function create a new movie clip and a new `BitmapData` instance, attaching the `BitmapData` to the movie clip. The last line of the `onEnterFrame` draws the displacement map with the Perlin noise onto the background image. Test your movie to see the results.

Figure 9-36. The displacement map made visible

What you need in order to keep the bottom of the flame stationary while the top of the flame flickers is to not have the Perlin noise as active at the bottom of the displacement map as it is at the top. You can accomplish this by drawing an alpha gradient over the image to lessen the noise.

13. Add the following bold lines to the ActionScript editor:

```
function initStage():Void {
  displaceImage = new BitmapData(imageWidth, imageHeight, ➥
false, 0xFFFFFFFF);
  createEmptyMovieClip("gradient_mc", 50);
  var matrix:Matrix = new Matrix();
  matrix.createGradientBox(imageWidth, imageHeight, Math.PI/2, 0, 0);
  gradient_mc.beginGradientFill("linear", [0x000000,0x000000], ➥
[0,100], [0,215], matrix);
  gradient_mc.lineTo(imageWidth, 0);
  gradient_mc.lineTo(imageWidth, imageHeight);
  gradient_mc.lineTo(0, imageHeight);
  gradient_mc.lineTo(0, 0);
  gradient_mc.endFill();
  gradientImage = new BitmapData(imageWidth, imageHeight, ➥
true, 0x00FFFFFF);
  gradientImage.draw(gradient_mc, new Matrix());
  gradient_mc.removeMovieClip();
  createEmptyMovieClip("background_mc", 0);
```

```
    backgroundImage = new BitmapData(imageWidth, imageHeight, ➥
false, 0xFF000000);
    background_mc.attachBitmap(backgroundImage, 0);
}
function onEnterFrame():Void {
    for (var i:Number = 0; i < 2; ++i){
        offsets[i].y += phaseRate;
    }
    displaceImage.perlinNoise(50, 30, 2, seed, ➥
false, false, 1, true, offsets);
    displaceImage.copyPixels(gradientImage, imageRect, new Point(), ➥
gradientImage, new Point(), true);
    var dMap:DisplacementMapFilter = ➥
new DisplacementMapFilter(displaceImage, ➥
new Point(), 1, 1, 10, 20, "clamp");
    flame_mc.filters = [dMap];
    backgroundImage.draw(displaceImage, new Matrix());
}
```

So what's happening here? In the `initStage` function, you're creating a new movie clip and drawing into it a gradient that goes from black at 0% opacity to black at 100% opacity. Note the use of the `createGradientBox` method of the new `Matrix` class, which makes it easy to create the `matrix` parameter required for `MovieClip`'s `beginGradientFill`.

Once the gradient is drawn, you create a new `BitmapData` object and draw the gradient into it, after which you can dispose of the movie clip since it's no longer needed.

Finally, in the `onEnterFrame`, you use `copyPixels` to copy the gradient image into the displacement map image. The end result is that the top of the Perlin noise will be perfectly visible, but the bottom will be obscured by the gradient. This will have the effect of displacing the top of the flame while maintaining the position of the bottom. Test your movie now to see this.

Figure 9-37. The displacement map with the gradient drawn over it lessens the displacement of the bottom of the flame.

The flame effect is now complete. You could just remove background_mc from the stage, but I liked the look of it so much that I decided to scale it up as an animated background for the flame.

14. Add or change the following bold lines of code. This is all of the final code for this exercise.

```
import flash.filters.*;
import flash.geom.*;
import flash.display.*;

init();
function init():Void {
  initVars();
  initStage();
  onEnterFrame();
}
function initVars():Void {
  phaseRate = 5;
  offsets = [new Point(), new Point()];
  seed = Math.random();
  imageWidth = flame_mc._width;
  imageHeight = flame_mc._height;
  stageWidth = Stage.width;
  stageHeight = Stage.height;
  imageRect = new Rectangle(0, 0, imageWidth, imageHeight);
  stageMatrix = new Matrix();
  stageMatrix.scale(stageWidth/imageWidth, stageHeight/imageHeight);
  colorTransform = new ColorTransform(1, 1, 1, .1, -100, 0, 0, 0);
}
function initStage():Void {
  flame_mc.swapDepths(30);
  candle_mc.swapDepths(20);
  table_mc.swapDepths(10);
  displaceImage = new BitmapData(imageWidth, imageHeight, ➥
false, 0xFFFFFFFF);
  createEmptyMovieClip("gradient_mc", 50);
  var matrix:Matrix = new Matrix();
  matrix.createGradientBox(imageWidth, imageHeight, Math.PI/2, 0, 0);
  gradient_mc.beginGradientFill("linear", [0x000000,0x000000], ➥
[0,100], [0,215], matrix);
  gradient_mc.lineTo(imageWidth, 0);
  gradient_mc.lineTo(imageWidth, imageHeight);
  gradient_mc.lineTo(0, imageHeight);
  gradient_mc.lineTo(0, 0);
  gradient_mc.endFill();
  gradientImage = new BitmapData(imageWidth, imageHeight, ➥
true, 0x00FFFFFF);
  gradientImage.draw(gradient_mc, new Matrix());
```

```
      gradient_mc.removeMovieClip();
      createEmptyMovieClip("background_mc", 0);
      backgroundImage = new BitmapData(stageWidth, stageHeight, ➥
    false, 0xFF000000);
      background_mc.attachBitmap(backgroundImage, 0);
    }
    function onEnterFrame():Void {
      for (var i:Number = 0; i < 2; ++i){
        offsets[i].y += phaseRate;
      }
      displaceImage.perlinNoise(50, 30, 2, ➥
    seed, false, false, 1, true, offsets);
      displaceImage.copyPixels(gradientImage, imageRect, new Point(), ➥
    gradientImage, new Point(), true);
      var dMap:DisplacementMapFilter = ➥
    new DisplacementMapFilter(displaceImage, ➥
    new Point(), 1, 1, 10, 20, "clamp");
      flame_mc.filters = [dMap];
      backgroundImage.draw(displaceImage, stageMatrix, colorTransform);
    }
```

After storing the stage height and width, you create a new `Matrix` that will scale a rectangle the size of the displacement map up to the size of the stage. You also create a `colorTransform` object that will lessen the red of the background by an offset value of –100, giving a nice cyan color. You then need to add these two new objects to the final line in the `onEnterFrame`. The only other new lines of code are in the `initStage` function, which swaps your three graphic clips to above the background_mc. In addition, you size the background image up at the end of the `initStage`, passing in `stageWidth` and `stageHeight` instead of `imageWidth` and `imageHeight`. Test it out to see it in all its glory!

Figure 9-38. The displacement map is scaled and colored to cover the entire stage.

Tileable patterns with bitmap fills

The final effect you'll explore in this chapter takes advantage of the new begin➡
BitmapFill method of the MovieClip object. This works just like it does in the authoring environment when you fill a shape with a bitmap fill, allowing you to tile the bitmap
across the entire shape. beginBitmapFill is merely the ActionScript equivalent. This,
in combination with the BitmapData pixel-manipulation methods, opens up so many
doors for filling shapes with tileable patterns randomized and generated at runtime. Here
you'll explore just a few options, but the number of effects that can be achieved with these
is truly staggering.

1. Create a new Flash document with a background color of #660033. Save it as
   pattern_1.fla.

2. Select frame 1 of the default layer and open your ActionScript editor. Add the
   following code:

```
import flash.display.*;
import flash.geom.*;
import flash.filters.*;

function drawPattern(definition:Array):BitmapData {
  var w:Number = definition[0].length;
  var h:Number = definition.length;
  var pattern:BitmapData = new BitmapData(w, h, true, 0x00FFFFFF);
  var c:Number;
  for (var r:Number = 0; r < h; r++) {
    for (c = 0; c < w; c++) {
      pattern.setPixel32(c, r, definition[r][c]);
    }
  }
  return pattern;
}
```

Here's a function that can be used for a number of scenarios. It needs to be passed
a multidimensional array that represents rows and columns of an image, with each
value holding a 32-bit color for a pixel. The width and height (w and h) of the
image are determined based on the length of the arrays. pattern will hold
the bitmap data of the pixel pattern. The two for loops run through the rows and
columns and set the pixel in the pattern based on the corresponding values in the
arrays. The finished pattern is returned.

To use this function, you need to create a multidimensional array and a movie clip
to draw into. Let's start things off easy with a checkerboard.

3. Add the following lines to the ActionScript editor right below the code entered in the previous step:

```
definition =
[
[0xFF000000, 0xFFFFFFFF],
[0xFFFFFFFF, 0xFF000000]
];

var w:Number = Stage.width;
var h:Number = Stage.height;

with (createEmptyMovieClip("background_mc", 0)) {
    beginBitmapFill(drawPattern(definition), new Matrix(), true);
    lineTo(w, 0);
    lineTo(w, h);
    lineTo(0, h);
    lineTo(0, 0);
    endFill();
}
```

`definition` here has two rows and two columns with alternating black and white colors, making a simple checker pattern. You then create a new movie clip named `background_mc` and use `beginBitmapFill`, passing in the `BitmapData` returned from `drawPattern`. The third parameter, `true`, sets the fill to tile across the shape, which you set to cover the whole stage. Test your movie to see the results. Since the checker pattern is so small, be sure to zoom in a bit to see it.

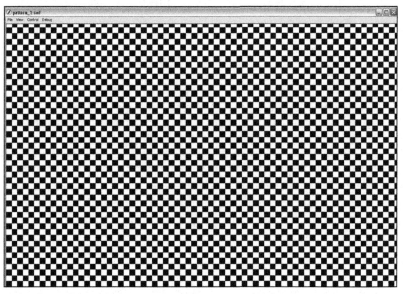

Figure 9-39. The zoomed-in version of the checker pattern

4. With this framework in place, try to pass in different pixel values for the definition. You can pass in any color for the pixels, but for monochromatic patterns, I find it's easier to draw white and black at low alphas over the color you wish to be dominant. Try this definition of one column with six rows, which produces horizontal bars across the stage. Notice that the bottom four rows are completely transparent, revealing the color underneath.

```
definition =
[
[0x33000000],
[0x22FFFFFF],
[0x00000000],
[0x00000000],
[0x00000000],
[0x00000000]
];
```

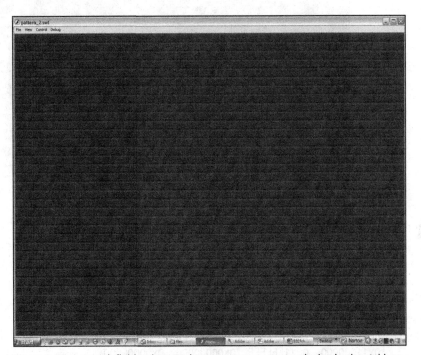

Figure 9-40. A new definition is passed to drawPattern, producing horizontal bars.

5. It's so easy to try different effects simply by altering the definition's value. This next one uses one row to draw vertical bands of varying white and black transparency over the background color (consider how you can also do this over a bitmap image for interesting effects).

321

```
definition =
[
[0x33000000, 0x33000000, 0x33000000, 0x00000000, 0x00000000,
0x22FFFFFF,0x22FFFFFF, 0x00000000, 0x00000000, 0x00000000,
0x22FFFFFF, 0x33000000, 0x33000000, 0x00000000, 0x44FFFFFF,
0x44FFFFFF, 0x44FFFFFF, 0x00000000, 0x00000000, 0x44FFFFFF,
0x00000000]
];
```

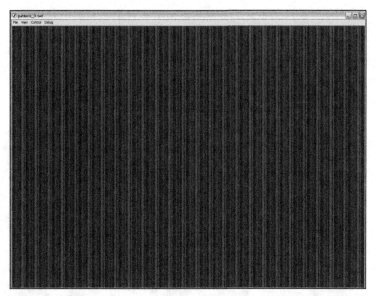

Figure 9-41. A new definition is passed to `drawPattern`, producing vertical bars.

6. Definitions can be as simple or as complex as you wish. Here's an example of a slightly more complex pattern that creates beveled tiles across the stage.

```
definition =
[
[0x11000000, 0x11000000, 0x11000000, 0x11000000,
  0x11000000, 0x11000000, 0x11000000],
[0x11000000, 0x11FFFFFF, 0x11FFFFFF, 0x11FFFFFF,
  0x11FFFFFF, 0x11FFFFFF, 0x11FFFFFF],
[0x11000000, 0x11FFFFFF, 0x00000000, 0x00000000,
  0x00000000, 0x00000000, 0x05000000],
[0x11000000, 0x11FFFFFF, 0x00000000, 0x00000000,
  0x00000000, 0x00000000, 0x05000000],
[0x11000000, 0x11FFFFFF, 0x00000000, 0x00000000,
  0x00000000, 0x00000000, 0x05000000],
[0x11000000, 0x11FFFFFF, 0x00000000, 0x00000000,
  0x00000000, 0x00000000, 0x05000000],
[0x11000000, 0x11FFFFFF, 0x05000000, 0x05000000,
  0x05000000, 0x05000000, 0x05000000]
];
```

Figure 9-42. The zoomed-in effect of the beveled tile pattern.

7. As I said, definitions can be as simple or as complex as you wish. Creating the dents pattern shown in Figure 9-43 required 15 × 15 arrays. The definition won't be shown here, but you can find it in the file pattern_5.fla.

Figure 9-43. The zoomed-in effect of the dents pattern, requiring a 15 × 15 array

8. Of course, you can just as easily randomize your patterns using ActionScript. These next lines of code create random colors that will tile into vertical stripes on the stage.

```
definition = [[]];
for (var i:Number = 0; i < 150; i++) {
  definition[0].push(
    0x6633CCCC | Math.random()*0x33 << 8 | Math.random()*0x33
  );
}
```

This adds 150 random colors to the definition, keeping the colors in the blue-green range. With 150 colors defined, tiling is less obvious.

Figure 9-44. The vertical randomized color lines

9. After seeing these stripes, I thought it might be nice to add another touch to the patterns—namely a bit of visual distortion to the clean lines. Add the following code to the end of your pattern code (put it after *all* the previous code) to cause some irregularities in the pattern.

```
var displaceImage = new BitmapData(w, h, false, 0xFFFFFFFF);
displaceImage.perlinNoise(5, 15, 1, ➥
Math.random(), false, false, 1, true);
background_mc.filters = [new DisplacementMapFilter(displaceImage, ➥
new Point(), 1, 1, 10, 10, "clamp")];
```

If you went through the last exercise, these should be familiar to you. A new `BitmapData` instance is used for a displacement map of the pattern. `perlinNoise` is used to introduce the irregularity, and then it's applied to the background as a displacement filter. This gives you a cool, random pattern in place of the vertical bars—with only three new lines of code!

Figure 9-45. The same vertical randomized color lines with a displacement map applied

You'll look at one last function in this section on patterns—one that will either fill a pixel or not, rather than taking a different color for each pixel. This will enable more complex patterns to be defined more easily.

1. Create a new Flash document name `pattern_8.fla` (if you've been following the different versions through these exercises). Make its background #660033.

2. Add the following code to your ActionScript editor, in the first frame of the default layer:

```
import flash.display.*;
import flash.geom.*;
import flash.filters.*;

function drawBitmapPattern(definition:Array, color:Number):BitmapData {
  var w:Number = definition[0].length;
  var h:Number = definition.length;
  var pattern:BitmapData = new BitmapData(w, h, true, 0x00FFFFFF);
  var c:Number;
  for (var r:Number = 0; r < h; r++) {
    for (c = 0; c < w; c++) {
      if (definition[r].charAt(c) == "1")
        pattern.setPixel32(c, r, color);
    }
  }
  return pattern;
}
```

This works similarly to the `drawPattern` in the previous exercise, but instead of being passed a multidimensional array of many colors, this function takes a one-dimensional array of strings and a single color. It then uses the same looping structure to go through columns and rows of an image, but uses String's `charAt` method to determine if the character in the string is a 1 or a 0. If it's a 1, it colors the pixel in the pattern with the color specified in the function.

3. Now you need to create a pattern definition in this new format. You can copy and paste these numbers from the file `pattern_8.fla`. Place the following code at the end of the code from the previous step.

```
definition =
[
"000110101010100100101010110001",
"001000000000100010000000001000",
"010000000000010100000000000100",
"100000000000000010000000000011",
"100000000000000101000000000010",
"010000000000010001000000000100",
"010000000000010000010000000100",
"001110000001000100010000000111000",
"000001000000010000010000001000000",
"000001000000001000100000000100000",
"000100000000010101010000000010000",
"000100111001000100010011100010000",
"001011000110000100001100001101000",
"010001000001100100110000001000100",
"100000100000010101000000010000010",
"000100010000111011100001000010001",
"100000100000010101000000010000010",
"010001000001100100110000001000100",
"001011000110000100001100001101000",
"000100111001000100010011100010000",
"000100000000010101010000000010000",
"000001000000001000100000000100000",
"000001000000010000010000001000000",
"001110000001000100010000000111000",
"010000000000010000010000000000100",
"010000000000010001000000000000100",
"100000000000000101000000000000010",
"100000000000000010000000000000011",
"010000000000000101000000000000100",
"001000000000010001000000000001000",
"000110101010100100101010110001",
"100101010101001110010101010011"
];
```

Could you imagine trying to define each of those individual colors using the `drawPattern` function in the last exercise? No, thanks! Don't test the movie yet, as right now the code won't actually do anything visually. That comes next.

4. To use the pattern to actually render something on-screen, you'll use nearly the same code as in the previous exercise. Enter the following at the end of your code:

```
var w:Number = Stage.width;
var h:Number = Stage.height;

with (createEmptyMovieClip("background_mc", 0)) {
  beginBitmapFill(
    drawBitmapPattern(definition, 0x22FFFFFF),
    new Matrix(),
    true
  );
  lineTo(w, 0);
  lineTo(w, h);
  lineTo(0, h);
  lineTo(0, 0);
  endFill();
}
```

The only difference in this code is that you're calling `drawBitmapPattern` instead of `drawBitmap`, and passing in the color you want drawn. If you test your movie now, you'll see the pattern you created using that definition. That's pretty sweet!

Figures 9-46. A more complex pattern, zoomed in, using strings to determine which pixels are turned on or off

Summary

This chapter has introduced just a small sampling of the effects that are now possible with Flash 8 and a bit of creativity, both through the enhancements in the IDE as well as ActionScript. Spend some time exploring and getting to know the new filters, blend modes, animation tools, and bitmap manipulation capabilities in ActionScript, and you'll have toys to entertain you for a good long while. Then with your toy box filled, you'll have an arsenal of useful effects to apply to your real-world work whenever you may need it.

10 EXTERNAL INTERFACE

Rollover me

Also rollover me

clickrollc

/Users/M

Wednesd

44 kHz S

Export setti

Device sound:

Macromedia Flash Play

The following local ap

/Users/Mills/Apress

is trying to communica

/Users/Mills/Apress

To let this application
You must restart this

by Glen Rhodes and Craig Swann

When you embed an SWF file in a web browser, it helps to think of the browser as the host for Flash Player, which then in turn loads your SWF file. Flash Player is simply a plug-in, which can be embedded into any number of different hosts. In the sense that Flash itself has components you embed and use, you can think of Flash Player as a component that can be made use of in *other* applications.

For example, it's possible to embed a Flash Player ActiveX control in a Visual Basic application, giving your application some added pizzazz and flair with all that a SWF brings to the experience. Or, you could create a program in C# that allows users to catalog their DVD collections—and instead of having a plain-text title at the top of the page, you could use a Flash Player ActiveX control to embed a cool animated title. To end users, it's transparent—they don't realize it's Flash.

But wouldn't it be even cooler if somehow your C# application could *talk* to the embedded SWF and make it do things based on the user's actions in the host application? For example, imagine you're making the DVD catalog program, but now when you enter the title of a DVD, that title is automatically displayed on a spinning, animated DVD on-screen. That spinning DVD is actually a SWF running inside the embedded Flash Player, but users don't see it like that—they just see this application that has really great animation. The question is, how do you make your C# program *tell* the embedded SWF what text to display on its spinning animation? You need a way to bridge the communication gap between host and embedded player.

Not a C# programmer? No problem. It should be noted that embedding Flash Player in a web page (as you've likely done hundreds of times) is exactly the same—the web browser is the host application and Flash Player is embedded within it.

In Flash MX 2004 and earlier, `FSCommand` was used as the method of communicating with the application hosting Flash Player. Using `FSCommand`, you could tell Flash to call functions that exist in the host, and the host could also call functions defined in your Flash movie. It worked, but the system was convoluted and somewhat difficult to implement.

Enter the new `flash.external` package, and specifically, the `ExternalInterface` class. With `ExternalInterface`, you now have a single object through which you can perform all host/player communication. The `ExternalInterface` class can act as a callback listener to handle calls from the host, and it can also be used to *call* functions that are on the host.

In this chapter, you're not going to be getting into C#, Visual Basic, or any other full application development systems, as that would take far too long and be beyond the scope of this book. Instead, you're going to be looking at all your examples through a web browser and HTML, and all of your host code is going to be written in JavaScript. This at least gives you an idea of what it's all about, and how it works—enough information to go boldly forth and create some cool applications of your own!

As always, the code for the examples included in this chapter is available for download from www.friendsofed.com.

A simple example

The first example you're going to look at is an example that simply passes a text string from the embedded Flash player into the host browser, and vice versa.

The SWF

To start with, let's make your SWF. In the end, it will look something like this:

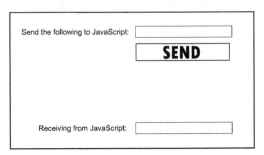

Send the following to JavaScript:

SEND

Receiving from JavaScript:

Figure 10-1. Layout of the SWF file for communicating to the browser via `ExternalInterface`

If you look at the image in Figure 10-1, you'll see that there are two text boxes. In the top text box, you'll type any text that you want to be passed into JavaScript (up into the host). Any text that's sent from JavaScript into the SWF will be placed in the bottom box when it's received. Begin as follows:

1. Open Flash and start a new Flash movie with dimensions of 400 × 300 pixels.

2. Create a new layer so there are two layers. Call the top one code and the bottom one ui. Lock the code layer.

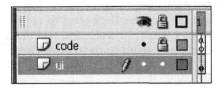

Figure 10-2.
Flash Timeline layout separating the code layer from the ui layer

3. Select the ui layer and draw two static text fields, placed like the two message text fields in Figure 10-1. In the top text field, write Send the following to JavaScript:, and in the bottom text field, write Receiving from JavaScript:. This book's example uses 12-point Arial.

4. Create an input text field next to the top message, Send the following to JavaScript:, and give it the instance name outText. This should also be 12-point Arial.

5. Create another 12-point Arial input text field, and place it next to the bottom message, Receiving from JavaScript:. Give this the instance name inText.

6. Beneath the outText text field, draw a white rectangle with a black stroke around it, and put text on top of it that says SEND. Position and size it similar to the screenshot.

7. Select the whole square and SEND text, and press *F8* to convert to a button. Set the behavior as Button, and give it the name sendButton. Click OK.

8. Select the newly created button, and give it the instance name sendButton.

You now have the user interface built to perform the Flash side of your example. The movie is now ready to have code added to it. Select the first frame of the code layer, and if it's not already, open the Actions window by pressing *F9*. In the code window, enter the following code:

```
import flash.external.*;
```

That's the first line of code, and it tells Flash that you're going to be making use of the flash.external package. The flash.external package only has one class, the ExternalInterface class. Continue by entering the following code below the first line:

```
function myFromJS(str:String)
{
        inText.text = str;
}
```

This is the myFromJS function, which is called when (you guessed it) text gets passed from JavaScript. The function takes one parameter, a string called str, and it sets the text property of the inText text field to that string. This will cause Flash to display on the screen whatever's passed in. Continue, adding the following code below what you've already added:

```
ExternalInterface.addCallback("fromJS", this, myFromJS);
```

Here, you're telling the ExternalInterface class to listen up. You're letting it know that the external host is going to be asking for something called fromJS. That's the first parameter. The next two parameters tell ExternalInterface what to call when that method is requested. You're saying to call the function myFromJS, and that the function is located on the root (indicated with this, as this refers to the root when the line of code is on the root timeline).

The format of the addCallback method is like so:

```
ExternalInterface.addCallback(methodName, instance, method)
```

> *Note that* ExternalInterface *uses static methods, and therefore you don't create an instance of the* ExternalInterface *class.*

Continue, entering the following code:

```
sendButton.onRelease = function()
{
        ExternalInterface.call("fromAS", outText.text);
}
```

This is the other side of the coin. This is the function that you call when the SEND button is pressed (well, released, technically); and here you're triggering the call method of the ExternalInterface class. You're telling ExternalInterface to call the fromAS function on the host, and to pass to it the contents of the outText text field.

The format of the call method is as follows:

```
ExternalInterface.call(methodName, argument1, argument2, argumentN)
```

The methodName is the method you want to call, and then can pass in as many arguments as you want.

Save this movie and call it example1.fla. Press CTRL+ENTER to run the movie. You'll see something that looks like the following:

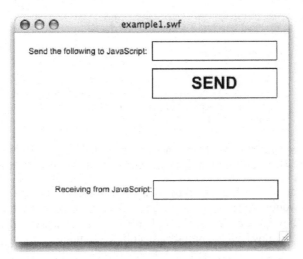

Figure 10-3. Example of what the SWF should look like after testing the movie from the Flash environment

There's no functionality at this point. Clicking the button or typing text will do nothing—this isn't yet running within the context of a host.

The HTML

Now that you've got the SWF ready, you must write the JavaScript and HTML code to make it active. The HTML aspect (the host) of this example will contain your embedded SWF, as well as two HTML text fields and a submit button, which will behave exactly like the Flash text fields and button. Your final HTML page will look like so:

Figure 10-4. Screenshot of generated HTML containing SWF file and HTML form

The top half is the embedded SWF, and the bottom half is HTML with two forms, the first containing a text field and button, and the second containing only a text field.

Most of this is standard HTML, and thus won't be explained—but the JavaScript will be explained. If you would like to know more about HTML, you can visit the World Wide Web Consortium (W3C) website at www.w3.org. A link to example1.html and EMBED tags can be found at www.w3.org/TR/REC-html40/struct/objects.html#h-13.3.

The first thing is to create a new HTML file and open it in an HTML editor. You can use any text editor you want for this. Create the new file and call it ExternalInterfaceExample.html.

In your text editor, enter the following code first:

```
<HTML>
  <HEAD>
  <META http-equiv="Content-Type"
    content="text/html; charset=ISO-8859-1">
  <TITLE>External Interface example 1</TITLE>

  <SCRIPT LANGUAGE="JavaScript">
```

This is the top of the HTML file, and at the end of that you're opening your JavaScript section. Enter the following code:

```
function thisMovie(movieName)
{
  if (isIE())
  {
    return window[movieName];
  }
  else
  {
    return document[movieName];
  }
}
```

This function simply returns a reference to an embedded object specified in movieName. Netscape and Microsoft Internet Explorer (IE) refer to embedded objects differently. Netscape addresses them via the document object, while IE looks for them in the window object (this function thanks to www.moock.org). Continue with the following code:

```
function isIE()
{
  return navigator.appName.indexOf ("Microsoft") != -1;
}
```

This function was called from the thisMovie function. This simply checks to see if the browser is IE or not. Continue with this code:

```
function makeCall(str)
{
  thisMovie("ExternalInterfaceExample").fromJS(str);
}
```

This is the function that will be called when the user hits the Send to AS button beneath the first HTML text field. This method receives a single string, str. First you establish a reference to an object called ExternalInterfaceExample, and call a method of that object called fromJS. You pass the value of str into fromJS. The object ExternalInterfaceExample is going to be the ID name you use to call your embedded Flash Player, which we'll discuss shortly. Continue with this code:

```
function fromAS(str)
{
  document.inForm.inField.value = str;
}
```

If you think back to your ActionScript, `fromAS` is the name of the function you called when the user hit the SEND button.

```
sendButton.onRelease = function()
{
        ExternalInterface.call("fromAS", outText.text);
}
```

> *The preceding code is a recap of the ActionScript from earlier, for reference only. Do not enter it into the HTML file.*

Into `fromAS`, you pass one parameter, `str`, which will contain the contents of the input text field `outText`, from the Flash movie. When this `fromAS` function is triggered, you set the value of the text field `inField` to `str`. This is a text field sitting in a form called `inForm`. You'll see that shortly. Next, enter the following code:

```
</SCRIPT>
</HEAD>
<BODY>
```

You're now ready to begin your main HTML body.

```
<OBJECT classid="clsid:D27CDB6E-AE6D-11cf-96B8-444553540000"
        codebase="http://download.macromedia.com/pub/shockwave/
                    cabs/flash/swflash.cab#version=8,0,0,0"
      width="400" height="300" id="ExternalInterfaceExample">
     <PARAM name="allowScriptAccess" value="always" />
     <PARAM name="movie" value="example1.swf" />
     <PARAM name="quality" value="high" />
    <param name="bgcolor" value="#ffffff" />
  <EMBED src="example1.swf" quality=high
        bgcolor=#FFFFFF width="400" height="300"
        name="ExternalInterfaceExample" swLiveConnect="true"
        allowscriptaccess="always"
        type="application/x-shockwave-flash"
        pluginspace="http://www.macromedia.com/go/getflashplayer">
   </EMBED>
 </OBJECT>
```

That's a big chunk of code to enter. Most of that's the standard code automatically generated by Flash when you publish a movie. The key parts to notice are highlighted in bold. The most important thing is that you set the `id` and `NAME` parameters to `ExternalInterfaceExample`, because this is what was referred to earlier in the JavaScript code. You also set the value of `swLiveConnect` to `true` to allow Netscape browsers (those earlier than Netscape 6.2) to talk to Flash Player. The `allowScript➡` `Access` parameter must also be set to `always` in order for Flash to be able to communicate with the scripts on the host. Continue by entering the following code:

```
<H4>External Interface Example: Javascript side</H4>

<FORM name="outForm" method="POST"
action="javascript:makeCall(document.outForm.outField.value)">
    Sending to ActionScript<BR>
    <INPUT type="TEXT" name="outField" value=""><BR>
    <INPUT type="SUBMIT" value="Send to AS">
</FORM>
```

After displaying the heading External Interface Example: Javascript side, proceed with your first form, which is called `outForm`. When the form is posted, you call the `makeCall` function that you created earlier. You pass into it the value of the outField text field. You then create the outField text field, and then below that create a SUBMIT button, with the label Send to AS. Next, enter the following code:

```
<FORM name="inForm" method="POST" action="">
    Receiving from ActionScript<BR>
    <INPUT type="TEXT" name="inField" value""><BR>
</FORM>
```

This second form is the form referred to earlier from your `fromAS` JavaScript function. This form, `inForm`, has no post action because it contains no SUBMIT button. It contains only one item; a text field called inField, which is initially empty, but is filled when `fromAS` is called from Flash. Enter these last two lines of code:

```
    </BODY>
</HTML>
```

To recap, here's the entire source of the HTML code:

```
<HTML>
  <HEAD>
  <META http-equiv="Content-Type"
    content="text/html; charset=ISO-8859-1">
  <TITLE>External Interface example 1</TITLE>

  <SCRIPT LANGUAGE="JavaScript">

    function thisMovie(movieName)
    {
      if (isIE())
      {
        return window[movieName];
      }
      else
      {
```

337

```
      return document[movieName];
    }
  }

  function isIE()
  {
    return navigator.appName.indexOf ("Microsoft") != -1;
  }

  function makeCall(str)
  {
    thisMovie("ExternalInterfaceExample").fromJS(str);
  }

  function fromAS(str)
  {
    document.inForm.inField.value = str;
  }

</SCRIPT>
</HEAD>
<BODY>

<OBJECT classid="clsid:D27CDB6E-AE6D-11cf-96B8-444553540000"
        codebase="http://download.macromedia.com/pub/shockwave/
                  cabs/flash/swflash.cab#version=8,0,0,0"
      width="400" height="300" id="ExternalInterfaceExample">
      <PARAM name="allowScriptAccess" value="always" />
      <PARAM name="movie" value="example1.swf" />
      <PARAM name="quality" value="high" />
<PARAM name="bgcolor" value="#ffffff" />
<EMBED src="example1.swf" quality=high
      bgcolor=#FFFFFF width="400" height="300"
      name="ExternalInterfaceExample" swLiveConnect="true"
      allowscriptaccess="always"
      type="application/x-shockwave-flash"
      pluginspace="http://www.macromedia.com/go/getflashplayer">
</EMBED>
</OBJECT>

<H4>External Interface Example: Javascript side</H4>
```

```
    <FORM name="outForm" method="POST"
action="javascript:makeCall(document.outForm.outField.value)">
        Sending to ActionScript<BR>
        <INPUT type="TEXT" name="outField" value=""><BR>
        <INPUT type="SUBMIT" value="Send to AS">
    </FORM>

    <FORM name="inForm" method="POST" action="">
        Receiving from ActionScript<BR>
        <INPUT type="TEXT" name="inField" value""><BR>
    </FORM>

    </BODY>
</HTML>
```

That's the end of the HTML file. Once you've done that, open the HTML file in a browser. It doesn't matter what you use, but you have to make sure your security settings are such that your browser allows you to run local active content. To do this in IE, open IE and select Tools ➤ Internet Options. Go to the Advanced tab, scroll down to the Security section, make sure that Allow active content to run in files on My Computer is selected, and click OK.

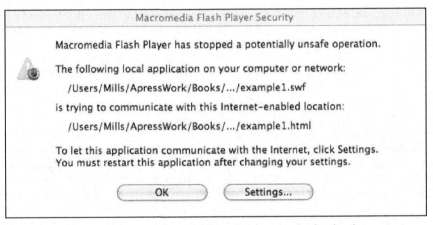

Figure 10-5. The security prompt from the browser when running local active content

We found the best results using Mozilla Firefox. When you run it, try typing some text in the text fields and hitting the SEND buttons. You should see things being passed back and forth properly.

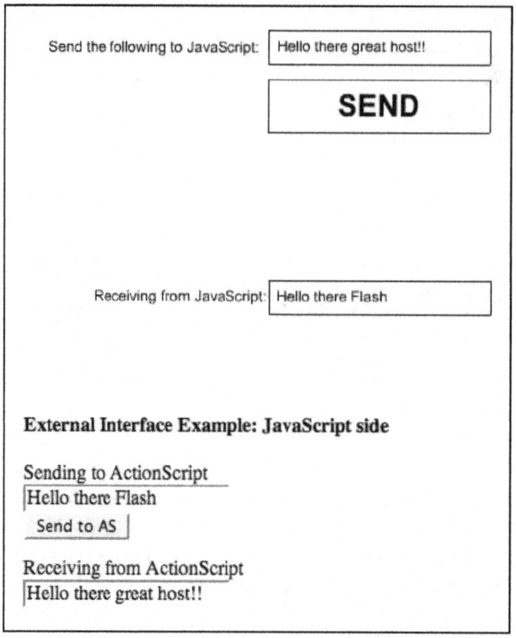

Figure 10-6.
The HTML with inputted and displayed text in the SWF file and JavaScript forms

That's it! That was a lot of code for a very simple example, but that's due to the fact that when using `ExternalInterface`, you have to program in two different environments: Flash and the host.

RollOver sound example

The second example you're going to make will embed a Flash movie in a web page that's actually hidden to the user. The Flash movie has one purpose only; to play a sound when a function is called. What will this allow you to do? It will allow you to take standard HTML elements like links and give them the ability to trigger a sound when the user moves the mouse over them. This isn't something that HTML can typically do on its own, but it can be accomplished using Flash.

The SWF

1. The first thing to do is create a new Flash movie. It can be any size, as it's not going to be seen.

2. Open Flash and import a sound into the library (File ➤ Import ➤ Import to Library). Any sound will do, but something like a short beep would be best.

3. From the library, open the Sound Properties dialog box by right-clicking on the clickrollover sound in the library. Give the sound the instance name clickrollover and set its compression quality to raw. This means that the sound will not be compressed whatsoever, but will be embedded in the SWF at full byte-for-byte quality. Click OK.

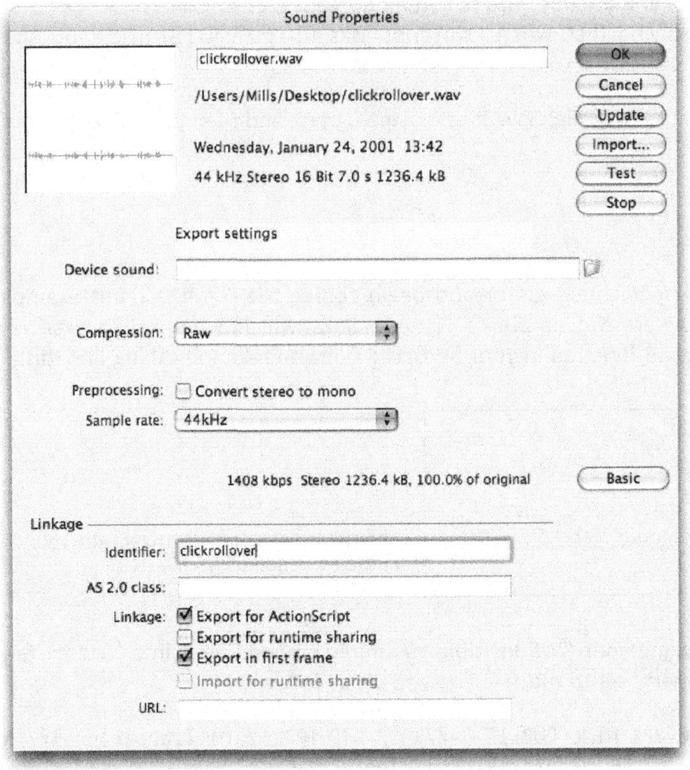

Figure 10-7. The Sound Properties dialog box for the clickrollover.wav sound

That's all the preparation this movie requires. The rest is code. Click on frame 1 of layer 1, and open the code window (*F9*). Enter the following code:

```
import flash.external.*;

s = new Sound(this);
s.attachSound("clickrollover");
```

First, you tell Flash you're going to be using the flash.external package. You then create a new sound object, s, and attach the clickrollover sound to it. Continue by entering the following code:

```
function playUISound()
{
    s.start(0,0);
}
```

This function, playUISound, is a function whose sole purpose is to tell the s sound object to play, therefore triggering the beep. Continue with the following:

```
ExternalInterface.addCallback("playUISound", this, playUISound);
```

That's the last line of code. You're setting up your `ExternalInterface` callback function by specifying that when JavaScript asks for `playUISound`, you should call the function `playUISound`.

That's the entire SWF file! Save it as example2.fla, and then press *CTRL+ENTER* to create the file example2.swf.

The HTML

Once again, open a text editor and begin coding the HTML for this example. All you're going to show are two simple <A href> links, which, when rolled over, will trigger the `playUISound` function in your SWF. The output looks something like this:

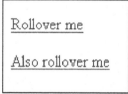

Figure 10-8.
The HTML links that will trigger the sound in the embedded SWF file

You'll be making your SWF invisible by simply embedding it in a <DIV> tag that has its visibility property set to hidden. The code is as follows:

```
<!DOCTYPE HTML PUBLIC "-//W3C//DTD HTML 4.01 Transitional//EN"
"http://www.w3.org/TR/html4/loose.dtd">
<HTML>
<HEAD>
    <TITLE>Example 2 - rollover sound</TITLE>
    <META CONTENT="text/html; charset=iso-8859-1"
     HTTP-EQUIV="Content-Type">
    <SCRIPT LANGUAGE="JavaScript">
```

That's the header of the HTML file. You've opened the script tag, so you can begin entering your JavaScript. The first two functions are identical to before:

```
function thisMovie(movieName)
{
  if (isIE())
  {
    return window[movieName]
  }
  else
  {
    return document[movieName]
  }
}
```

```
function isIE()
{
    return navigator.appName.indexOf ("Microsoft") != -1;
}
```

The preceding code gets a reference to the object specified in movieName. Enter the following function:

```
function makeCall()
{
    thisMovie("ExternalInterfaceExample2").playUISound();
}
```

The makeCall function is what you use to call the playUISound method of the movie specified by the id ExternalInterfaceExample2. This is what you'll be embedding your movie as. Continue, entering the following code:

```
    </SCRIPT>
</HEAD>
<BODY>
<DIV id="Layer1" style="position:absolute; visibility: hidden;">
    <OBJECT classid="clsid:D27CDB6E-AE6D-11cf-96B8-444553540000"
            codebase="http://download.macromedia.com/pub/shockwave➥
/cabs/flash/swflash.cab#version=8,0,0,0"
            height="400" ID="ExternalInterfaceExample2" width="550">
        <PARAM name="movie" value="example2.swf">
        <PARAM name="allowScriptAccess" value="always" />
        <PARAM name="quality" value="high">
        <EMBED src="example2.swf" quality="high"
pluginspage="http://www.macromedia.com/go/getflashplayer"
type="application/x-shockwave-flash" width="550" height="400"
NAME="ExternalInterfaceExample2" swLiveConnect="true"
ALLOWSCRIPTACCESS="always">
        </EMBED>
    </OBJECT>
</DIV>
```

After closing the script tag and the head tag, you open the body of your HTML file. You create a new DIV layer, and by setting its style to position:absolute, visibility:hidden, it won't be seen at all and won't have any physical effect on anything else on the page, but it will still exist on the page. Everything else is the same as the embedding in the previous example, except your id and NAME tags are ExternalInterfaceExample2, and you've embedded example2.swf rather than example1.swf. Below this, enter the following lines of code:

```
<P><A href="http://www.macromedia.com" onMouseOver="makeCall();">
        Rollover me</A></P>
<P><A href="http://www.macromedia.com" onMouseOver="makeCall();">Also
rollover me </A></P>
```

This will create the two links on the words Rollover me and Also rollover me. Right now they're set to go to http://www.macromedia.com, but they can be set to go anywhere. The magic here is on the `onMouseOver` tag. This is set to the value `makeCall();`. This means that when the mouse moves over these tags, the `makeCall` function will be called, which will in turn call the `playUISound` method in your SWF movie. What will happen then? Your sound will play! Close out the HTML file with the last two lines of code:

```
</BODY>
</HTML>
```

That's all there is to it. Save this HTML file as `example2.html`, and then launch it in a browser. Keep in mind the security issues mentioned earlier. If all is working well, you should immediately notice that when you roll the mouse over the two text links, you'll hear the sound that you embedded in your SWF file. Just like that, you've given plain-old HTML the ability to produce sound when something simple like a rollover occurs.

Summary

So where do you go from here? What else can you do with the `ExternalInterface` class in Flash? Well, realistically, the power doesn't lie with `ExternalInterface`, but rather what you *do* with it. Your imagination and your knowledge of JavaScript (or whatever host application you choose to use) is your only limit. As the previous example has shown, you can use Flash for a task that isn't even visual! The ideas are endless. You could

- Create a page that talks when certain titles and links are rolled over.
- Embed a Flash movie that loads and displays JPEG images when the JPEG images are chosen from an HTML drop-down box in the same page. This would allow you to generate your content dynamically with HTML, but make use of Flash to display and update the interactive part of the experience.
- Use an HTML configurator to allow users to build something dynamically (e.g., choosing toppings on a pizza), and use a Flash window to dynamically update price, total, or even generate a *picture* of what your pizza will look like.

A **FLASH 8 EXAMPLES**

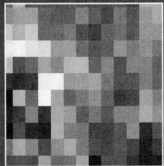

by Stephen Downs

This chapter focuses on giving you working examples for some of the features that have been previously covered (or not covered) in this book. This should give you more of an understanding of the new features and how to use them in real projects. In all the examples in this chapter, all content in the library is exported for ActionScript, leaving the stage empty until the movie is played. All examples have been built using ActionScript 2.0 and external classes. You can access the settings for exporting a library item for ActionScript or linking a library item to an external class by right-clicking (⌘-clicking on the Mac) and selecting linkage.

There are four examples that cover different features and functionality newly available in Flash 8. Each will have an overview to explain its purpose, and then the FLA and ActionScript file(s) that create the example will be walked through to explain how it works. There will be lots of familiar code mixed in with some of the new classes available in Flash 8.

All the source files for each example can be downloaded from www.friendsofed.com.

DeskTop

This example uses some of the new classes in Flash 8 to create a realistic desktop with items you can drag around. It uses a drop shadow filter that's updated dynamically to change the shadow effect depending on the item's position and distance from the desk surface and its distance from the light source. The light source is passed as an object with an x and y value, and defines the central point of the light for each object. Also, to add the effect of light being shined onto the desk, a movie clip blend mode is applied to a movie clip that's on a higher depth than the other movie clips in the example.

Figure A-1 shows the completed movie.

Figure A-1. The finished movie in action

The following are the new Flash 8 classes, methods, and properties used in this example:

- `MovieClip`
  - `MovieClip.attachBitmap()`
  - `MovieClip. blendMode`
- `flash.display.BitmapData`
  - `BitmapData.loadBitmap()`
- `flash.display.Point`
  - `Point.distance()`

The FLA file

Figure A-2 shows the library from the FLA. An explanation of each item follows.

Figure A-2.
Library window from `DeskTop.fla`

- `DragEnabledDynamicDropShadowMovieClip`: This is a blank movie clip. It's linked to the class `DragEnabledDynamicDropShadowMovieClip` and is exported for ActionScript with the linkage identifier `DragEnabledDynamic→ DropShadowMovieClip`.
- `DynamicDropShadowMovieClip`: This is a blank movie clip. It's linked to the class `DynamicDropShadowMovieClip` and is exported for ActionScript with the linkage identifier `DynamicDropShadowMovieClip`.

- items (folder): This contains the four images that will be used to create the items on the desktop. Each of the images are exported for ActionScript and have a unique linkage identifier that matches their displayed name in the library without the file extension.

- light: This is a movie clip that contains a radial gradient that has been cropped to a rectangle the size of the stage. It will be used to give the appearance of light shining on the desktop and is exported for ActionScript with the linkage identifier light.

- wood.jpg: This image is the size of the stage and is exported for ActionScript with the linkage identifier wood. This will be used as the surface of the desktop.

- DeskTop: This is the movie clip that's linked to the ActionScript 2.0 class DeskTop and has the linkage identifier DeskTop. It's an empty movie clip.

On frame 1, there are three lines of code used to attach the DeskTop movie clip from the library to the stage.

```
//import classes
import DeskTop;
//define the object 'deskTop_mc'
var deskTop_mc:DeskTop;
//attach an instance of the 'DeskTop' object to the Stage and give
// it the instance name 'deskTop_mc'
this.deskTop_mc = this.attachMovie("DeskTop", "deskTop_mc",➥
this.getNextHighestDepth());
```

Figure A-3 shows the timeline for DeskTop.fla.

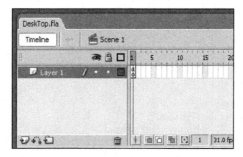

Figure A-3.
The timeline from DeskTop.fla

The ActionScript files

There are three ActionScript files that make up this example. In this section, I'll go through and explain how each one works. I haven't included a line-by-line description of each file, as that would take too long. Look to the source code if you want to follow the code along with my explanations.

DynamicDropShadowMovieClip.as

This is the class that creates the drop shadow filter on the movie clips. All movie clips that are linked to this class (or a class that extends this class) will automatically have a drop shadow filter added to its filter list. First, the `DropShadowFilter` class is imported using the `import` keyword and the fully qualified class name. If a class isn't imported, you have to refer to it by its fully qualified name throughout the rest of the code. Once imported, you can refer to the class by its class name. You can see this as a shortcut for typing less code.

```
//import classes
import flash.filters.DropShadowFilter;
import flash.geom.Point;
```

Then the class is declared, the internal variables are set up, and a constructor invokes `super()` and then invokes the `init()` method.

```
public function DynamicDropShadowMovieClip()
{
  super();

  this.init();
}
```

`init()` sets the variable `_z_num` to 0, which represents the clip's height from the surface the shadow will be cast on. It also creates a new `Point` object, which will be used as the light source for the shadow. Both of these are defaults.

```
//define default Point object for the light source
this._lightSource = new Point(0, 0);
```

`getAngle()` is used to find out the angle of the movie clip from the `_lightSource` `Point` object. Its return value is passed as the second parameter to the `updateDrop➡ Shadow()` method when it's invoked inside the `update()` method.

```
//invoked by 'update()' when passed as a parameter to
//'updateDropShadow()'
private function getAngle(x_num:Number, y_num:Number):Number
{
  //calculate and return the angle of the point passed from the Point
  //object '_lightSource'
  return Math.atan2 (y_num - this._lightSource.y, x_num - ➡
  this._lightSource.x) * (180 / Math.PI);
}
```

The drop shadow filter is applied in the `updateDropShadow()` method. This is invoked by the `update()` method and passed the numbers returned by `getDistance()` and `getAngle()`. It then creates a new drop shadow filter using these numbers to calculate the `distance`, `angle`, `alpha`, `xBlur`, and `yBlur` parameters passed to the constructor. This is added to the movie clip's filter list and the new shadow is rendered on the screen (as shown in Figure A-4).

```
//invoked by 'update()'
private function updateDropShadow(distance_num:Number, ➥
angle_num:Number):Void
{
//create/replace the DropShadow filter using the parameters passed
//and '_z_num'
  this.filters = [new DropShadowFilter((distance_num / 100) * ➥
  this._z_num, angle_num, 0x000000, 1 -   (distance_num / 600), ➥
  ((distance_num / 100) * this._z_num) / 5, ((distance_num / 100) * ➥
  this._z_num) / 5, 0.5, 3, false, false)];
}
```

Figure A-4. The change in the drop shadow filter as its distance and angle change from the specified x and y points defined in the lightSource object

There are then five public methods, as follows:

```
update()
set lightSource()
get lightSource()
set _z()
get _z()
```

update() is invoked each time you want to update the shadow. So if you've changed the movie clip's _x, _y, or _z properties, you need to invoke this function so that the changes are made in the shadow seen on-screen. It invokes the updateDropShadow() method and passes it two parameters. The first parameter is returned by the static method Point.distance(). This method takes a new Point object (which is the registration point of the movie clip), the _lightSource Point object, and returns the distance between them. The second parameter passed to `updateDropShadow()` is the number returned by the `getAngle()` method.

```
//first parameter is the distance between the registration point of
//this instance and the _lightSource Point object
//second parameter is the angle between this instance registration
//point and the _lightSource Point object
this.updateDropShadow(Point.distance(new Point(this._x, this._y), ➡
 this._lightSource), this.getAngle(this._x, this._y));
```

The setter `lightSource()` allows you to pass a new `Point` as the center for the light source. Once a new `Point` is passed, the `update()` method is invoked and the new drop shadow filter is created.

Its counterpart, `get lightSource()`, returns the current `Point` being used as the light source.

`set _z()` changes the distance the movie clip is from the target surface, and therefore how the drop shadow filter is created and viewed. The new drop shadow filter isn't created and applied when this method is invoked—you must invoke the `update()` method to see any changes in what's rendered on-screen.

The getter `_z()` returns the current value used as the distance of the movie clip from the targeted surface.

DragEnabledDynamicDropShadowMovieClip.as

What a mouthful! This class extends the `DynamicDropShadowMovieClip` class, which means it inherits all the properties and methods of that class.

```
class DragEnabledDynamicDropShadowMovieClip extends ➡
DynamicDropShadowMovieClip
```

It adds the functionality of being able to click an item on the desktop and drag it around. When an item is clicked, it's scaled and has its `_z` property (which represents its distance from the desktop) changed.

All the classes that are required are imported at the top of the file.

```
//import classes
import flash.geom.Point;
```

The class is then declared and a constructor invokes `super()` and then invokes the `init()` method.

```
public function DragEnabledDynamicDropShadowMovieClip()
{
  super();

  this.init();
}
```

The init() method changes the _xscale and _yscale of the instance created. This is done so that when the instance is clicked, it can be scaled up to 100%. If scaled over 100% it would lose quality, so it's best to scale the item down first, and then scale up to 100% max. The init() method also sets the variable _z_num to 0 and creates a new Point, which will be used as the light source for the shadow. These are both defaults, and are required because the method DynamicDropShadowMovieClip.init(), with which these are created, has been replaced with this init() method.

Then there's an onPress() method, invoked when the user clicks the movie clip. When clicked, the movie clip is scaled to 100% and its _z property is changed to 10. The update() method is then invoked so that its shadow is updated to reflect the change in the value of the _z property. The startDrag() method is then invoked so that the user can drag the movie clip around the screen. As the instance is moved around the screen,

the shadow also needs to update, so onMouseMove() is set to invoke the update() method inherited from the DynamicDropShadowMovieClip class. The movie clip's depth is then changed to ensure that it's on top of any other items on the desktop. Figure A-5 shows an example.

Figure A-5.
One of the instances of a
DragEnabledDynamicDropShadowMovieClip
object when the user clicks it

The onRelease() method really does the opposite of the onPress() method. It sets the movie clip's _xscale and _yscale back to 80% and its _z property back to 0. The update() method is then invoked again so that the shadow on-screen reflects the

changes made (see Figure A-6). The stopDrag() method is invoked so that the movie clip no longer follows the user's mouse around the stage, and the onMouseMove() method is deleted to stop the update() method from being continually invoked unnecessarily.

Figure A-6.
One of the instances of a
DragEnabledDynamicDropShadowMovieClip
object when it's released by the user

DeskTop.as

This is the main class that creates everything else in the movie. First, the required classes are imported.

```
//import classes
import flash.display.BitmapData;
import flash.geom.Point;
import mx.transitions.easing.Regular;
import mx.transitions.Tween;
```

Then the class is declared, the internal variables are set up, and a constructor invokes `super()` and then invokes the `init()` method.

```
public function DeskTop()
{
  super();

  this.init();
}
```

The `init()` method first creates a new `BitmapData` object by loading the image from the library, and attaches it to the instance.

```
//create a new BitmapData object by loading the 'wood' image directly
// from the library
newBitmap = BitmapData.loadBitmap("wood");
//attach 'newBitmap' to this
this.attachBitmap(newBitmap, this.getNextHighestDepth());
```

A blank movie clip called `_deskContents_mc` is then created. This will be the movie clip that contains all the items that appear to be on the desk surface. A `Point` object that represents the center of the stage is then created, and will be used as the light source for each item on the desktop.

```
//create a new Point
lightSource = new Point(400, 300);
```

A new `BitmapData` object is then created by loading the card image from the library. A new instance of `DragEnabledDynamicDropShadowMovieClip` is then created inside `_deskContents_mc` by attaching it from the library, and a blank movie clip is created inside it with the instance name `_holder_mc`. The `BitmapData` object is then attached to `_holder_mc`, and it's positioned so that it's centered. The instance of `DragEnabled➥ DynamicDropShadowMovieClip` is then moved to a random position and given a random `_rotation` property. The `lightSource` `Point` object is then passed as a parameter to the `lightSource()` method of `DragEnabledDynamicDrop➥ ShadowMovieClip`. The photo is then created in the same way, and the paper clips are created using the same concept, but in a `for` loop so that more than one paper clip is created.

```
//create a new BitmapData object by loading the 'card' image directly
//from the library
newBitmap = BitmapData.loadBitmap("card")
//attach an instance of 'DragEnabledDynamicDropShadowMovieClip' inside
// '_deskContents_mc' and give it the instance name 'card_mc'
newItem_mc = this._deskContents_mc.attachMovie➡
("DragEnabledDynamicDropShadowMovieClip", "card_mc",➡
this._deskContents_mc.getNextHighestDepth());➡
//create an empty MovieClip inside '_deskContents_mc.card_mc' with the
//instance name '_holder_mc'
newItemHolder_mc = newItem_mc.createEmptyMovieClip("holder_mc",➡
newItem_mc.getNextHighestDepth());
//attach 'card' to '_deskContents_mc.card_mc.holder_mc'
newItemHolder_mc.attachBitmap(newBitmap, 1);
//center '_deskContents_mc.card_mc.holder_mc' inside ➡
'_deskContents_mc.card_mc'
newItemHolder_mc._x = -newBitmap.width / 2;
newItemHolder_mc._y = -newBitmap.height / 2;
newItem_mc._x = Math.floor(Math.random() * 300);
newItem_mc._y = Math.floor(Math.random() * 300);
//give '_deskContents_mc.card_mc' a random position and rotation
newItem_mc._rotation = Math.floor(Math.random() * 180) - 90;
//pass the 'lightSource' Point to the setter 'lightSource()'
newItem_mc.lightSource = lightSource;
newItem_mc.update();
```

The pen now needs to be added. Again, a new `BitmapData` object is created by loading the image directly from the library, but this time, a new instance of `DynamicDropShadowMovieClip` is created inside _deskContents_mc, instead of a `DragEnabledDynamicDropShadowMovieClip`.

```
//create a new BitmapData object by loading the 'pen' image directly
//from the library
newItem_mc = this._deskContents_mc.attachMovie➡
("DynamicDropShadowMovieClip", "pen_mc", ➡
this._deskContents_mc.getNextHighestDepth());
```

A blank movie clip is then created inside pen_mc with the instance name _holder_mc. The `BitmapData` object is then attached to _holder_mc, and _holder_mc is centered. pen_mc is then positioned off the stage and given a random rotation. Its lightSource() setter method is then invoked, passing the lightSource Point object to it. Its _z() method is invoked and set to 20 so that pen_mc will appear to be raised off the surface.

_light_mc is then attached and the movie clip blend mode overlay is specified. This gives the effect of a light shining on all the objects and the desktop itself. Figures A-7, A-8, and A-9 successively show the desktop without _light_mc attached, with _light_mc attached but with no blend mode applied, and with _light_mc attached and the blend mode set to overlay.

```
//attach an instance of 'light' and give it the instance
//name '_light_mc'
this._light_mc = this.attachMovie("light", "_light_mc", ➥
this.getNextHighestDepth());
//set the blendMode of '_light_mc' to "overlay"
this._light_mc.blendMode = "overlay";
```

Figure A-7. The desktop and contents without `_light_mc` attached

Figure A-8. The desktop and contents with `_light_mc` attached, but no blend mode applied

Figure A-9. The desktop and contents with _light_mc attached and its blend mode set to overlay

Notice that pen_mc is an instance of the DynamicDropShadowClassMovieClip class, unlike the other instances that were created inside _deskContents_mc, which are instances of the DragEnabledDynamicDropShadowMovieClip class. This means that the user won't be able to click and drag the item, and therefore it won't move anywhere. Therefore, a timer is set up so that pen_mc is moved after a certain amount of time has passed. The variable _penTime_num is set to represent the current time, and _penTargetTime_num is set to the target time. An interval is then created to invoke the penTimer() method once every second. Figure A-10 shows a highlighted example of pen_mc as it's tweened across the screen.

The penTimer() method checks to see if the variables _penTime_num and _penTargetTime_num are equal. If they're not equal, it increments _penTime_num. If they are equal, then two tweens are created. One moves pen_mc across the stage and into view, and the other rotates pen_mc as it passes across the stage. The instance of the created DeskTop is then set up as a listener for the tween.

onMotionChanged() is invoked every time the position of pen_mc is changed by the tween. It gets passed an object that contains a variable obj. This stores a reference to pen_mc, so the update() method is invoked and the shadow is updated.

Figure A-10. The desktop and contents with `pen_mc` highlighted as it's tweened across the screen

Summary

Hopefully this example will have shown you how to use filters and blend modes, and how to update a filter dynamically.

Any movie clip in a Flash 8 movie can be attached inside an instance of `DynamicDrop`➥ `ShadowMovieClip` using `MovieClip.attachMovie()`, or linked directly to the class `DynamicDropShadowMovieClip` from the library, to add a drop shadow filter to the movie clip that updates depending on its `_x`, `_y`, and `_z` properties and defined `lightSource Point` object. If you wanted the user to be able to drag the movie clip around the screen and have a drop shadow filter that updates, you could attach it inside an instance of `DragEnabledDynamicDropShadowMovieClip` or link the movie clip to `DragEnabledDynamicDropShadowMovieClip` directly from the library.

You may also want to change the calculation within the `DropShadowFilter` constructor to change how the shadow is rendered.

ColoringBook

You may have seen Flash coloring books in the past. These were previously achieved by having separate movie clips for each area of color. When each movie clip was clicked, its color was then changed to the required color, using the `Color` object and `setRGB()`. This wasn't very dynamic, and each time you wanted to add a new image, the IDE would need to be opened and all the clips created for each area of fill.

This example uses the new `BitmapData` object available to Flash 8 that gives you methods to get data about images and make changes to images at runtime. The `BitmapData.floodFill()` method fills the surrounding area that has the same color as the start point of the fill. Using a GIF that's made up of a black outline, white fills, and a transparent background, you can detect the white areas and allow the user to `floodFill()` them with their chosen color.

The clown illustration used in this example was supplied by Michael Lawrence (www. thatblokemike.com).

The finished movie is shown in Figure A-11. The source files can be downloaded from www.friendsofed.com.

Figure A-11. The finished movie in action

The new Flash 8 classes, methods, and properties used in this example are as follows:

- `MovieClip`
  - `MovieClip. attachBitmap()`
  - `MovieClip.loadMovie()` – new ability to load GIF's at runtime

- `MovieClip.filters`
- `MovieClip.scale9Grid`
- `MovieClip.transform`
- `flash.display.BitmapData`
  - `BitmapData.draw()`
  - `BitmapData.dispose()`
  - `BitmapData.getPixel32()`
  - `BitmapData.floodFill()`
- `flash.filters.DropShadowFilter`
- `flash.geom.ColorTransform`
- `flash.geom.Rectangle`

The FLA file

Figure A-12 shows the library from the FLA. An explanation of each item in the library follows.

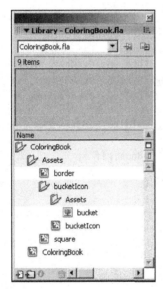

Figure A-12.
Library window from `ColoringBook.fla`

- `border`: This is the frame for the image. The swatches will be positioned on the left of this frame, and the frame will be resized depending on the size of the image loaded.
- `bucketIcon`: A movie clip that contains `bucket.gif`. It's exported for ActionScript with the identifier `bucketIcon`.

- `square`: This is a simple, white 25 × 25-square-pixel vector. It's exported for ActionScript and has the identifier `square`. This will be used to draw the swatches.

- `ColoringBook`: This is the movie clip that's linked to the ActionScript 2.0 class `ColoringBook`. It contains an instance of the movie clip border and is exported for ActionScript with the identifier `ColoringBook`. It also has the title FLASH 8 COLORING BOOK written on it.

On frame 1, there are seven lines of code. First, an instance of the `ColoringBook` movie clip is attached from the library and positioned on the stage. An array of hexadecimal colors are then passed to the instance of the `ColoringBook` movie clip (these will be the colors the user has to choose from), and finally a string is passed to the instance of `ColoringBook`, which is the path to the GIF to be loaded.

```
//import classes
import ColoringBook;
//define the object 'coloringBook_mc'
var coloringBook_mc:ColoringBook;
//attach an instance of the 'ColoringBook' object to the Stage and
//give it the instance name 'coloringBook_mc'
this.coloringBook_mc = this.attachMovie("ColoringBook", ➡
"coloringBook_mc", this.getNextHighestDepth());
this.coloringBook_mc._x = 10;
this.coloringBook_mc._y = 10;
//pass an array of 32 bit hexidecimal color values to the
//setter 'swatches()'
this.coloringBook_mc.swatches = [0xFFF9EBD9, 0xFFF3D9B7, 0xFFC0B288, ➡
0xFF685934, 0xFF456834, 0xFF62C332, 0xFF69E0D6, 0xFF4385D7, ➡
0xFF2C358B, 0xFFCFBEE4, 0xFF684570, 0xFFC02C64, 0xFFF41F6F, ➡
0xFFCE1313, 0xFFDDEB40, 0xFFF1F406];
//pass the path of the external GIF to be displayed to the setter
// 'loadGif()' as a String
this.coloringBook_mc.loadMovie("ColoringBook.gif");
```

Figure A-13 shows the timeline for `ColoringBook.fla`.

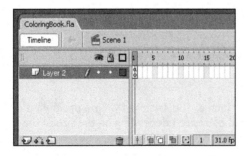

Figure A-13.
The timeline from `ColoringBook.fla`

The ActionScript file

Again, it's a good idea to have the ActionScript file open so that you can follow along with my explanation, as I haven't included every line of code.

ColoringBook.as

All the classes that are required are imported at the top of the file.

```
//import classes
import flash.display.BitmapData;
import flash.filters.DropShadowFilter;
import flash.geom.ColorTransform;
import flash.geom.Rectangle;
import mx.utils.Delegate;
```

Then the class is declared, the internal variables are set up, and a constructor invokes `super()` and then invokes the `init()` method.

```
public function ColoringBook()
{
  super();

  this.init();
}
```

The first line in the `init()` method sets up the `scale9Grid` property for your border movie clip. The property enables you to split the movie clip into nine regions used for scaling.

```
//define a Rectangele for the scale9Grid property of '_border_mc'
this._border_mc.scale9Grid = new Rectangle(220, 15, 5, 210);
```

A rectangle is passed with the x position, y position, width, and height of the area you want to scale, using normal rules. This results in the grid shown in Figure A-14.

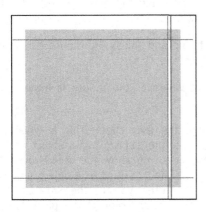

Figure A-14.
The `scale9Grid` applied to _border_mc

Now when you change the width and height of this movie clip, it will scale according to the regions you've set up. All the corners of the grid will remain the same size. Only the height of the center-left and center-right regions will be affected, and only the width of the center-top and center-bottom regions will be affected. However, the width and height of the white region will be affected. This is shown in Figure A-15.

Figure A-15. scale9Grid comparison: on the left, _border_mc is resized to twice its width and height *with* scale9Grid applied. On the right, _border_mc is resized to twice its width and height *without* scale9Grid applied.

A drop shadow filter is then applied to _border_mc, and three movie clips are created. _bitmapHolder_mc has its visible property set to false and another movie clip attached inside it. This internal movie clip will hold the GIF image once it's loaded, but the user will never see it because the clip it resides within has its _visible property set to false. _bitmapDisplay_mc is used to hold the instance of the BitmapData object once you've created it. This is the clip the user will see, and therefore it's positioned on the stage in the correct position and given an onRollOver() and onRollOut() action. When rolled over, the showBucket() method is invoked; and when rolled out, the hideBucket() method is invoked. _bucketIcon_mc is just an instance of the bucketIcon movie clip in the library—it's attached and then hidden.

The showBucket() method hides the mouse cursor and shows the bucket icon. It's invoked when _bitmapDisplay_mc is rolled over.

The hideBucket() method hides the bucket icon and shows the mouse cursor. It's invoked when _bitmapDisplay_mc is rolled out.

The onMouseMove() method makes sure that wherever the mouse is moved, the bucket icon follows.

The onMouseDown() method runs every time the user clicks. This is when the floodFill() method is used to apply new colors to the BitmapData object. First, it checks to see if _bucketIcon_mc is visible. If it is, you know the user is over the BitmapData object. Once you know the user is over the BitmapData object, you find out the color of the pixel underneath the cursor. To do this, you use the getPixel32 method of the BitmapData object. This returns a 32-bit color of the pixel directly underneath the mouse cursor.

```
//get the color of the pixel under the Mouse
pixelColor_num = ➡
this._bitmap.getPixel32(this._bitmapDisplay_mc._xmouse,➡
this._bitmapDisplay_mc._ymouse)
```

You then check to make sure that the color returned isn't black or totally transparent. These are the two areas of the BitmapData object that you don't want the user to be able to fill—that is, the background of the image and the outline of the drawing. If the user hasn't selected one of these two areas, the floodFill() method is invoked and passed the position of the target pixel and the hexadecimal value of the currently selected swatch.

```
//check that the color returned isn't transparent or black
if(pixelColor_num != -16777216 && pixelColor_num != 0)
{
    //fill the area under the mouse which the color of the
    //selected swatch
    this._bitmap.floodFill(this._xmouse - this._bitmapDisplay_mc._x, ➡
    this._ymouse -    this._bitmapDisplay_mc._y,➡
    this._swatches_array[this._currentSwatch_num]);
}
```

Figure A-16 shows the functionality that you've built up so far.

Figure A-16. With the fill bucket shown, the large rectangular area behind the shape is filled with the red color selected.

The hexTo32() method returns an array that contains the redOffset, greenOffset, blueOffset, and alphaOffset, relative to the 32-bit hexadecimal color passed to the method.

The swatchSelected() method is invoked when a swatch is clicked. It invokes the updateCurrentSwatch() method and passes it the number that's stored inside the selected swatch. This number corresponds to the position of the hexadecimal color that the swatch represents in the array of colors passed to the instance of the object on line six of the code in the FLA.

updateCurrentSwatch() stores the number passed to it in the variable _currentSwatch_num so that it can be used in the floodFill() method. It also changes the color of the _currentSwatch_mc using the new ColorTransform object, to clearly indicate to the user what color they've selected (see Figure A-17). Every movie clip has a transform property (which is a Transform object), and every Transform object has a colorTransform property (which is a ColorTransform object).

```
//create an Object with argb values from a 32 bit hexidecimal value
color_obj = this.hexTo32(this._swatches_array[index_num]);
//set the color of '_currentSwatch_mc' to match the color of the last
//selected swatch
this._currentSwatch_mc.color_mc.transform.colorTransform =➡
new ColorTransform(0, 0, 0, 1, color_obj.redOffset, ➡
color_obj.greenOffset, color_obj.blueOffset, color_obj.alphaOffset);
```

Figure A-17.
The large rectangular swatch at the bottom is updated to match the color of any square swatch that's clicked.

The updateSwatches() method is what draws the swatches on the screen. Each time a new array of swatches is passed to the set swatches() method, this function is invoked. It removes the holder movie clip that contains the swatches and also removes _currentSwatch_mc. A new holder movie clip is then created for the swatches and positioned. A for loop then creates a blank movie clip for each swatch and gives each one a unique index_num ID value that corresponds to its position in the grid. The swatch is then positioned. Two instances of the square movie clip in the library are then attached inside each swatch movie clip—one for the background of the swatch and one for the color area of the swatch. These are both positioned and resized, and color_mc has its color changed to match the swatch it represents. A drop shadow filter is also applied to each swatch and given an onPress(), so that when a swatch is pressed, it invokes the swatchSelected() method. _currentSwatch_mc is then created in the same manner, positioned, and its color set to the first hexadecimal color value. Finally, the variable _currentSwatch_num is set to 0 so that when floodFill() is invoked, it will fill using the first hexadecimal color value in the array (which is set with set swatches()).

Figure A-18 shows what the movie looks like after the swatches have been created.

Figure A-18.
The movie, after the swatches have been set and created. Notice _border_mc doesn't resize itself until the GIF is loaded.

Each time a new GIF has fully loaded, `update()` is invoked. This resizes `_border_mc` using the width and height of the movie clip that contains the GIF. It then disposes of the current `BitmapData` object shown on the user's screen, and immediately creates a new `BitmapData` object of the required size. The movie clip that the GIF was loaded into is then drawn onto the new `BitmapData` object using `BitmapData.draw()`. The `BitmapData` object is then attached to the `_bitmapDisplay_mc` movie clip using `MovieClip.attachBitmap()`, which displays it in position on-screen.

```
//invoked by 'onLoadInit()'
private function update():Void
{
//resize '_border_mc' using the width and height properties of the
//movie clip that holds the GIF
this._border_mc._width = this._imageHolder_mc._width + 240;
this._border_mc._height = this._imageHolder_mc._height + 30;

//dispose of the current BitmapData object
this._bitmap.dispose();

//create a new BitmapData object the height and width of
//'_imageHolder_mc'
this._bitmap = new BitmapData(this._bitmapHolder_mc._width,➡
this._bitmapHolder_mc._height, true, 0);
//draw '_imageHolder_mc' onto '_bitmap'
  this._bitmap.draw(this._bitmapHolder_mc);

  //attach '_bitmap' to '_bitmapDisplay_mc'
this._bitmapDisplay_mc.attachBitmap(this._bitmap, 1);
}
```

The `onLoadInit()` method is invoked when the GIF passed through the `loadGif()` method has fully loaded. This is invoked by the `MovieClipLoader` set up in the `loadGif()` method. Although there's no load progress information displayed on-screen, this functionality is required to make sure the GIF has fully loaded before it's drawn onto the `BitmapData` object. If it isn't fully loaded, the `BitmapData.draw()` method draws a blank movie clip onto the `BitmapData` object, and the user never sees the image.

There are then three public methods.

```
loadGif ()
set swatches ()
get swatches ()
```

The first, `loadGif()`, supplies you with a way of passing a GIF to the class. It uses `MovieClipLoader.loadClip()` to load the image into your movie clip positioned off the stage. First, it removes the listener from the previous `MovieClipLoader` object. The `MovieClipLoader.loadClip()` method is then invoked, and the instance of the class is then set up as a listener. Once the image has fully loaded, the `onLoadInit()` method is invoked.

The setter method `swatches()` enables the colors for the swatches to be passed to the class. It stores a copy of the array internally and invokes `updateSwatches()`, which removes the current set of swatches and adds a new set to represent the new array of hexadecimal color values.

The getter method `swatches()` provides you with a method to get the array of hexadecimal color values currently in use.

Summary

In this example, we've really only touched upon a few of the methods of the new `BitmapData` object.

To add different images, you just need to pass the path to the external image to the `loadGIF()` method. Remember that the image will need to be a transparent GIF with a black outline in the places you don't want the user to fill in. To change the swatches, you just need to pass an array of the colors you want to the setter `swatches()`.

You could also add to this example by supplying a selection of images to choose from using thumbnails and a different array of colors for each image.

PixelTransition

The concept of this example is to create an eye-pleasing transitional effect from one image to another. It uses `BitmapData.getPixel32()` to sample the pixels of the image it's transitioning from and to. The transition can be split into three main parts. First, a grid of colored cells are created on top of the current image until it's completely covered. The image is then swapped and the colors on the grid are changed to reflect the new image. Once all the cells have changed to represent the colors from the new image, the new image is revealed by filling the cells with a completely transparent color.

All the images used in the example are supplied by Mimi Mollica (www.mimimollica.com).

Figure A-19 shows the finished movie in action. The source files can be downloaded from www.friendsofed.com.

Figure A-19. The finished movie in action

The new Flash 8 classes, methods, and properties used in this example are as follows:

- `MovieClip`
  - `MovieClip.attachBitmap()`
- `flash.display.BitmapData`
  - `BitmapData.fillRect()`
  - `BitmapData.getPixel32()`
  - `BitmapData.dispose()`
- `flash.geom.Rectangle`

The FLA file

Figure A-20 shows the library from the FLA, followed by an explanation of each item.

Figure A-20.
Library window from `PixelTransition.fla`

- `button`: This is the button that will be used to move forward and backward through the images. It contains a text field with the instance name `text_txt` and an instance of the `square` movie clip, named `bg_mc`. This movie clip is then exported for ActionScript with the identifier `button`.

- `square`: This is a simple, white 100 × 100-square-pixel vector. It's exported for ActionScript, has the identifier `square`, and is used inside the `button` movie clip. It's also attached in the instance of the class as the background.

- `PixelTransition`: This is the movie clip that's linked to the ActionScript 2.0 class `PixelTransition` and has the linkage identifier `PixelTransition`. It's an empty movie clip.

- images (folder): This contains the five images that will be used in the example. Each of these images are exported for ActionScript and have a unique linkage identifier such as `image01.jpg`, `image02.jpg`, `image03.jpg`, etc.

On frame 1, there are six lines of code. First, an instance of the `PixelTransition` movie clip is attached from the library and positioned. Then an array containing the linkage identifiers for the contents of the images folder is passed to the `PixelTransition` instance.

```
//import classes
import PixelTransition;
//define the object 'pixelTransition_mc'
var pixelTransition_mc: PixelTransition;
//attach an instance of the 'PixelTransition' object to the Stage and
```

```
//give it the instance name 'pixelTransition_mc'
this.pixelTransition_mc = this.attachMovie("PixelTransition",➥
  "pixelTransition_mc", this.getNextHighestDepth());
this.pixelTransition_mc._x = 10;
this.pixelTransition_mc._y = 10;
//pass an array of linkage identifiers of the images in the library to
//be used in the movie
this.pixelTransition_mc.images = ["image01.jpg", "image02.jpg",➥
  "image03.jpg", "image04.jpg", "image05.jpg"];
```

Figure A-21 shows the timeline for `PixelTransition.fla`.

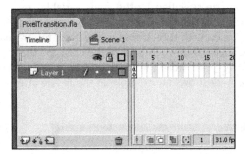

Figure A-21.
The timeline from `PixelTransition.fla`

The ActionScript file

Again, it's a good idea to have the file open from the source code to follow along with my explanation, as I haven't included every line of code.

PixelTransition.as

All the classes that are required are imported at the top of the file.

```
//import classes
import flash.display.BitmapData;
import flash.geom.Rectangle;
import mx.utils.Delegate;
```

Then the class is declared, the internal variables are set up, and a constructor invokes `super()` and then invokes the `init()` method.

```
public function PixelTransition()
{
  super();

  this.init();
}
```

The `init()` method attaches everything you need for the display. First, an instance of the `square` movie clip from the library is attached and resized for use as the background. The two buttons are then attached, positioned, resized, and their text set. They're then given a method to invoke when they're clicked. The `_bitmapContainer_mc` is then created and positioned. This is the movie clip that will hold and display the `BitmapData` object that will contain the images attached from the library. Another blank movie clip is created and named `_pixelGrid_mc`. This movie clip will hold the `BitmapData` object that the pixel grid will be created in each time a transition takes place. The `BitmapData` object is then created and attached to `_pixelGrid_mc`.

```
//create a new BitmapData object with the instance name '_pixelBitmap'
this._pixelBitmap = new BitmapData(IMAGE_WIDTH, IMAGE_HEIGHT, true);
//attach '_pixelBitmap' to '_pixelGrid_mc'
this._pixelGrid_mc.attachBitmap(this._pixelBitmap, 1);
```

The `BitmapData` object is created at the size specified by the static variables defined before the constructor, and the transparent parameter is set to `true`. It needs to be `true` so that you can fill areas of `BitmapData` with total transparency, therefore revealing the image underneath. Three variables that will be used later in the class are then set. `_pixelWidth_num` and `_pixelHeight_num` store the width and height of a single cell in the grid that will be created. Figure A-22 shows an example of the movie after the `init()` method has been invoked.

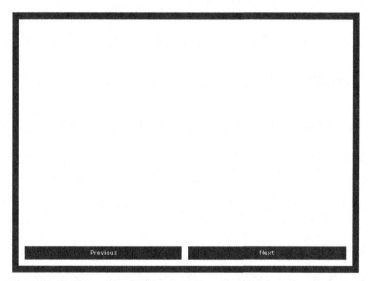

Figure A-22. The movie after the `init()` method has been invoked

The `createTransitionArray()` method does exactly what is says. It creates an array the length of the number of cells in the grid used in the transition. Each element in the array stores a number that corresponds to the element's position.

`pixelTransitionIn()` is invoked after the user has requested the next or previous image. It first clears the transition interval. This is to make sure that there's only ever one interval running at once. It then invokes the `createTransitionArray()` method, which creates a new array for use in the transition process. An interval is then created to invoke the `showPixels()` method and start the transition process of covering the current image with a grid of colored cells. A string is also passed as a parameter, which is used to invoke a method once this first part of the transition process is complete.

Once the current image has been covered with the grid of colored cells, the `pixelTransitionChange()` method is invoked. This method isn't much different from the `pixelTransitionIn()` method, except that it changes the current image by attaching the newly requested one from the library. First, the transition interval is cleared and `createTransitionArray()` is invoked. The new image is then attached.

```
//dispose of the old BitmapData object
this._bitmap.dispose();

//create a new BitmapData object by loading an image directly from the
//library
this._bitmap = BitmapData.loadBitmap(this._images_array➡
[this._currentImage_num]);
//attach '_bitmap' to '_bitmapContainer_mc'
this._bitmapContainer_mc.attachBitmap(this._bitmap, 1)
```

The old `BitmapData` object is disposed of and a new one is then created by passing the linkage identifier of the image to attach from the library to the static method `loadBitmap()`. This returns a new `BitmapData` object that contains the image, which is then attached to the `_bitmapContainer_mc` movie clip using `attachBitmap()` to render the image on-screen. As with the `pixelTransitionIn()` method, a new interval that invokes `showPixels()` is then created. This time, a different string is passed as the parameter so that `pixelTransitionOut()` is invoked once this part of the transition is complete. This `pixelTransitionChange()` method is also run when the array of images are passed to the instance of the class. In this case, there's no need to remove the previous image as there isn't one. Figure A-23 shows the screen as `pixel➡TransitionChange()` is invoked.

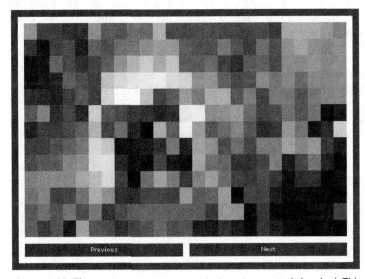

Figure A-23. The screen as `pixelTransitionChange()` is invoked. This occurs between the first and second phase of the transition from image 0 to image 1.

pixelTransitionOut() is the final part of the transition process. It clears the transition interval, invokes the createtransitionArray() method to create a new array, and then starts another interval. This time, the interval is set up to invoke the hidePixels() method. Figure A-24 shows the screen as pixelTransitionOut() is invoked.

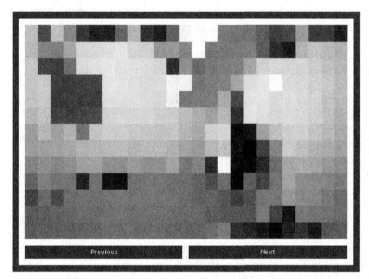

Figure A-24. The screen as pixelTransitionOut() is invoked. This occurs between the second and third phase of the transition from image 0 to image 1.

The showPixels() method is invoked on an interval and is the method that draws the colored cells. It's invoked for the first and second part of the transition using setInterval. Each time the method is invoked, it removes a random element from _pixelGridTransition_array by invoking getRandomPixel() which returns a number. This number is then used to locate a pixel and sample its color. Once this length of _pixelGridTransition_array is 0, the transition is complete.

```
//invoked by '_transition_interval' created in 'pixelTransitionIn()',
// 'pixelTransitionChange()'
private function showPixels(callback:String):Void
{
  var randomPixel_num:Number, pixelXPos_num:Number,➥
  pixelYPos_num:Number, color_num:Number;

  //store a Number which represents a random cell in the grid by
  //invoking 'this.getRandomPixel()'
```

```
      randomPixel_num = this.getRandomPixel();
      //calculate the position of the top left hand corner of the random
    cell
        pixelXPos_num = this._pixelWidth_num * (randomPixel_num - (COLUMNS *➥
          Math.floor(randomPixel_num / COLUMNS)));
        pixelYPos_num = this._pixelHeight_num * Math.floor(randomPixel_num /➥
          COLUMNS);

        //store the color of the pixel in the image that is in the center
        //position of the random cell
        color_num = this._bitmap.getPixel32(pixelXPos_num +➥
        (this._pixelHeight_num / 2), pixelYPos_num +➥
        (this._pixelWidth_num / 2));

        //fill the area of the random cell with the color
        this._pixelBitmap.fillRect(new Rectangle(pixelXPos_num,➥
        pixelYPos_num, this._pixelWidth_num,   this._pixelHeight_num),➥
        color_num);

        //check to see if all the cells are full
        if(this._pixelGridTransition_array.length == 0)
        {
          clearInterval(this._transition_interval);
          //invoked callback method passed as a String
          this[callback]();
        }
      }
    }
```

First, all the variables that are used in the method are defined. A random number that represents a random cell in the grid is then returned and stored by invoking the method getRandomPixel(). This also removes the random element from the _pixelGrid➥ Transition_array so you don't get the same element more than once. The x and y positions of this random cell are then calculated. BitmapData.getPixel32() is then used to return the color of the pixel from the image, located in the center of the random cell. Once the color is returned, BitmapData.fillRect() is then used to draw a rectangle of this color at the correct size and position onto _pixelBitmap. To do this, a rectangle is passed to the BitmapData.fillRect() method as the first parameter specifying the x, y, width, and height of the square to be drawn, and then the variable color_num is passed as the color to fill the rectangle. The array's length is then checked to see if there are any cells left to change. If there are, the method continues to run; if not, the interval is cleared and the callback invoked. Figures A-25, A-26, and A-27 give examples of the screen at three different stages at which showPixels() is running.

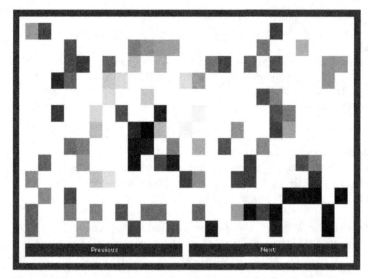

Figure A-25. showPixels() partway through running for the first time. This is the second phase of the transition, as there's no first phase required the first time the movie is run.

Figure A-26. showPixels() partway through running. This is the first phase of the transition from image 0 to image 1.

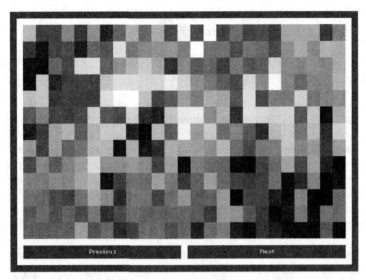

Figure A-27. showPixels() partway through running. This is the second phase of the transition from image 0 to image 1.

The hidePixels() method is very much like showPixels(). It's invoked as the third and final part of the transition, and makes each of the cells transparent to reveal the new image that follows.

```
//invoked by '_transition_interval' created in 'pixelTransitionOut()'
private function hidePixels():Void
{
  var randomPixel_num:Number, pixelXPos_num:Number,➥
  pixelYPos_num:Number;

  //store a Number which represents a random cell in the grid by
  //invoking 'this.getRandomPixel()'
  randomPixel_num = this.getRandomPixel();
  //calculate the position of the top left hand corner of the random
cell
  pixelXPos_num = this._pixelWidth_num * (randomPixel_num - (COLUMNS *➥
  Math.floor(randomPixel_num / COLUMNS)));
  pixelYPos_num = this._pixelHeight_num * Math.floor(randomPixel_num /➥
  COLUMNS);

  //fill the area of the random cell with a fully transparent color
  this._pixelBitmap.fillRect(new Rectangle(pixelXPos_num, ➥
  pixelYPos_num, this._pixelWidth_num,   this._pixelHeight_num),➥
  0x00000000);
```

```
            //check to see if all the cells are full
            if(this._pixelGridTransition_array == 0)
            {
              clearInterval(this._transition_interval);
            }
        }
```

As with `showPixels()`, a random element is returned, stored, and removed from `_pixelGridTransition_array` using `getRandomPixel()`. The position of this cell is then calculated—but there's no need to find the color of the pixel under the center of the cell, as you want to turn the cell transparent. To do this, `BitmapData.fillRect()` is used in the same way, but `0x00000000` is passed as the color value, which is a totally transparent hexadecimal color value. The length of `_pixelGridTransition_array` is then checked, and if there are no more cells, the interval is cleared. Figure A-28 shows the screen when `hidePixels()` is in the third and final phase of the transition.

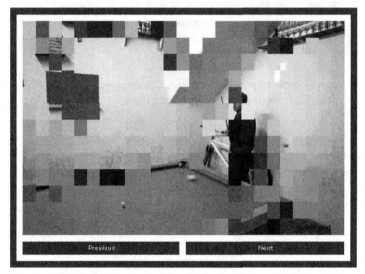

Figure A-28. `hidePixels()` partway through running. This is the third and final phase of the transition from image 0 to image 1.

`getRandomPixel()` is the method used to return a random element from the array that was set up for the transition. As well as returning the random number that represents the random cell to fill, it also removes the element from the array so that no number representing a cell can be returned more than once. This is also used to tell when a transition part is complete, as the length of the array is then 0.

The `showPrevious()` method is invoked when the Previous button is pressed by the user. It checks to see if the user is currently viewing the first image. If so, it sets the variable `_currentImage_num` to represent the position of the last image in the array of images passed to the instance of the class. If the user isn't currently viewing the first image, the variable `_currentImage_num` is set to represent the position of the previous image.

showNext() is invoked when the Next button is pressed by the user. It checks to see if the current image is the last image. If so, it sets the variable _currentImage_num to represent the first image. If not, it sets the variable _currentImage_num to represent the position of the next image in _images_array.

Finally, there's a getter and setter. The set images() setter lets the user pass an array of linkage identifiers of images in the library to the instance of the class. It stores this array, sets _currentImage_num to 0 to represent the first element in the array, and then invokes pixelTransitionChange(). This starts to display the grid of colors for the first image.

The getter, get images(), gives you a way to retrieve the array of linkage identifiers that are currently in use in the instance of this class.

Summary

In this example, you've looked at a few more methods of the new BitmapData object, and also used it to load images that have been exported for ActionScript directly from the library.

You may want to experiment with using different images or creating different patterns of color to represent the color of the pixels in the images beneath the colored grid.

FileReferenceExample

The FileReference object hasn't been covered in this book up until now, but it's something that many developers have been requesting. It enables the user to open an OS window and select files, and then upload them using a server script configured to accept uploads. It also enables the user to select a location to save a file on their computer, and then download the file directly through Flash to their hard drive. There are currently a few projects/components that are capable of doing this, but unlike FileReference, none are cross-platform, and none of them feed back the important information about the progress of the task taking place.

In this example, when you click the Upload button in the movie, you can browse for any SWF or JPG files on your hard drive. Once you've selected a file, the movie will display the name, type, size, date created, and date last modified of the file. You can then upload it to the server. When uploading, it feeds back information on the progress of the upload, and tells you when it's complete and whether there are any errors. The server-side script used in this example is PHP, and it uploads the files to a directory called uploadedFiles, which needs to be created in the same directory in which the SWF and PHP are run.

When you click the Download button in the movie, you're able to select where on your hard drive you want to save the file. Once a destination has been confirmed, the file will start to download and update you with the progress of the download, and again tell you when it's complete or if there were any errors.

Figure A-29 shows four states of the finished movie in action. The source files can be downloaded from www.friendsofed.com or by clicking on the Download button in the online example.

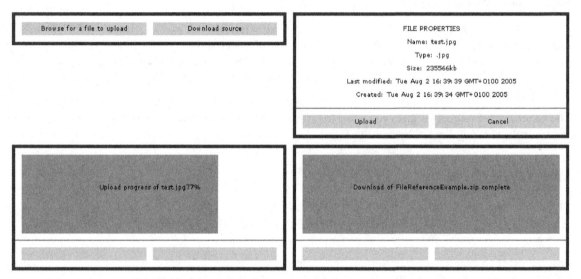

Figure A-29. Four states of the finished movie in action

Following are the Flash 8 classes, methods, and properties used in the example:

- MovieClip
  - MovieClip.transform
- FileReference
  - FileReference.name
  - FileReference.type
  - FileReference.size
  - FileReference.modificationDate
  - FileReference.creationDate
  - FileReference.browse()
  - FileReference.upload()
  - FileReference.download()
  - FileReference.onOpen()
  - FileReference.onProgress()
  - FileReference.onComplete()
  - FileReference.onSecurityError()
  - FileReference.onIOError()

- `FileReference.onHTTPError()`
- `FileReference.onCancel()`
- `FileReference.onSelect()`

The FLA file

Figure A-30 shows the library from the FLA, followed by an explanation of each item.

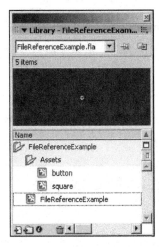

Figure A-30.
Library window from `FileReferenceExample.fla`

- `square`: This is a simple, white 100×100-square-pixel vector. It's exported for ActionScript and has a linkage identifier named `square`.

- `button`: This contains an instance of the square clip that has been tinted to `0xA5EF39`. On the layer above is a single-line text field. The text field is positioned vertically so that it's centered in the square below. It's exported for ActionScript and has the linkage identifier `button`.

- `FileReferenceExample`: This is a blank movie clip that's exported for ActionScript and has the linkage identifier `FileReferenceExample`. This clip is also linked to the ActionScript 2.0 class `FileReferenceExample`.

On Frame 1, there are three lines of code that attach the `FileReferenceExample` movie clip in the library to the stage.

```
//import classes
import FileReferenceExample;
//define the object 'FileReferenceExample_mc'
var FileReferenceExample_mc:FileReferenceExample;
//attach an instance of the 'FileReferenceExample' object to the Stage
//and give it the instance name 'FileReferenceExample_mc'
this.FileReferenceExample_mc = ➡
this.attachMovie("FileReferenceExample", "FileReferenceExample_mc", ➡
this.getNextHighestDepth());
```

Figure A-31 shows the timeline for `PixelTransition.fla`.

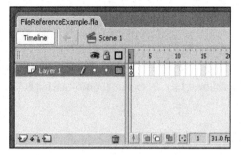

Figure A-31.
The timeline from `PixelTransition.fla`

The ActionScript file

As before, it's a good idea to open up the ActionScript file so you can follow along with my explanation, as I haven't included every line of code.

FileReferenceExample.as

All the classes that are required are imported at the top of the file.

```
//import classes
import flash.net.FileReference;
import flash.geom.ColorTransform;
import mx.utils.Delegate;
import mx.transitions.Tween;
import mx.transitions.easing.Regular;
```

Then the class is declared, the internal variables are set up, and a constructor invokes `super()` and then invokes the `init()` method.

```
public function FileReferenceExample()
{
  super();

  this.init();
}
```

The `init()` method is what sets up your class and creates the display for the user. First, it defines a new `MovieClip` object inside the method that will be used further on in the code. The `FileReference` object is then created and a listener is added to it, so that the events that it dispatches can be received. The `FileReference` class itself is used as the listener.

```
//create a new FileReference object with the instance name ➥
'_FileReference'
this._FileReference = new FileReference();
this._FileReference.addListener(this);
this._FileReference.addListener(this);
```

The path to the server script that accepts and handles the uploads is then stored inside the variable _uploadURL_str as a string. A blank movie clip is then created and given the instance name _fileProperties_mc. An instance of the square movie clip from the library is attached inside _fileProperties_mc to be used as a mask. The mask is set to the required width and height, and then set as the mask for _fileProperties_mc. A white square background is then created inside _fileProperties_mc. The square clip from the library is again used for this, and set to the required size. The progress bar is then added. A blank movie clip is created inside _fileProperties_mc and given the instance name _loader_mc. The square movie clip in the library is then attached inside _loader_mc, given the instance name bg_mc, and resized to represent 100%. The color of _bg_mc is then changed using ColorTransform. The reason for not simply attaching the square movie clip from the library as the loader itself is that it wouldn't scale correctly when loading, as it already has a predetermined size.

```
//set the color of '_fileProperties_mc._loader_mc.bg_mc'
this._fileProperties_mc._loader_mc.bg_mc.transform.colorTransform =➥
new ColorTransform(0, , 0, 1, 165, 239, 67, 0);
```

A small for loop is then created to attach the movie clips that will display the information about the file that's uploading/downloading. In each iteration of the loop, the button movie clip from the library is attached, positioned, and resized, and the visible property of bg_mc inside each button is set to false. This is so that you can see _loader_mc behind the lines of text created.

```
//create the MovieClips that will display file and upload/download
//information
for(var i = 0; i < 6; i++)
{
    //attach an instance of 'button' inside '_fileProperties_mc' and give
    //it an instance name based on its position in the list of MovieClips
    //that will display information
    newProperty_mc = this._fileProperties_mc.attachMovie("button", ➥
    "property" + i + "_mc",➥
    this._fileProperties_mc.getNextHighestDepth());
    newProperty_mc._x = 10;
    newProperty_mc._y = (20 * i) + 10;
    newProperty_mc.bg_mc._visible = false;
    newProperty_mc.text_txt._width = 400;
}
```

First, a single pixel strip is created by attaching the square movie clip from the library inside _control_mc, and it's given the instance name _pixelGap_mc. This is used to stop _control_mc and _fileProperties_mc from merging together when _fileProperties_mc is being shown or hidden. It's then resized and positioned as required. The new ColorTransform object is then used to change the color of pixelGap_mc to match the stage.

```
//set the color of '_control_mc.pixelGap_mc'
this._control_mc.pixelGap_mc.transform.colorTransform = ➥
new ColorTransform(0, 0, 0, 1, 165, 239, 67, 0);
```

Another instance of the square movie clip in the library is then attached inside _control_mc. This will be the background of this clip, and the buttons will sit on top of it. Again, it's resized to the required dimensions. The two buttons that the user interacts with are then attached. The button movie clip from the library is used and positioned, and then the movie clip and text field inside the button movie clip are also resized. Now that _control_mc is complete, you can turn your attention to the movie clip that will give the user information about the files you upload/download and the progress of the action taken. The setupStart() method is then invoked (you'll take a look into this method a little later).

The next method is tweenClips(). This takes two parameters, the first of which is the _y position of _control_mc. This is the movie clip containing the buttons that the user interacts with; the other represents the visible height of _fileProperties_mc, which is the clip that displays file information and information about the progress of the task. The two tween objects are first stopped, and then new tween objects are created that position _control_mc and change the height of the movie clip that's applied as a mask to _fileProperties_mc.

startDelay() is next. This simply clears an interval, disables the two user buttons, resets _delayCount_num to 0, and starts a new interval to run the delay() method once every second.

The delay() function gets invoked every second if startDelay() is invoked. delay() checks the value of _delayCount_num to see if the correct amount of time has passed. If _delayCount_num is less than the number specified, it's incremented and the method will be invoked again on the next interval. If the time specified has passed, the interval is cleared and the elusive setupStart() function is invoked.

Two setup methods, setupStart() and setupUpload(), follow. These are used to set the two main states of the movie. setupStart() gives the user buttons the text to display on-screen and the methods to invoke when each is pressed. The enabled properties of both of the buttons are then set to true, the loader's _xscale is set to 0, and tweenClips() is invoked (which will position _control_mc correctly and tween the height of the mask inside _fileProperties_mc to 0 so that it's not visible). This is the start state of the movie (see Figure A-32)—the method was invoked from the init() method, which was run by the constructor.

Figure A-32. The on-screen display in the start state of the movie

The setupUpload() method is invoked once the user has selected a file to upload and the second state of the movie has therefore been reached. It changes the text displayed in the buttons and the action taken when each button is clicked. When the left button is clicked, the startUpload() method is invoked, and when the right button is clicked, the onCancel() method is invoked. _fileProperties_mc is also set up to display information about the file selected. Once the OS window has been opened and a file is selected successfully, the `FileReference` object is populated with the data about the file, which is accessed here.

```
//display the properties of the file selected to upload
this._fileProperties_mc.property1_mc.text_txt.text = "Name: " + ➥
this._FileReference.name;
this._fileProperties_mc.property2_mc.text_txt.text = "Type: " + ➥
this._FileReference.type;
this._fileProperties_mc.property3_mc.text_txt.text = "Size: " + ➥
this._FileReference.size + "kb";
this._fileProperties_mc.property4_mc.text_txt.text = ➥
"Last modified: " + this._FileReference.modificationDate;
this._fileProperties_mc.property5_mc.text_txt.text = "Created: " + ➥
this._FileReference.creationDate;
```

`tweenClips()` is then invoked to move the `_control_mc` position and change the height of the mask of `_fileProperties_mc` so that it's displayed on-screen. Figure A-33 shows the screen when a file has been selected for upload and the `setupUpload` method is invoked.

Figure A-33. The display on-screen when a file has been selected to upload and the `setupUpload` method is invoked

There are now two start methods, one for each of the movie's functions. `startUpload()` is invoked when the user presses the Upload button. It disables both buttons and removes any text displayed in them by invoking `disableButtons()`. The text inside `_fileProperties_mc` is then updated to inform the user that the upload has started, and the name of the file is displayed by accessing the instance of `_FileReference`. The `upload()` method of the `FileReference` object is invoked, and the path to the server-side script is passed as a parameter. This method is invoked when the Upload button is pressed. Figure A-34 shows the screen when `startUpload()` is invoked.

```
//invoked by '_control_mc.leftButton_mc.onPress()'
private function startUpload():Void
{
    this.disableButtons();

    //inform the user the upload process has started
```

```
this._fileProperties_mc.property0_mc.text_txt.text = "";
this._fileProperties_mc.property1_mc.text_txt.text = "";
this._fileProperties_mc.property2_mc.text_txt.text = "Uploading "➥
 + this._FileReference.name;
this._fileProperties_mc.property3_mc.text_txt.text = "";
this._fileProperties_mc.property4_mc.text_txt.text = "";
this._fileProperties_mc.property5_mc.text_txt.text = "";

//upload the file
this._FileReference.upload("upload.php");
}
```

Figure A-34. The display on-screen when `startUpload()` is invoked

The `startDownload()` method disables both buttons and removes the text displayed in them by invoking `disableButtons()`. It then updates _fileproperties_mc to inform the user that the file has begun to download. `tweenClips()` is then invoked to show _fileProperties_mc. Figure A-35 shows the screen when `startDownload()` is invoked.

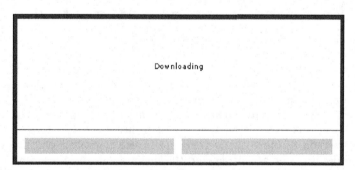

Figure A-35. The display on-screen when `startDownload()` is invoked

Two `openDialog` methods follow. These methods are invoked if either of the buttons are pressed when the movie is in its start state. `openUploadDialog()` sets the variable that internally stores the state of the movie to `Upload`, and then invokes the `browse()`

method of the `FileReference` object. The browse method opens an OS window for the user to select a file. You can pass parameters to this method specifying the allowed file types and a description of that group of file types. Flash movies (SWF) and a selection of image files (JPG, GIF, and PNG) are passed as parameters so that these will be the only file types that are shown in the system browse window, and therefore the only file types the user can select. If this parameter is omitted, all files types will be shown. If the OS window isn't successfully opened, the `FileReference.browse()` method returns `false`, both buttons are disabled, and the user is informed that the upload has failed. If the OS window is successfully opened, it returns `true`. More information on how the `FileReference.download()` method can fail can be found in the help documents that come with Flash 8. Figure A-36 shows the screen when the OS window fails to open when `FileReference.browse()` is invoked.

```
//invoked by '_control_mc.leftButton_mc.onPress()'
private function openUploadDialog():Void
{
  var success:Boolean;

  this._state_str = "Upload";

  //open OS window and specify a description for each group and the
  //file types allowed in that group
  success = this._FileReference.browse([{description: "Image files",➡
  extension: "*.jpg;*.gif;*.png", macType: "JPEG;jp2_;GIFF"}, ➡
  {description: "Flash Movies", extension: "*.swf", macType: "SWFL"}]);

  //if the OS window failed to open
  if(success == false)
  {
    this.disableButtons();

    //inform the user the upload process failed
    this._fileProperties_mc.property0_mc.text_txt.text = "";
    this._fileProperties_mc.property1_mc.text_txt.text = "";
    this._fileProperties_mc.property2_mc.text_txt.text = "Upload➡
    failed";
    this._fileProperties_mc.property3_mc.text_txt.text = "";
    this._fileProperties_mc.property4_mc.text_txt.text = "";
    this._fileProperties_mc.property5_mc.text_txt.text = "";

    this.tweenClips(141, 140);

    this.startDelay();
  }
}
```

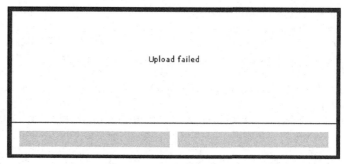

Figure A-36. The display on-screen if the OS window fails to open when `FileReference.browse()` is invoked

`openDownloadDialog()` sets the internal state of the movie to `Download`. Here, the `download()` method of the `FileReference` object is invoked, and the path to the file that will be downloaded is passed in the first parameter. The second parameter is optional and specifies the file name the user will see in the OS window when downloading the file. If this parameter isn't used, the full path to the file will be shown in the dialog box. If the OS window isn't successfully opened, the `FileReference.download()` method returns `false`, both buttons are disabled, and the user is informed that the download has failed. If the OS window is successfully opened, it returns `true`. More information on how the `FileReference.download()` method can fail can be found in the help documents that come with Flash 8. Figure A-37 shows the screen when the OS window fails to open when `FileReference.download()` is invoked.

```
//invoked by '_control_mc.rightButton_mc.onPress'
private function openDownloadDialog():Void
{
  var success:Boolean;

  this._state_str = "Download";

  //open OS window and specify the path to the file to download and the
  // file name that will be displayed
  success = this._fileReference.download("FileReferenceExample.zip", ➡
  "FileReferenceExample.zip");

  //if the OS window failed to open
  if(success == false)
  {
    this.disableButtons();

    //inform the user the download process failed
    this._fileProperties_mc.property0_mc.text_txt.text = "";
    this._fileProperties_mc.property1_mc.text_txt.text = "";
    this._fileProperties_mc.property2_mc.text_txt.text = "Download ➡
    failed";
```

```
    this._fileProperties_mc.property3_mc.text_txt.text = "";
    this._fileProperties_mc.property4_mc.text_txt.text = "";
    this._fileProperties_mc.property5_mc.text_txt.text = "";

    this.tweenClips(141, 140);

    this.startDelay();
  }
}
```

Figure A-37. The display on-screen if the OS window fails to open when `FileReference.download()` is invoked

`disableButtons()` disables both buttons. It also removes all text from both buttons so that they're blank. It's called by various methods when a process of displaying information—or uploading/downloading a file—has started.

Finally, we come to the events that are broadcast by the `FileReference` object, and that you've set your class up to listen for. `onOpen()` is broadcast from the `FileReference` object when an upload or download starts. In the class, the loader's `_xscale` is set to 0 and all text is removed except one line. This one line uses the variable that stores the state of the movie (either `Upload` or `Download`) and the name of the file, which is accessed through the `FileReference` object, to inform the user the action has started and the progress is 0%. The `tweenClips()` method is also called to make sure `_control_mc` is in the correct position and `_fileProperties_mc` is visible. Figure A-38 shows the screen when the upload process starts and the `onOpen` method is invoked. Figure A-39 shows the screen when the download process starts and the `onOpen` method is invoked.

```
    //invoked by the FileReference object '_FileReference'
    private function onOpen():Void
    {
      this._fileProperties_mc._loader_mc._xscale = 0;

      //inform the user the upload has started and show "0%" and the➥
      progress
      this._fileProperties_mc.property0_mc.text_txt.text = "";
      this._fileProperties_mc.property1_mc.text_txt.text = "";
```

```
    this._fileProperties_mc.property2_mc.text_txt.text =
this._state_str➡
      + " progress of "  + this._FileReference.name + " 0%";
    this._fileProperties_mc.property3_mc.text_txt.text = "";
    this._fileProperties_mc.property4_mc.text_txt.text = "";
    this._fileProperties_mc.property5_mc.text_txt.text = "";

    this.tweenClips(141, 140);
}
```

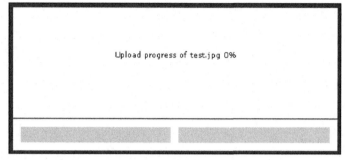

Figure A-38. The display on-screen when the upload process starts and the onOpen method is invoked

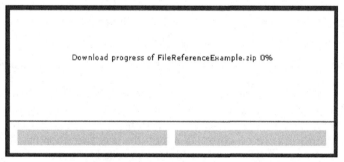

Figure A-39. The display on-screen when the download process starts and the onOpen method is invoked

onProgress() is invoked periodically during the upload/download process. This method also has three parameters: the first is the FileReference object itself, the second is the number of bytes transmitted, and the final parameter is the total number of bytes required to transmit to complete the process. _loader_mc is scaled to represent the percentage of the process completed, and the line of text that was set in the onOpen() method is updated to show the progress with a percentage calculated using the number of bytes transmitted and the total number of bytes to transmit. If the number of bytes transmitted cannot be determined, -1 will be returned. A check is performed to see if this is the case, and if so, the text is updated to inform the user that the progress of the process can't be determined. Figure A-40 shows the screen during the upload process as onProgress is invoked, and Figure A-41 shows the screen during the download process as onProgress is invoked.

```
//invoked by the FileReference object '_FileReference'
private function onProgress(fileRef:FileReference, loaded_num:Number,⇥
total_num:Number):Void
{
  //check that the size in bytes of the file being uploaded can be
  //determined by the FileReference object
  if(total_num != -1)
  {

    //scale '_fileProperties_mc._loader_mc' so the user can see the
    //progress
    this._fileProperties_mc._loader_mc._xscale = ⇥
    Math.round((loaded_num / total_num) * 100);
    //inform the user of the progress made by the upload/download
    //process
    this._fileProperties_mc.property2_mc.text_txt.text = ⇥
    + " progress of " +     this._FileReference.name + " " +⇥
    this._fileProperties_mc._loader_mc._xscale + "%";
  }
  else
  {
    //inform the user that we're unable to show the progress of the
    upload/download process
    this._fileProperties_mc.property2_mc.text_txt.text =⇥
    "Unable to determine " + this._state_str + " progress of " ⇥
    + this._FileReference.name;
  }
}
```

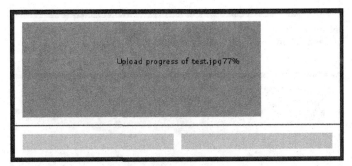

Figure A-40. The display on-screen during the upload process as onProgress is invoked

Figure A-41. The display on-screen during the download process as `onProgress` is invoked

The next method is invoked when an upload or download is complete. The right on-screen button (previously set as Cancel) is disabled so that no buttons are enabled. The text is updated to inform the user the process is complete and the loader's `_xscale` is set to 100%. The `startDelay()` function is then invoked. This creates a short delay so the user can take in the information before the movie is set back to its start state. Figure A-42 shows the screen when a file has been uploaded successfully and `onComplete` is invoked, and Figure A-43 shows the screen when a file has been downloaded successfully and `onComplete` is invoked.

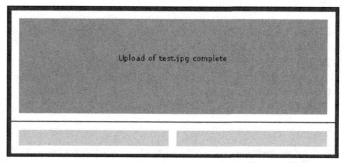

Figure A-42. The display on-screen when a file has been uploaded successfully and `onComplete` is invoked

Figure A-43. The display on-screen when a file has been downloaded successfully and `onComplete` is invoked

There are then three methods that are invoked when various errors take place. You can find more specific information on these errors in the ActionScript 2.0 Language Reference found in the help files included with Flash 8. Each method disables the right button, and the text is updated to inform the user of the error. The `startDelay()` function is then invoked to give the user time to take in the information shown before the movie is set back to its start state.

```
//invoked by the FileReference object '_FileReference'
private function onSecurityError():Void
{
  this._control_mc.rightButton_mc.enabled = false;

  //inform the user there was a security error with the
  //upload/download process
  this._fileProperties_mc.property2_mc.text_txt.text = ➡
   this._state_str + " security error for " + ➡
   this._FileReference.name;

  this.startDelay();
}

//invoked by the FileReference object '_FileReference'
private function onIOError():Void
{
  this._control_mc.rightButton_mc.enabled = false;

  //inform the user that the upload/download is unable to be completed
  this._fileProperties_mc.property2_mc.text_txt.text = "Unable to ➡
  complete " + this._state_str + " of " + this._FileReference.name;

  this.startDelay();
}

//invoked by the FileReference object '_FileReference'
private function onHTTPError(fileRef:FileReference, ➡
  httpError_num:Number):Void
{
  this._control_mc.rightButton_mc.enabled = false;

  //inform the user there was a http error with the upload/download
  //process and provide the error number
  this._fileProperties_mc.property2_mc.text_txt.text =
this._state_str➡
    + " error " + httpError_num + " for " + this._FileReference.name;

  this.startDelay();
}
```

onCancel() is invoked by the FileReference object if the user dismisses the OS window opened when FileReference.browse() or FileReference. download() have been invoked. It's also invoked if the user presses the Cancel button when a file to upload has been successfully selected. The text is updated to inform the user the process has been canceled, and tweenClips() is invoked to make sure _control_mc is in the correct position and _fileProperties_mc is visible. The startDelay() function is then invoked to give the user time to take in the information shown before the movie is set back to its start state. Figure A-44 shows the screen when the user dismisses the system dialog box that's opened when selecting a file to upload, and Figure A-45 shows the screen when the user dismisses the system dialog box that's opened when selecting a file to download.

Figure A-44. The display on-screen when the user dismisses the system dialog box that's opened when selecting a file to upload and onCancel() is invoked

Figure A-45. The display on-screen when the user dismisses the system dialog box that's opened when selecting a file to download and onCancel() is invoked

Finally, the last method in the class is onSelect(). This is invoked by the FileReference object when a file has been selected to upload, or a location to download a file to has been specified. The method checks the internal state to see if the user is currently uploading or downloading, and invokes the appropriate method.

Summary

Using the code base in this example, you could try to build your own UI for a custom `FileReference` movie.

I've covered all the properties and methods of the `FileReference` object except the `FileReference.creator` property, which retrieves the Macintosh creator type of the file. This was purposely left out, as it will always return null on Windows—but you may want to experiment with it.

You may also want to look into the new `FileReferenceList` object, which enables users to upload multiple files in one go, and is used with `FileReference`.

INDEX

Printed in the United States
By Bookmasters